Quantitative Analysis
for Planning Decisions

QUANTITATIVE ANALYSIS FOR PLANNING DECISIONS

K. HOWARD
*Senior Lecturer in Management Science at University
of Bradford Management Centre*

MACDONALD & EVANS LTD.
8 JOHN STREET, LONDON WC1N 2HY

First published July 1975

©

MACDONALD AND EVANS LIMITED
1975

ISBN: 0 7121 1701 6 (hard case)

ISBN: 0 7121 1702 4 (paperback)

Filmset by Keyspools Limited, Golborne, Lancs.
Printed by Tinling (1973) Limited, Prescot, Merseyside.

PREFACE

The purpose of this book, which is directed at practising managers and students of management, is to indicate how decision making may be made more efficient by the adoption of a quantified and analytical approach. It does not seek to claim that the whole or even most of decision making can be reduced to a mechanistic base, but it suggests that much of the complexity of the decision process can be removed by appropriate analysis, enabling greater attention to be focussed on non-quantifiable factors.

The main concern running through the chapters is with the problem of uncertainty confronting managers in making decisions of a planning nature. It is accepted that in practice a good deal of uncertainty exists with respect to ongoing activities, and there are numerous examples in the literature of techniques and methodologies directed towards their solution. There are for example many solutions, ranging from a practical to a theoretical nature, proposed for the purpose of increasing the efficiency of stock control. Or again much has been written about the optimisation of distribution systems and machine schedules. In a sense, decisions in this area are of a *design* rather than a *planning* nature and are the subject of writings in the field of traditional operational research and production management.

The author in his contacts with students of management and management in organisations in the public and private sector has frequently been confronted by requests for references to works which are comprehensible to non-mathematicians and which describe the quantitative analysis relevant to the planning type of decision. This book was written in view of the evident absence of other works with this theme.

It should be stressed that the reader will find little which is new in theory or techniques in the various chapters. It is in fact pointed out in Chapter 9 that most of the theory and techniques which are currently in use have been available for some two decades, and it is difficult to forecast new approaches which may be developed. This is one of the reasons why in various parts of the world (notably the United States of America) managers have become disenchanted with decision processes involving mathematical or statistical analysis. For as basic techniques have been adopted as routine, specialists within organisations have been motivated towards the development of more sophisticated and abstruse analyses, often with little practical relevance.

Insofar as organisational decision making is concerned, it is the author's opinion that greater efficiency will be achieved by the adoption of a multi-disciplinary approach rather than a series of fragmented approaches, possibly at different levels of sophistication. Therefore, while this book is concerned with quantified analytical methods, frequent reference is made to the place of these within the total process of decision making.

Some understanding of basic mathematics and statistics is inevitably required, but in this respect the book attempts to be self-contained. Readers are in the first instance recommended to read Appendix I which has been compiled in recognition of the fact that unless the symbolism and jargon of mathematics and statistics is understood much of what is written will be incomprehensible. Instead however of covering the necessary mathematics and statistics in the first Chapter, this is reserved for Chapter 3. The aim then of Chapter 1 is to create in the reader an appreciation of the implications of uncertainty and the attendant risk. This is followed in Chapter 2 with a study of the planning process and the use which may be made within it of models of the real life situation. In particular, the potential role of the mathematical model is examined.

Having in the first three chapters, it is to be hoped, created within the reader a "feeling" for this approach to problem solving and having equipped him with the fundamental mathematical skills, Chapters 4–8 are concerned with the manner in which decision models are constructed and used.

Nearly every planning decision involves uncertainty, that is variables which most probably will be outside the control of the decision maker (e.g. demand, debt charges, skilled manpower) and thus if the framework for decision making is to be set, estimates of these variables must be made. Chapter 4 is devoted to a study of some important methods of forecasting variables which must be quantified if analysis is to proceed.

Again, if decision making involves a complex sequence of activities some means is required of estimating the timing of important events. Network analysis which became well known in building and construction management some fifteen years ago, is now beginning to be used in the planning of organisational activity in the more corporate sense, and it is with this orientation that Chapter 5 is written.

Chapters 6 and 7 deal with two approaches to uncertainty which are becoming more widely adopted by management in order to study uncertain and risky situations. Decision trees will be shown to be of value in helping management to structure a problem logically, even if no further analysis is undertaken, and the attractiveness of being able to experiment on a model of the real life situation by the process of simulation is widely recognised.

During the past decade, interpretation of the aims of quantified decision making has changed. At the beginning of this period managers were being "sold" the idea that analytical procedures could indicate optimum strategy. The fact that in general they failed to do so is another reason why some managers have become disillusioned with the general quantitative approach. The idea that the decision should be taken out of their hands did not appeal and the "What-if?" opportunity afforded by simulation came in general to be preferred. Nevertheless, with the continuing difficulty of allocating resources in order to achieve an organisation's objectives in an efficient and an effective manner, the author feels that it is necessary to study further the potential of the optimising approach. It will be deduced from reading Chapter 8 that the techniques of optimisation may be able to make a significant contribution towards decision making if they are not viewed as providing definitive solutions to problems.

In Chapter 9, the current extent of the quantified analytical approach is examined and the future assessed. Specific reference is made, as in many places throughout the book, to the role of this approach at the corporate level. Although current usage may in no way be described as being extensive, particularly in the case of planning decisions, it is increasing and it is suggested that the potential is considerable. This book attempts to discuss comprehensively the techniques and methodologies which it is to be hoped will enable more of this potential to be realised.

I should like to express my particular thanks to Mrs. Marjorie Richards, whose secretarial assistance and general support reduced the uncertainty surrounding the completion of this book to manageable proportions.

CONTENTS

Page

PREFACE

v

LIST OF ILLUSTRATIONS

xi

LIST OF TABLES

xiii

Chapter

1   THE INFLUENCE OF UNCERTAINTY ON
     DECISION MAKING   1
        Introduction; Risk and uncertainty; The basis of deci-
        sion making; A general discussion of utility; Utility
        "quantified;" The form of the utility curve—personality
        implications; General comments and summary.

2   THE PLANNING PROCESS AND THE ROLE OF
     THE MODEL   21
        Introduction; The decision making process; Deciding
        what?—The need for planning; Objectives and goals;
        The basis of the logical decision—the model; The
        mathematical model—interpretation and construction;
        A classification of mathematical models; The role of the
        computer in model building and usage; General
        comments and summary.

3   BASIC MATHEMATICS AND STATISTICS   54
        Introduction; Required mathematics; Statistics; De-
        scriptive statistics; Inferential statistics.

4   FORECASTING VARIABLES FOR PLANNING
     DECISIONS   93
        Introduction; The basis of forecasting; A classification
        of forecasting methods; The classical approach to fore-
        casting; Tracking methods; Non-linear trend curves;
        General comments and summary.

5   NETWORK ANALYSIS AND DECISION MAKING   128
        Introduction; The network: origins and construction;
        Analysis of the network; The allocation of resources;
        Activity durations which may be varied or are un-
        certain; The C.P.M. time-cost procedure; The PERT
        approach towards uncertainty; General comments and
        summary.

6   DECISION TREES   152
        Introduction; Selecting the alternative using expected
        values; The value of perfect and imperfect information;
        The effect of utility on the selection of the alternative;
        Further aspects of decision trees; Summary.

7   THE ROLE OF SIMULATION IN DECISION
      MAKING   176
          Introduction; An example of deterministic simulation;
          An example of probabilistic simulation; Simulation and
          the analysis of risk; Simulation in practice; General
          comments and summary.

8   THE OPTIMISING APPROACH TO PLANNING
      DECISIONS   209
          Introduction; The framework for optimisation; Opti-
          mising techniques; An example of linear programming;
          The manager and linear programming in practice;
          Linear programming extensions: non-linear program-
          ming; The objective function; Optimisation by experi-
          ment (hill climbing); General comments and summary.

9   QUANTITATIVE ANALYSIS AND PLANNING
      DECISIONS—PRESENT AND FUTURE   245
          Introduction; Current usage of quantitative methods
          within organisations; Problems associated with the
          quantitative approach to planning decisions; Future
          developments; Developments based on existing meth-
          ods; Other quantitative and analytic aids to planning
          decisions; Some final comments on the needs of
          management in the future.

APPENDIX I. SYMBOLS AND TERMINOLOGY   271

APPENDIX II. A TABLE OF RANDOM NUMBERS   276

INDEX   279

LIST OF ILLUSTRATIONS

Figure		Page
1	The decision/outcome relationship	2
2	Minimum and maximum utility of project outcomes	12
3	The utility function of the decision maker	15
4	Utility functions of different decision makers	16
5	Utility functions of different forms	18
6	The corporate planning framework	26
7	The position of the corporate planning group	27
8	A general classification of models	32
9	Total and company market for a product "explained" by the black box	39
10	Extrapolation of different functions	40
11	Graphical representation of an inequality	58
12	The graphical representation of the non-linear relationship $g = 200q - 0.05q^3 - 2000$	60
13	Histogram of transactions by value	71
14	Frequency polygon of transactions by value	72
15	Cumulative frequency distribution of transactions by value	73
16	Comparison between distributions	73
17	The normal distribution	81
18	The distribution of means of a sample of random numbers	83
19	The distribution of the mean of a sample size n taken from a population of arbitrary form	84
20	Relationships between two variables x and y	86
21	New axes drawn through the means of the x and y values	86
22	The effect of uncertainty in slope, m	101
23	The cyclical effect	107
24	The forecasting procedure	109
25	The effect of trend	110
26	"Tests" for forecasting methods	118
27	The time series of actual data in Table IX	120
28	The life cycle of a commodity or service	121
29	An activity with start and end events	130
30	The use of a dummy activity to achieve unique coding	131
31	The use of a dummy to indicate a constraint	131
32	A network analysed for E.E.T.s and L.E.T.s	133
33	Bar chart arising from analysis of the network shown in Fig. 32 and showing total float (hatched)	135
34	Demand for a resource. Activities commenced as early as possible	138
35	Resource demand smoothed by re-scheduling	139
36	The relationship between cost and time for a single activity	142

37	Optimisation using normal and crash times	142
38	Possible probability distributions of activity durations	144
39	An activity with three-time estimates of duration	146
40	Part of a network, indicating three-time activities	146
41	Normal distribution of E.E.T. of event 33 of Fig. 40 according to the upper and lower paths	148
42	The decision tree for two alternative products	154
43	The decision tree for two alternative products with chance outcomes	159
44	The effect of perfect information	164
45	The effect of imperfect information	165
46	The decision maker's utility function	169
47	Continuous and discrete representation of demand for product A	171
48	The timing of contribution (Fig. 43. Product A—home and abroad alternative)	173
49	An evaluation of best, worst and most likely combinations of demand and labour and materials costs (£000)	185
50	The cumulative probability of demand	191
51	An output distribution of contribution	193
52	Cumulative distributions of I.R.R. for two projects A and B	197
53	Choosing between two projects A and B	198
54	Ten alternatives summarised by their means and coefficients of variation	199
55	The ideal method of setting objectives	210
56	A resource-service matrix	211
57	Graphical representation of the linear programme	220
58	Piecewise linear functions	231
59	Two dimensional combinations with constraint	238
60	Optimisation by experiment	240
61	A local optimum X	241
62	An activity broken down into three alternatives depending on the quantity of resource consumed	257
63	The nine (3×3) paths through a probabilistic network of two activities	258

LIST OF TABLES

Table		Page
I	A comparison of 4 possible outcomes	5
II	A classification of the approach to decision making	8
III	Value of transactions through sixty distributors during a six month period	70
IV	The raw data of Table III placed in groups	70
V	U.K. production of nuclear electricity	99
VI	An example of fitting a straight line to arithmetic and logarithmic data	100
VII	Determination of seasonal effects	104
VIII	Interpreting seasonal factors	104
IX	Forecasting on the basis of exponential smoothing—smoothing constant 0.1 throughout	115
X	Selection of a trend curve by a study of slope transforms	124
XI	The probability distribution of a resource to meet a specific activity time	143
XII	Calculation of $E(t)$ and $V(t)$ from three-time estimates	147
XIII	Estimated annual contributions—from marketing at home and abroad, years 3–6 inclusive	158
XIV	The effect of discounting at 10 per cent per annum on the certainty equivalents of Fig. 43	173
XV	Probability distributions for demand, direct labour cost per unit and material cost per unit	184
XVI	Allocation of random numbers to the various levels of the input variables	187
XVII	Twenty simulations with an evaluation of gross profit in each case	188
XVIII	The output probability distribution of gross profit	189
XIX	Allocation of random digits to the various levels of demand	192
XX	The conditional relationship between production cost and quantity produced	194
XXI	Calculation of selection boundaries	201
XXII	The consequences of operating at the optimum and other feasible points (nearest whole number of models) (*See* Fig. 57)	221
XXIII	The initial basis tableau	226
XXIV	The optimum basis tableau	227
XXV	The flexibility of models	269

Chapter One

THE INFLUENCE OF UNCERTAINTY ON DECISION MAKING

INTRODUCTION

The purpose of this book is to define and describe procedures which are involved in making "logical" decisions (as defined shortly) at higher levels in organisations. The emphasis will be on the forward looking planning type of decision with which senior management is chiefly concerned. Broadly, most organisations may be seen to operate at three levels. The highest of these is necessarily the corporate level and the lowest the operational or tactical level. The area between the two may be described as the sub-corporate level. Decisions at the operational level are often taken in some isolation, in the sense that although it may be acknowledged that action based on the decision will have implications in other parts of the organisation, the effects may not be significant. Also decisions are often concerned with the reallocation of existing resources and as such are not part of an overall planning procedure. For example, many techniques have been found to be of value at the operational level to resolve problems of stock and production control, distribution, promotional effectiveness, and so on. In fact, some of the techniques which have been developed to aid decision making at the lower level will be used in this book, but in a different context.

It might be thought that the complexity of a decision (implying the amount of detail involved) would be related to its importance and would increase the higher the level at which it is made. At the present time this is not necessarily true, as whether the organisation be a company, a public body, or a national economy the stage is only just being reached when corporate decisions may in any sense be described as logical. As means of handling and analysing information improve, high level decisions will be able to take all relevant detail into account, but inevitably aggregation will continue to be necessary at this level to prevent decision makers being submerged in detail.

1

There remain the sub-corporate areas into which numerate analysis is penetrating and in which decisions influence significantly other activities within the organisation. It is quite possible that logical decision making will be applied here after it has been adopted at both the corporate and operational levels. For it is likely that in many instances senior management will accept the potential of appropriate analytical procedures at the corporate level and not wish to wait for the final stages of a lengthy "bottom-up" process in which one analytical brick is placed upon another. A corollary of this is that as senior managers become more experienced in the use of the decision aiding procedures which are described in this book they will seek further insight into the workings of their organisation through a "top-down" process in which the procedures will increasingly be adopted in sub-corporate areas.

Although this book is not concerned specifically with corporate planning, frequent references will be made to the procedure. Corporate objectives will be discussed, together with various sub-objectives and goals which emerge from them. It is recognised that in some quarters corporate decisions are seen to be largely political in nature, entirely dominating other considerations. If by political is implied "off-the-cuff," "intuitive" or "entrepreneurial" then there would seem little purpose in the holders of such views trying to familiarise themselves with the contents of this book. If on the other hand it is accepted that political considerations will be weighted no more than any other form of consideration, then these will be seen as just another, albeit important, set of constraints within which the organisation must operate. Furthermore if after careful analysis the alternative suggested is rejected on political or any non-economic grounds the relative cost of the policy adopted will be indicated. A few high costs arising from action of this nature may well tend to lessen the frequency of purely "political" decisions within an organisation.

Before proceeding to a study of procedures and techniques on

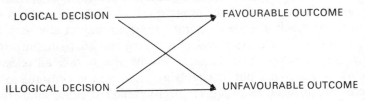

FIG. 1. The decision/outcome relationship.

which logical decisions are based, some thought must be given to the nature and consequences of decisions themselves. The prime responsibility which a manager must be prepared to accept is decision making. If in general the outcomes of decisions which he takes are favourable to the organisation by which he is employed the manager will be deemed to be successful. If not, his position must ultimately become untenable. The decision/outcome relationship may be summarised as in Fig. 1.

If we put aside for the moment the question of how logical decisions and favourable outcomes may be defined, but accept that they and their antitheses exist, a point of great significance may be made. This is that there is no guarantee when future uncertainty exists that on the one hand logical decisions lead to favourable outcomes and on the other that illogical decisions lead to unfavourable outcomes. In particular, nothing can be done for the "accident-prone" manager who despite painstaking analyses is seen in retrospect always to have taken the "wrong" decision. Similarly there exists the manager who seems always to be able to analyse the most complex of situations in a few moments, and consistently is seen to have made a decision which results in outcomes which are classed as favourable. The concern of this book is not with either of the aforementioned categories but with the large majority of decision makers who fall into neither group. It will be seen that in fact there can be no guarantee of a specific outcome if a planning decision of any realism is taken. It is however suggested that *on average* the proportion of favourable outcomes will be increased if logical decisions are taken.

RISK AND UNCERTAINTY

To a very large degree the future is unpredictable. High level decisions involving perhaps the major portion of an organisation's assets must be made against this background. It is necessary at the outset to consider the implications of making decisions when no specific outcome can be guaranteed. Current writings on managerial decision making contain a liberal scattering of the word "risk," frequently in conjunction with "uncertainty." Traditionally, a distinction has been made between risk and uncertainty on the grounds that in the former case the probability of the various possible outcomes was assumed known, whereas in the latter case the probabilities were unknown. Thus for example a gamble on the toss of a coin would take place under conditions of risk as equal probabilities would be intuitively applied to the two possible outcomes, whereas a gamble on the proportion of defective items produced by a brand new machine would occur under conditions of uncertainty. However, as there is an increasing tendency to apply probabilities to all possible outcomes, some writers see fit to use the words interchangeably.*

Again, other writers propose their own definitions† by which quite separate meanings are implied. Both risk and uncertainty are words used widely in everyday speech, and usually the former is associated with hazard or the consequences of mischance. It is suggested that it is of advantage to use this interpretation of risk in a managerial environment. A number of organisations may however claim that they operate under risk-free conditions. In the case of the small company, management may feel so confident of an assured and continuing market that favourable outcomes will inevitably arise from the decisions which are taken. A large organisation may feel that the sheer bulk of their operations will provide so much momentum that providing management maintain current efficiency the effect of a few loss ventures may be shrugged off. And although national governments may be very conscious of the risk factor, local government may feel suitably buttressed against risk, at least in a financial sense, by the income generating and fund raising procedures at its disposal. Perhaps intuitive notions of mischance serve to make the occasional unsatisfactory venture almost welcome on the grounds that "things would be too good to be true if every project were successful." Of course, in all of these cases, management is inefficient. The future cannot be ignored nor should general acceptance of the inevitability of success or failure be part of planning philosophy. Unfavourable outcomes will of course occur and before making any decisions the consequences of mischance should be taken into account. In order to do this a distinction is made between uncertainty and risk, which are defined in the following way:

UNCERTAINTY: A situation in which the state of an individual or organisation is subject to change, as a result of which more than one possible outcome may arise.

* See IRA HOROWITZ, *Decision Making and the Theory of the Firm*, Holt, Rinehart and Winston, Inc., New York, 1970, p. 86.

† See T. R. DYCKMAN, S. SMIDT, A. K. MCADAMS, *Management Decision Making under Uncertainty*, Macmillan, London, 1969, pp. 31, 424.

RISK: Acknowledgment of the fact that the state of an individual or organisation measured by any criterion may become relatively less acceptable due to the occurrence of a particular outcome.

It is important to note that in defining risk, reference is made to outcomes which are *relatively* less acceptable. In other words, in addition to those outcomes which are positively unfavourable, such as the occurrence of a loss, favourable outcomes of differing degree must be compared. If change from the present asset position is considered and the estimated worth of alternative outcomes listed in Table I are compared it will be seen that C and D appear favourable, A unfavourable, and B of no advantage (B may have been the

TABLE I: A COMPARISON OF FOUR POSSIBLE OUTCOMES

Outcome	Change from present asset position
A	−£10,000
B	0
C	£15,000
D	£20,000

outcome arising from having taken no action at all). In everyday parlance, A and possibly B would be seen to involve risk whereas C and D would not. In the sense of the above definition C also involves risk; namely the risk (or opportunity cost) of £5000, by which the increase in assets falls short of outcome D.

A problem exists in evaluating outcomes. It is preferable to consider the net liquid asset position of the organisation arising from each possible outcome. Cash flows should therefore be amended to the anticipated equivalent net liquid asset position at the completion of the project. Here, change from the current net liquid asset position will be employed. This is felt to be more appropriate, as it is desirable that major decisions should be evaluated quite specifically and independently. Such decisions will not be made with great frequency and each must be considered in the light of the impact on the asset position of the organisation up to the planning horizon.

One further semantic point before proceeding. In the precise sense of the above definitions of risk and uncertainty, it may be concluded that whilst uncertainty does not necessarily imply risk, the acceptance of risk most definitely implies uncertainty. It is not difficult to think of occasions when an individual may find himself in situations of uncertainty to which no risk is attached. However, the reader may wish to exercise his imagination in order to suggest situations of uncertainty surrounding an *organisation's* actions which do not involve risk. Perhaps surprisingly at first sight, these situations transpire to be trivial. Even the state of the weather during the annual outing may have a significant effect on morale and hence on immediate future production! This of course supports the view of those who hold that risk and uncertainty amount to the same thing. The advantage claimed here is that by proposing two definitions, repeated emphasis can be given by the use of the word risk to the *relative* consequences of the different outcomes possible.

THE BASIS OF DECISION MAKING

On what basis are decisions being taken in organisations? One classification would list those which are claimed to be logical and those which appear illogical. It is not necessarily true, however, that these two categories should be described as mutually exclusive. In fact, the vast majority of planning decisions which are taken are a mixture of the logical and the illogical. In many instances, the illogical portion may be due to an unwillingness to commit additional expenditure for further analysis. For example, the cost of achieving a truly random sample in market research is often prohibitive, and strictly a decision which is taken on the basis of the sample results and in the knowledge that bias may be involved is an illogical one.

On the basis of the foregoing comments, it would seem appropriate to define a logical decision as follows:

> LOGICAL DECISION: A decision which is taken utilising all known and relevant methods of analysis and interpretation, up to the point when it is concluded that the extra expenditure incurred in making the analysis is not justified in terms of the increase obtained in the discriminatory power of the decision.

Again it is stressed that there is no definite relationship between a logical decision and an acceptable outcome. Many acceptable outcomes have arisen following decisions which are seen later to have been illogical, and of course the converse applies with equal force. Both have unfortunate consequences for the organisation. In the former case a manager's reputation may be enhanced unjustifiably, creating the opportunity for him to make a further decision in similar manner with disastrous consequences (how many companies would accept an Adolf Hitler as their Chief Executive?—a decade or so of brilliant intuition followed by the decision to invade Russia). The word "entrepreneur" carries its own mystique with overtones of glamour, and is associated by some with brilliant strokes of decision making. It would be interesting to learn how many current chief executives see themselves wholly as entrepreneurs. The latter certainly continue to exist and probably always will, but if a rather cynical description of an entrepreneur as "a person with a high probability of making an erroneous decision" is accepted, it would seem to be an unfortunate "profession" to embark upon: one not in great demand by a modern organisation of any size. The most unfortunate of men are of course managers who make logical decisions and continue to suffer the consequence of unacceptable outcomes. One would hope that their organisations are sufficiently tolerant to support them and that ultimately they will indeed achieve a favourable outcome. As implied earlier, the major proposition of this book is that management and their organisations will *in general* benefit by making logical decisions. Favourable outcomes arising out of illogical decisions and unfavourable outcomes arising out of logical decisions (the latter receiving no doubt some publicity) will it is claimed then form a smaller proportion of the total outcomes arising.

Managers *capable* of making planning decisions logically will increasingly be demanded by organisations, but there remains a very long way to go before the stage is reached when even a substantial proportion of decision makers actually *adopt* this approach. A major feature in delaying this desirable state is the lack of appreciation of the *need* by senior management. And even where the need is recognised, management is often constrained by lack of suitably qualified support personnel in service departments. Despite the fact that inevitable progress in management technique is universally accepted, many organisations, particularly those which are of a smaller size, seem unable to reach the point of take-off at which they commit themselves wholeheartedly to the task of making logical decisions. What environment, then, is necessary for the taking of logical decisions? A start must be made somewhere, and it is in this respect that corporate strategy and strategic planning are so vital.

There is of course a good deal of the chicken and the egg at this stage. Logical decisions are themselves necessary in order to determine what corporate strategy might be, and organisations may wish to operate in an iterative way so that an acceptable corporate policy is reached only after the passage of time. This approach is recommended by leading authorities as in many cases being the most appropriate method of introducing corporate planning. Thus although a current corporate objective may be known to be deficient in some respects, it is most important that once having been accepted all decisions made with reference to it should be logical in the sense defined above.

A list of decision approaches which qualify to be described as logical is given in Table II.

TABLE II: A CLASSIFICATION OF THE APPROACH TO DECISION MAKING

		Without utility consideration	With utility consideration
A	Objective but empirical		
B	Analytical but deterministic		
C	Analytical and probabilistic		

Category A is included in recognition of the fact that many decisions will continue to be made to a large degree intuitively on the basis of a summary of appropriate information. For example, in private industry the implications of dividend policy may be seen as so wide as to defy decision making which is other than empirical. And in the public sector, until social cost and output measurement may be acceptably included in analyses, empirical decisions based on the value judgments of individuals or committees will continue to be taken. The major part of this book will be concerned with the categories B and C, on the basis that there will be a continual trend from instinctive to analytical decision making and thus from category A to categories B and C as causal relationships become increasingly understood. Referring to Table II, decisions are further classified according to whether they are made with or without considerations of "utility." This is not the utility described in classical economics, and in fact some writers prefer to use the word "preference."

A GENERAL DISCUSSION OF UTILITY

Utility relating to organisational decisions is encountered in a number of contexts, including utility indices, utility functions, preference curves, etc.* The following general definition of utility is seen as being appropriate here:

UTILITY: A measure of the value attached by a decision maker to a range of possible alternative and exhaustive outcomes, one of which it is anticipated will arise by chance following a decision. The value is assessed in the light of corporate or individual circumstances likely to be contemporaneous with the outcome.

Although business executives are becoming increasingly aware of the need to possess some appreciation of the concepts of probability to deal with uncertainty, the logical step of specifically evaluating a range of possible outcomes has not yet received the same attention. Apart from the frequently expressed view that such considerations are automatically taken into account, an explanation for this omission is that although the principles of utility are easily understood it is difficult to include these explicitly in decision making. There is also the problem of realistic and consistent quantification of utility. If logical decisions are, however, to be made it is not sufficient to assume that the decision maker will intuitively take into account the effect on the organisation of the possible failure or success of a project. He will certainly be aware that if the organisation's position in respect of future funds is somewhat insecure, then high risk projects should not be undertaken. If on the other hand the organisation's financial position is very secure, then his attitude may be completely different and high risk projects may be undertaken with equanimity. However, between these extremes lies a whole range of decisions whose outcome is more or less significant to the organisation. The purpose of the utility approach is to attempt to quantify the attitude of the decision maker (or his organisation) towards the range of possible changes from the current asset situation.

The major concepts of utility theory can be introduced quickly. Consider the offer of a sale of a gamble to three individuals X, Y, and Z. The gamble is the outcome of a *single* toss of a penny. In the event of a head then a gain of £100 ensues and in the event of a tail a loss of £100 is involved. The three decision makers are confronted with a situation in respect of which two comments may be made. In the first place, many managers adopt a "long-run" (*i.e.* repeated)

---

* See T. R. DYCKMAN, S. SMIDT, A. K. MCADAMS, *Management Decision Making under Uncertainty*, Macmillan, London, 1969, pp. 308–313.

view of decisions under uncertainty, even though in general decisions are unique. Additionally in this hypothetical example, X, Y, and Z are involved in a situation in which their *personal* assets are assumed to be at stake. Suppose that the personalities of the three individuals are different: X is an ultra-cautious individual, Y sees himself as being very logical and Z is something of a gambler. It is possible that X and Y's initial decision will be different from Z, in that both will decline to take the gamble. In the world of business, however, it is not possible to postpone forever the taking of decisions without incurring some penalty. It is therefore proposed that all three are required individually to negotiate their participation in, or freedom from, the gamble. Individual X has been described as ultra-cautious, and as such is least likely to be desirous of participating in the gamble. In fact, he will be prepared to pay to be freed from it. How much he will pay will depend very much on his current asset position. If his current assets are low, then the level of these will set a limit on what he can afford to pay and of course as his assets rise the amount he is prepared to pay will also rise. Turning to Y, the logical decision maker, what is his attitude? He is aware that if the gamble were repeated over and over the average value would approximate to £0, but he is also aware of course that if after any number of gambles the cumulative gain is £0 then the next gamble will convert this into $+£100$ or $-£100$, so that this approach is not the complete answer when dealing with a single course of action. Nevertheless Y's attitude will be determined on the one hand by his thoughts that in the long run the gamble is worth nothing and on the other hand by the existing state of his assets. All one can say is that for a given level of initial assets Y will pay somewhat less than X to avoid being involved in the gamble. Our final individual, Z, is an entirely different character. He is encountered in all walks of life being prepared to gamble on anything from a frog jumping competition to an election. In business, with perhaps the one exception discussed below, he can be a menace, although as implied earlier many successful gamblers bear the description of entrepreneur. Individual Z is in fact actually prepared to pay for the privilege of participating in the gamble (although he is informed that this will take place once only). Speculation can lead to thoughts that Z might be prepared to pay more than £100, but realistically one would not expect anything approaching this sum to be involved. With reference to the exception case referred to above it must be accepted that even the most cautious decision maker may tend to become a gambler if his solvency is in jeopardy and in these cases such an approach may be accepted as being justifiable. Thus if X's assets are steadily being eroded he will tend to avoid the gamble until his assets become less than £100, when he will become under increasing pressure to participate. This general discussion has been developed at some length in order to stress the following points:

(a) Separate decision makers may view the same decision quite differently.
(b) For an individual decision maker, his decision will be influenced by the current asset position of himself or his organisation.
(c) Many planning decisions, probably the majority in business, refer to unique, non-repetitive situations.

UTILITY "QUANTIFIED"

It is necessary to attempt a quantification of utility in order to compare the attitudes of individual decision makers or the attitudes agreed by empowered decision making groups within organisations. The first bridge to be crossed is that linking the individual and his personal circumstances with the organisation. If the individuals X, Y, and Z mentioned above are characterised by the manner in which they conduct their personal affairs, will this apply also to their handling of the assets of their organisation? Further, will their attitudes remain constant over time? These questions are not at all easy to answer. As will be seen from the discussion which follows it is possible at any given time to quantify a decision maker's attitude to risk. It is difficult to disentangle attitudes towards changes in his own personal asset situation (which in most cases will be relatively stable) from attitudes which he holds towards changes in the asset position of his organisation (which are likely to be more variable). The problem is largely behavioural and one which has profound implications in respect of an organisation's operating effectiveness, but it is felt to be of sufficient importance to warrant devoting some space to quantified attitudes towards risk, on the understanding that these may well influence the ultimate "logical" decision which is taken. Some consideration will be given to the behavioural aspects involved following the example now to be developed.

Let us take the case of the manager who has authority to incur expenditure on projects up to the sum of £50,000 and who during a given time period will make one such decision of this nature. Assume that in relation to a particular project the present value (as defined in Chapter 3) of the most profitable outcome envisaged is £100,000 above the current asset position and of the least profitable outcome is £100,000 below the current asset position. Then this manager by his decisions will be responsible for a change in the asset position of the organisation by some amount in the range −£100,000– +£100,000. (It is of course necessary in a practical situation to take into account the value of any physical assets existing at the planning horizon involved, and some writers* go further and suggest the inclusion of allowances for non-monetary assets such as expertise and opportunities for expansion.) The two amounts −£100,000 and +£100,000 represent respectively minimum and maximum utility in respect of possible financial outcomes. This is shown graphically in Fig. 2.

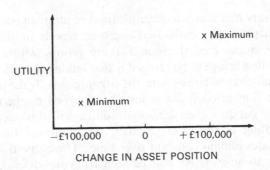

FIG. 2. Minimum and maximum utility of project outcomes.

Two questions are now raised:

1. What numerical values may be given to maximum, minimum and intermediate utilities?
2. How may changes from current asset position within the range −£100,000 to +£100,000 be evaluated in terms of utility?

Question 1 has been the subject of some discussion, but it is agreed generally that the most appropriate values are 1 for maximum

* *See*, for example, ROBERT SCHLAIFER, *Analysis of Decisions under Uncertainty*, McGraw-Hill, New York, 1969, pp. 45–49.

utility and 0 for minimum utility This suggests immediately a range of utility between 0 and 1 which in turn calls for some interpretation of a utility of, say, 0.8. It must be stressed that whatever interpretation is given to 0.8 this must not imply that a utility of this magnitude is twice as acceptable as a utility of 0.4. Utility is measured on an ordinal scale, and all that may be inferred is that an alternative possessing a utility of 0.8 is to be preferred to one of 0.4, which in turn is to be preferred to a utility of 0.2. It is Question 2 which is of major significance in relation to the performance of individual managers within an organisation. For example, faced with the possibility of undertaking a given project, how would three managers quite separately rate the utility of no change in current asset position?

It is appropriate at this point to suggest that writers on the theory of utility give insufficient prominence to the inevitable association of risk with utility. Assessment of utility only arises when a number of outcomes due to chance are possible, and thus in the case of making no change from the current situation the utility approach is of relevance only by an evaluation of the possible outcomes arising from undertaking alternative projects. Utility considerations may then be applied to the unchanged asset position but not for example to making no payment on power bills (when the outcome will be certain!). Or again, if one customer is prepared to pay £10,000 for certain goods whereas another customer will pay only £9,500, utility does not enter into these alternatives as no uncertainty is involved.

The answer to the problem posed of not proceeding with a project may be achieved in an indirect but simple manner, using again the 50:50 gamble involved in the toss of a coin. How much would a manager be prepared that his *organisation* should pay to participate in a gamble in which there was an equal chance of making a gain of £100,000 or a loss of £100,000? It is virtually certain that except in the case of possible bankruptcy, he would not wish his organisation to be involved at all. Suppose that he had to think in terms of the sum the organisation should pay to avoid being involved in the gamble. Now this may appear completely alien to the current thinking of management. The decision whether or not to go ahead with a project is customarily based on some financial criterion such as the estimated return on investment. If the project does not come up to minimum requirements or some other project is seen as being superior then it is not pursued. Because of this it may be easier for the manager to think along different lines and consider two 50:50 outcomes, one of which will result in a gain of £100,000 and the other a loss of £100,000 and for which insurance against the latter is sought. For the time period under consideration it may then be concluded that a premium of £10,000 would just be in order. Thus this definite amount of −£10,000 (*i.e.* £10,000 worse than current asset position) is given the utility which represents a 50:50 gamble for +£100,000 or −£100,000. This fixed and finite sum has been described as a "certainty equivalent."

> CERTAINTY EQUIVALENT: A change in asset position for which the decision maker is indifferent between accepting the change and being involved in a gamble.

The utilities allocated to the extreme amounts of +£100,000 and −£100,000 are 1 and 0 respectively and the required utility of the 50:50 gamble is 50 per cent of 1 plus 50 per cent of 0, that is 0.5 (this will be elaborated upon in Chapter 3). Therefore a utility of 0.5 attaches to a £10,000 decrease from current asset position, which is the certainty equivalent of the gamble. Furthermore, the change in current asset position corresponding to other utilities may be found by repeated application of the 50:50 gamble. Take the change in assets just mentioned of −£10,000 and assume that this amount or +£100,000 be determined by the outcome of the gamble. These two possible outcomes must together be worth some certain amount within the range −£10,000−+£100,000 which after due consideration may be assessed at £30,000. The utility of this amount will then be 50 per cent of the utility of −£10,000 (0.5) and 50 per cent of +£100,000 (1.0) and so will be 0.75. Extending the concept of insurance to equiprobable −£100,000 and −£10,000 (that is a loss of at least £10,000) this might suggest that an amount of −£60,000 will correspond to the utility of 0.25. Repeated use of this approach will enable the graph of Fig. 3 to be constructed. The general form of the curve which may be drawn through calculated utilities will be discussed below. It is assumed for now that the continuous curve ABC shown in Fig. 3 emerges. ABC is termed the utility function of our manager who has authority to incur expenditure on projects up to the sum of £50,000, which may lead to a change from current asset position of £100,000. The utility function ABC may be compared with the straight line joining A and B. The latter is the utility function which would arise if the decision maker adopted a "long-run" attitude (as individual Y earlier), as though the outcomes of many similar projects could be averaged. Thus a 50:50 gamble between −£100,000 and +£100,000 viewed in this way would suggest a certainty equivalent of £0. The difference of £10,000 between £0 and −£10,000 which for both certainty equivalents possess a utility of 0.5 might be termed the "risk premium" (BD in Fig. 3) and is a measure of a decision maker's "risk aversion."

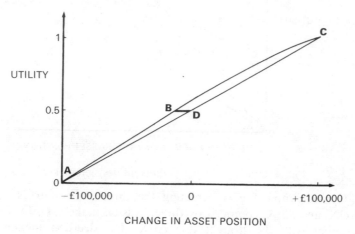

FIG. 3. The utility function of the decision maker.

THE FORM OF THE UTILITY CURVE—PERSONALITY IMPLICATIONS

It will be seen from Fig. 3 that the risk premium, being the horizontal distance between ABC and ADC, decreases as one moves further away from current asset position. This is consistent with intuitive attitudes towards risk. The points on the curve ABC are determined by successively taking two outcomes equivalent to converging asset positions. In practice only sufficient points (up to, say, nine) need be established to enable a reasonable curve to be drawn in. If the procedure were repeated the decision maker would ultimately be confronted near the upper extreme point with placing a value on a 50:50 chance of £100,000 or £99,000. Obviously the utility of this gamble would be a little different from a certain £100,000 or £99,000 or any intermediate value. Similar considerations would apply in respect of a 50:50 gamble involving −£100,000 and −£99,000 in which region points on ABC and ADC almost coincide. This must not however be taken as indicating symmetrical attitudes towards utility at each of the extreme ends of the range; quite the reverse. It can easily be shown by reference to the gradient of the utility function that the most rapid increase in utility for a given increase in asset position occurs at the lower extreme.

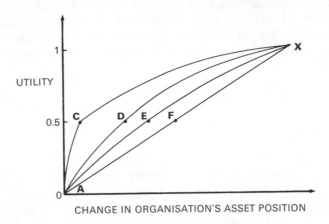

FIG. 4. Utility functions of different decision makers.

Consider now Fig. 4 depicting the three utility curves ACX, ADX, and AEX, compiled by three decision makers, C, D, and E, together with the straight line AFX. The decision makers are assumed to operate under identical circumstances. Note that at a utility of 0.5 the risk premium DF from curve ADX is greater than the risk premium EF from curve AEX, and that the same is true for these two curves at any utility. This means that the decision maker D is consistently a more risk averse individual as far as his organisation is concerned than decision maker E. Similarly C is more risk averse than both D and E. The purpose of including ACX is to permit consideration of the general form of the utility curve. C is a point of discontinuity on either side of which the risk premium decreases, the decrease being particularly sharp as utility increases. A point of discontinuity may feasibly occur in the loss region if for example the loss is of such an amount that certain financial require-ments are jeopardised, *e.g.* necessary retained earnings or the ability to pay a particular dividend. Similarly one may envisage points of discontinuity to the right of the present asset position when, say, a corporate target would be reached. In general, however, particu-larly in the larger organisation where the impact of individual projects would be relatively smaller one would expect continuous curves of the type ADX and AEX. In the event of "irregularities" which cannot be smoothed out or explained it would be necessary for the decision maker to reassess his calculations for consistency.

The problem of consistency has been discussed elsewhere at some length. Schlaifer* suggests that in addition to the 50:50 gamble reference gambles should be employed as an alternative means of constructing a utility curve. In our earlier example we saw that by using the 50:50 gamble a utility of 0.75 was given to the sum of £30,000. Without examining too deeply the implications of a reference gamble involving a 3 in 4 chance of gaining +£100,000 and a 1 in 4 chance of losing —£100,000 it may be accepted that the worth of this gamble will have the utility $(0.75 \times 1) + (0.25 \times 0)$, that is 0.75. If therefore the decision maker does not evaluate this reference gamble at £30,000 he is acting inconsistently. Methods exist which assist decision makers to assess the value to them of a reference gamble involving chances of say 3 in 4 and 1 in 4. Using cross-checking and iterative methods to build up a utility curve it would indeed be a source of much satisfaction if it could be assumed that a uniquely consistent curve would emerge. If a decision maker "refuses" to be consistent, however, how may he be "brought into line"? The use of leading questions is self-defeating. When one realises that the individual in addition to being inconsistent is also variable, in the sense that his attitudes vary from day to day as a result of his digestion, the weather, his relationship with his colleagues and so on, it may perhaps be questioned whether an entirely stable utility curve exists at all. Nevertheless, sufficient has been written about research into utility to assume that in general continuous curves are appropriate and reasonably stable. And as the 50:50 gamble is the easiest to handle conceptually it is felt that the use of this approach to determine the certainty equivalent of gambles at utilities of 0.25, 0.50, and 0.75 in addition to 0 and 1 is the best method of generating the function. If a smooth curve is not initially a good fit, then discussion with the decision maker, or decision making body should enable a more acceptable form to be achieved. This is not to suggest however that the curve should lie entirely to one side of the straight line joining the extreme outcomes. It is quite possible that a curve possessing a point of inflection will describe a decision maker's attitude, as for example AGX and AHX in Fig. 5. In both cases, at the present asset position, the curves lie above the straight line between A and X; in other words in this

---

* See ROBERT SCHLAIFER, *Analysis of Decisions under Uncertainty*, McGraw-Hill, New York, 1969, pp. 151–153.

region the decision makers G and H are risk averse (the curves are made to intersect above the current asset position for convenience of comparison). In the region of improvement on current asset position, however, G consistently places lower utility on additions to current asset position than does H and in fact in crossing the straight line AX adopts a position in which he is showing some indifference to additions to his organisation's assets. G in fact might view somewhat cynically the "extreme" outcome X. As far as he is concerned this may be placed so far to the right of the position indicated in Fig. 5 that utility barely increases as the asset position improves. It is of

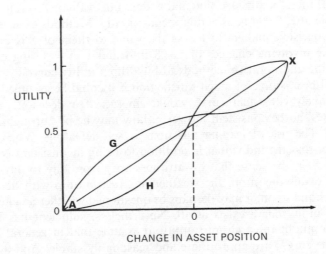

CHANGE IN ASSET POSITION

FIG. 5. Utility functions of different forms.

course unlikely that a decision maker possessing this attitude would commit his thoughts to paper (if indeed he were conscious of them) but such managers undoubtedly exist. Providing the project is profitable in any sense and in excess of some financial datum, they are content. At the same time, G is very averse to projects which may make a loss. In a large organisation G's activities, while not adding much to profitability, may attract little attention in respect of opportunity cost. In a small organisation, however, or for that matter in a larger organisation with a "corporate G-type attitude," there will be a tendency towards stagnation and missed opportunities.

The utility curve of H is the converse of that of G. In the region of addition to current assets H adopts the more "rational" attitude of placing a premium on risk, but for the major part of the loss range he assumes the gambler's attitude and places a much lower utility than G on individual loss values. This implies a degree of indifference to his organisation making a loss. It is difficult to imagine a curve in the form of AHX representing the attitude of a decision maker in a *large* company. In this case it would be expected that the "gambler's attitude" would apply across the full range of outcomes and the utility curve would lie below AX for all changes in asset position. It is however feasible to associate the preferences held by H with his deep involvement in a small organisation in considerable danger of insolvency. Prospective gains are viewed conservatively whereas losses because of their probably fatal consequences are viewed in rather cavalier fashion. For example, it may be considered that an insurance premium of only £10,000 would be set against a 50:50 gamble involving zero gain and a loss of £100,000.

GENERAL COMMENTS AND SUMMARY

The major aim of this chapter has been to prepare a foundation for the study and appreciation of the techniques and analytical procedures which follow. In particular, as planning decisions are concerned with the future, to which uncertainty and hence risk attach, an attempt has been made to pre-empt any notion that analysis (whether quantitative or not) will automatically dictate the decision to be taken. This situation will not exist until the response to stimuli of all things whether natural or physical is known with certainty. We are still some millennia from this (happy?) state of affairs.

Thus at the beginning of the Chapter it was stressed that outcomes entirely favourable to the organisation cannot be guaranteed, no matter what effort is put into making the decision. If a number of outcomes are possible "uncertainty" exists, and some at least of these outcomes will have relatively unfavourable consequences for the organisation (even if the risk is the opportunity cost of not having achieved a more favourable outcome). The contention is that decision makers in total should assume that a supernatural agency is not operating against their interests and should therefore adopt a "logical" decision making approach (with which ensuing Chapters will be concerned) with the expectancy that overall the proportion of favourable outcomes will be increased. If an unfavourable outcome follows a decision which has been made in a logical manner rather than by hunch a decision maker is entitled to feel disgruntled at the least if the experience is repeated on two or three occasions!

The discussion on utility was introduced in order that maximum account may be taken of the different attitudes of decision making bodies towards risk. The majority of high level decisions are non-repetitive and hence each needs to be analysed and considered in relation to the situation prevailing within an organisation at a specific moment in time. The circumstances within organisations should influence the utility attitudes of decision makers, but the personalities of individuals may lead to inconsistencies. Very large organisations with a high frequency of decision making should be able to tolerate, more than the small organisation, a "long-run" approach, particularly in the region of decrease from existing asset position. This would, for example, enable relatively greater research and development effort within the larger organisation. Alternatively, a small company in some danger of falling into financial difficulty would be likely to opt for the less risky of two alternative courses of action whereas a company actually in financial difficulty may well see a high risk, high return venture as being preferable to one with a low risk and a low return. As stated, however, there is no guarantee that the personal utility function of the decision maker will satisfy the needs of his organisation. For example, the necessity for a gamble to be taken is unlikely to be satisfied by a decision maker possessing extreme risk aversion. Although the implications of circumstances such as these are highly significant, they fall more within the purview of the behavioural specialist. This book must assume that consistency of utility attitude exists between decision makers and the organisations by which they are employed.

Chapter Two

THE PLANNING PROCESS AND THE ROLE OF THE MODEL

INTRODUCTION

In Chapter 1, in order to focus attention on certain implications of making decisions within an organisation, detailed consideration was not given to the decision process itself nor to the way in which the need to make decisions arises. After discussing briefly the nature and process of decision making, this Chapter will be concerned with the type of environment most conducive to logical decision making. The latter, it will be suggested, is stimulated by an organisational structure in which strategic planning in the operational and corporate sense is highly developed. Finally the fundamental role of the model as the basis for logical decision making will be developed.

THE DECISION MAKING PROCESS

Every time a manager exercises his judgment he is making a decision. This is true whether this relates to the time he will finish work for the day or whether he will authorise the expenditure of £50,000 on a project. Any judgment which he makes involving the interests of the organisation on whose behalf he is acting has therefore some significance. There must, however, be some point up to which intuitive decision making is acceptable on the grounds that the opportunity cost of the time taken up by the decision is apparently small and a high degree of discrimination is not required. This does not imply that such an intuitive decision is illogical; suitable account must be taken of a manager's ability to exercise the correct judgment in these circumstances as a result of experience and expertise. Our concern is with those decisions in respect of which both opportunity cost and possible outcomes (taking full account of utility) are significant and off-the-cuff judgments are therefore unacceptable.

A number of points arise from the definition of a logical decision given in Chapter 1. First, there is the suggestion that a logical decision normally requires considerable involvement of management over a period of time. It may well be that the final step will be a formality, but in general managerial contribution will have been required at specific points in the analysis. Managers should in fact be more concerned with the "process" of decision making rather than the final decision itself. If this were not so then given certain operating rules the situation would be reduced to one of automatic selection, obviating the need for a manager at all. This latter procedure will tend to occur increasingly, particularly at operational levels, as information systems and techniques of analysis become more sophisticated, leading to a steady conversion of what were originally time-consuming decisions into routine and automatic instructions. There will however continue to be the planning decision, often of increased complexity, which by its novelty and background of uncertainty will require the full attention and involvement of the manager. The taking of a decision should therefore be thought of not simply as the moment of time when resources are committed but rather the span of time between accepting that analysis should proceed and the actual resource committal. Another comment which has already been partly implied is that only those decisions which are based on realistic and relevant analysis (which need not necessarily be mainly quantitative) are our concern. This leads directly to the problem of deciding which decisions require analysis and what effort should be expended in the analysis. A general conclusion which barely needs substantiating is that very many major decisions are taken on the basis of little or no formal analysis of any kind. Accepting that managers themselves have insufficient time to devote to exhaustive analysis, who will undertake this task for them? A number of considerations apply: size and financial strength of the organisation, services available to management, and the nature of the decision itself. In some organisations there may be unwillingness to commit resources to assist the decision making process and at the other extreme there exist organisations which for a variety of reasons support analytical services to management but do not take full advantage of their potential contribution. A very rough and ready guide to reasonable expenditure in this direction in money terms is the "1 per cent rule" which suggests that 1 per cent of anticipated outlay on a venture is justified in planning what the appropriate course of action should be. For example £10 prior to purchasing a £1000 car, £100 prior to purchasing a £10,000 house and £10,000 in taking a decision on a £1,000,000 project. This aspect will not be pursued here. Suffice to state that for an annual expenditure of £25,000 a small management services group of four or five persons may be maintained. The emphasis is on directed service to management but it should be recognised that in addition to fulfilling this role the group is a potential source of ideas which may be worth much more to the organisation than the £25,000 apparent cost per annum.

A major purpose of this book is to attempt to acquaint the manager with a sufficient understanding and appreciation of basic quantitative methodology and analyses appropriate for the decision process. It is the firmly held opinion of the author that at the least the manager should have an appreciation of the methodology and analysis involved. And, according to the significance of the decision, he should be prepared to familiarise himself with each stage of the decision process. For high level planning decisions the suggestion is that a meaningful dialogue should be established between general and function managers, and planning and management service groups. This can only be achieved if each group have sufficient knowledge of a common language to enable effective communication to be established.

DECIDING WHAT?—THE NEED FOR PLANNING

Some space has been taken up in considering what constitutes a logical decision. What must now be considered are the circumstances in which such decisions arise. Given that a company is contemplating a new factory then where should this be located? Given that a local authority is considering an increase in the sum to be spent on road building then how should this be used? What must first be questioned is whether a new factory should be built at all, or might for example some of the expenditure on road building be more appropriately allocated to school building? To answer questions such as these one must consider an organisation's *raison d'être*. This must be either to make a profit or provide a service or some combination of both. In every case, investment decisions must be taken in respect of the resources over which the organisation has control. Decisions of this nature imply futurity and hence uncertainty. Therefore although an organisation understands (one would hope!) why it is in existence and what is its purpose in society it cannot state that its investment decisions *will* achieve certain results but only that the decisions are *aimed* at achieving those results. It will be argued in the early part of this Chapter that effective and efficient use of an organisation's resources can only be achieved by the adoption of some formal planning process.

It is pertinent to dwell upon the many aspects and descriptions of organisational planning. We have in addition to corporate planning, strategic, long range, short range, tactical and operational planning, to mention a few of the most widely used, in addition to the more specific functional planning (for example, financial) and the methodology involved (for example, optimising). Obviously there is much scope for confusion here. Ackoff* presents an excellent and lucid analysis, but one which this author feels does not conform completely with the approach adopted in this book. The main point at issue is the word "strategy," which Ackoff associates firmly with the long term. Here the following definition of strategic planning will be used:

STRATEGIC PLANNING: A course of action concerned with the setting and means of achievement of realistic objectives or major goals which within any set of constraints internally or externally imposed is accepted as being the best course possible.

Note that the strategic plan is defined in terms of being *accepted* as the best course of action rather than being that course of action which *is* the best. The difficulty of recognising the best course of action need not be emphasised. The concern of this book is with logical decisions which it is claimed will enable this ideal to be approached. It is suggested therefore that if in an organisation the decision making body feels unable due to shortage of time or resources to explore all the alternatives fully (and in how many organisations is this achieved?) then it is still entitled to describe its plans as being strategic. It must however be borne in mind that decision making bodies would only rarely claim that a best course of action leading to a corporate objective could be determined without appreciable discussion and analysis. Strategic planning, therefore, in which one sets out with a purpose and adopts an. approach which is seen as being the best among alternatives, may be used to qualify all other forms of planning. In particular, we

---

* *See* RUSSELL L. ACKOFF, *A Concept of Corporate Planning*, John Wiley & Sons, Inc., New York, 1970, Chapter 1.

can recognise two of these, namely, corporate and operational
planning, which can be defined in the following terms:

CORPORATE PLANNING: The determination of the action
necessary in respect of the allocation
and control of resources and, if
possible, control of the environment
to achieve organisational objectives
which are set, taking account of
internal and external factors.

OPERATIONAL PLANNING: The determination of the action
necessary in respect of the allocation
and control of resources and, if
possible, control of the environment, to achieve within areas of the
organisation objectives which may
or may not be consistent with the
corporate plan.

We are now in a position to describe the major planning processes
within an organisation. For example, corporate planning in which
a conscious search for the optimum is undertaken would be termed
strategic corporate planning, or perhaps preferably corporate
strategy. In the latter case we may then define long range and short
range corporate strategy. Short range operational strategy may for
example be concerned with establishing raw material input and
necessary production capacity to meet forecast demand during the
year ahead. As planning efficiency improves it is anticipated that
operational planning will increasingly become a sub-set of corporate
planning.

The implications of these definitions and the interaction between
corporate and operational planning may best be considered by
reference to Fig. 6, which outlines a model framework of suggested
general application. In this respect, whatever the type of organisation, the chief executive will define the upper boundary below which
decisions will be taken. In the private sector of industry corporate
planning in the strict sense can only be achieved if there is no down-
ward flow of resource control (other than environmental) through
the boundary. For example, a subsidiary company may only be
said to employ corporate planning if the parent company permits
absolute freedom of action, in which case the relationship between
the companies makes little sense. As soon as the subsidiary confronts

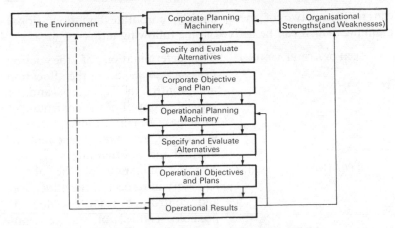

F<small>IG</small>. 6. The corporate planning framework.

its parent with a request for capital, the problem of resource allocation at corporate level arises. Despite this, many subsidiaries would
claim that corporate planning is meaningful in their context. Corporate planning in the public sector is not so easy to define. Strictly,
the government itself is the only body capable of planning at this
level. One would hope, however, that the huge nationalised industries could be viewed as adopting a corporate approach although
they themselves may object to the way their performance is evaluated
and to the unpredictability of political pricing decisions which they
must accept. The case of local authorities is more difficult. At least
the nationalised industries have their objectives, albeit imposed, but
local authorities must in many cases set their own objectives whilst
at the same time being uncertain as to the supply of long term funds.
There is a limit to the sums borrowed through the market and to the
extent to which local rates may be increased, and government grants
and loans cannot be forecast with any precision except in the short
term. Nevertheless if government action is viewed as an environmental factor (decreasing in significance from public to private
sector), it is possible to argue that corporate planning is feasible
within any type of organisation which possesses a reasonable degree
of autonomy.

Having suggested the possible universal applicability of corporate
planning, some thought must be given to the manner in which it
may function. By reference to Fig. 6 it will be seen that the corporate
planning machinery needs to take into consideration environmental

factors and operational planning submissions emanating from sub-corporate levels, and must make its own assessment of the strengths and weaknesses of its total operations. The chief executive, the board, or senior policy team should approve all major planning decisions and from what has been said it is apparent that appropriate time must be spent by the decision makers before this approval is given. As however the time necessary to study and assess all the factors involved in a major decision constitutes, in an organisation of any size, possibly man-years of analysis it is obvious that the chief executive must have appropriate support if strategic corporate planning as defined above is to be achieved. In many organisations corporate planning groups are being introduced and extended, increasingly becoming vital components of the machinery of corporate planning. Their ideally unique position of being able to take an objective view of the organisation's activities and aspirations enables the policy makers to be provided ultimately with corporate plans with which the stated objectives and goals of operating units (*e.g.* subsidiary company or local authority departments) may be compared. There are apparent line and staff problems here which can be demonstrated by reference to Fig. 7 in which the corporate

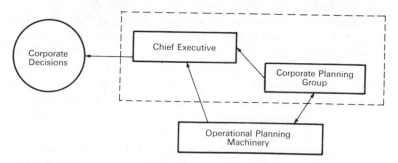

FIG. 7. The position of the corporate planning group.

planning machinery, included in a single box in Fig. 6, is now shown as comprising, organisationally, two parts. The first is the chief executive (representing an individual, board, committee, etc.) and the second the advisory corporate planning group. It is the latter which in consequence of being an entirely new appendage in the organisational structure is creating many behavioural problems.*

* *See* ERWIN VON ALLMEN, "Setting up Corporate Planning," *Long Range Planning*, Vol. 2, No. 1, 1969, p. 5.

The major problem is the extent to which traditional application to the chief executive by the operational or departmental units in respect of corporate resource allocation should be affected by recommendations of the corporate planning group.* The solution may seem easy; operational planning for each unit should be carried out with the assistance and final "blessing" of the corporate planning group. This however would result, in effect, in the latter moving into a line position, a situation quite intolerable to the senior managers of the operational units. But in consequence of growing experience and expertise, corporate planners will be able more and more to adopt the "total" approach and to assess the implications of operational unit plans in relation to the corporate plan. Inevitable inconsistencies due to the particular origin of planning are likely and hence friction will arise. Perhaps this is the price that organisations must pay for the innovation. Certainly the chief executive will have a vital role to play in assessing and controlling the contribution of the corporate planners. Ideally one would hope that both the chief executive and the operational units will recognise the corporate planning group as a centre of objective planning excellence and through the establishment of proper channels for dialogue ensure that situations of unresolved conflict are minimised.

A conclusion of vital importance which emerges at this point is that the chief executive must be prepared to devote a considerable amount of time to formalised corporate planning, particularly at its inception, and from then on at an appropriate level of involvement. Whether the members of the corporate planning group come from within or without the organisation such committal is essential. In the event of the planning group consisting wholly or mainly of persons from within the organisation support must be given to them until senior management come to accept and appreciate their role. It is not enough for a chief executive to introduce a corporate planning group, define its terms of reference and then leave it to make its own impact on the organisation. Conflicts of purpose and personality may quickly create an impossible situation. On the other hand, corporate planning demands powers of analysis and an ability to communicate which may simply not be available from within the organisation. In this case, the chief executive must be prepared to give proper support to the corporate planner who is brought into the

---

* See K. HOWARD AND R. C. LUCKING, "Corporate Planning after Reorganisation," *Local Government Chronicle*, No. 5534, 6th April, 1973, pp. 385–387.

organisation. If corporate planning is to live up to its name the chief executive must in addition accept that his *modus vivendi* will inevitably change. Whereas, hitherto, objectives may sometimes have been set in cavalier style over lunch, decisions to expand or divest or diversify will now only be based on time-consuming appraisal of analyses. And appraisal of analysis implies that the concepts and procedures involved in the analysis are appreciated. In other words a decision should not be seen as being almost instantaneous but as a cycle of involvement, a point which was made earlier in this Chapter. To maintain the proper role in the corporate planning machinery demands much therefore of the chief executive. He must continually resist on the one hand an inclination to revert to the intuitive decision making which probably helped him to reach the apex of the hierarchy and on the other hand he must avoid the temptation to become a rubber stamp to proposals from the corporate planning group. These situations may become difficult to avoid if in the first case a series of logical decisions have unfavourable outcomes and in the second case if acceptance of a series of "best alternatives" as indicated by the corporate planning group all lead to very favourable outcomes.

OBJECTIVES AND GOALS

Reference was made earlier to "objectives" and "goals," words which appear frequently in planning literature and which are often given different meanings. The definitions which follow are broadly in accord with majority usage:

OBJECTIVE: A fundamental outcome or state which an organisation aims to achieve within a given planning horizon.

GOAL: The precise and timed specification of the situation which an organisation must reach by allocation of its resources in order to meet the implications of a given objective.

It is apparent therefore that defined in this way goals are dominated by objectives. For example, a company may have as an objective an increase in market share of 1 per cent per annum for each of the next five years. In order to achieve this, the goal for an ensuing year may be to increase turnover by £200,000. Again, one objective of a local authority may be to rehouse all tenants of sub-standard dwellings within a decade. The first year's goal may then be the construction of

5000 new dwellings. The "broader" an objective then the larger in general will be the number of goals necessary to satisfy it. An objective of national government may be to contain inflation within a rate of 4 per cent per annum. Annual goals in this respect will need to be defined in respect of prices, incomes, money supply, investment, tax revenues, and so on.

In order that goals and objectives shall be established meaningfully, corporate strategy is a prerequisite, and fundamental to corporate strategy is the adoption of logical decision making procedures. Although not a major concern of this book, some thought must be given to the situations which necessitate the taking of strategic corporate decisions. The chief executive may be likened to the captain of a space craft. He is piloting his organisation (through a continuum of time) with a momentum which may be deceptive. If resources are not injected in the right manner and to the proper extent he will either crash or become lost forever in organisational space (a metaphorical take-over!). If he wishes only to maintain current momentum he must inject limited resources (perhaps wastefully) and will assume an orbit, from which he may later move in either direction, but in which he will rapidly become unexceptional and probably unnoticed. If, however, he is to have any chance of reaching the stars he must aim to increase the momentum of the organisation to the maximum by availing himself of every opportunity and allocating his resources in the optimal way. Although a general objective may be to reach the stars there will be a particular star which on account of its position and the resources thought necessary to reach it, will be nominated as a matter of policy. But in this case a good deal of ingenuity may need to be exercised in order to reach the target. At this point our metaphor becomes a little thin although the possibility of developing a new and more efficient fuel through the flight may be taken as being analogous to the development of a new product or methodology. In practice, management at all levels and in all types of organisation is continually searching for means whereby the gap between aspiration and expectation may be bridged. Governments may alter exchange rates and regroup local resource control. Businesses search for new products and markets and appropriate acquisitions and mergers. Quite obviously the selection of a limited number of objectives can be exceedingly complex.

The mixture of the general and the specific in corporate objectives calls for further comment. Organisations frequently include each type. For example, an objective of achieving a sales level of £4,000,000 in five years may be concurrent with an objective of achieving the leading company position by that time. Further, one company may specify an increase in profit of 10 per cent per annum whereas the objective of another company may be "simply" to maximise profit. A response to the latter alternative may be that every organisation aims to optimise something. Hence "maximisation" is not especially profound, whereas a quantified objective suggests that its feasibility has been established on the basis of analysis. The latter may or may not be the case.* During the early years of corporate planning much of the chicken and egg situation applies. Are quantified corporate objectives indicated by study of the alternative ways of allocating resources, or are resources allocated in such a way that possibly arbitrarily quantified corporate objectives are met? It is easy enough to state that the former is more closely akin to the optimum approach but until corporate planners have gained sufficient experience and expertise within their organisations it is likely that quantified corporate objectives of some measure of arbitrariness will continue to be set.

Objectives of a corporate nature will emerge from and initiate strategic decisions which are taken within the organisation. As mentioned, quantitative analysis has its part to play in selecting these objectives but it must be recognised that other factors of a socio-economic, ethical or even philanthropic nature may be of overriding significance. Thus an organisation may decide not to build its new plants in the South East of England but will search for appropriate new town locations in the Midlands˙ where it will attempt to integrate and co-operate with the developing community to achieve "optimum," but difficult to quantify, "welfare."

It should be recognised that a quantified corporate objective does not preclude the imposition of constraints arising from apparently non-quantifiable considerations. For example, acknowledgment of the need for community development or aesthetically acceptable design of works may involve extra cost necessary to meet minimum acceptable standards. Costs of this type may be brought into the analysis and influence the choice of alternative. Corporate decisions therefore may be made on grounds which are recognisably logical or on grounds which although not illogical *per se* may be illogical

* See HARRY P. HATRY, "*Criteria for Evaluation in Planning State and Local Programs,*" in IRA M. ROBINSON, ed., *Decision-Making in Urban Planning*, Sage Publications, Inc., Beverly Hills, 1972, Chapter 10, p. 214.

in pure money terms. The role of analysis in aiding the former category in total or the latter category in part will find frequent mention in the ensuing Chapters. On whatever basis corporate decisions are taken and objectives set the *goals* so defined will require logical decision procedures at all levels in the organisation.

THE BASIS OF THE LOGICAL DECISION—THE MODEL

A "logical decision" as defined earlier in this Chapter is seen to involve a judgment based on the analysis of alternatives. The analytical problems inherent in planning decisions, involving as they do the complex interaction of resources under uncertainty, do not, except by chance, yield to instinct, and some fundamental aid to decision making is necessary. This aid is the *model*, which is defined as follows:

> MODEL: A representation of all or certain facets of a real life situation (actual or planned) expressly constructed for the purpose of studying the consequences of altering the real life situation or the inputs to it and hence aiding decision making.

It is immediately apparent that a model is capable of assuming many different forms. A classification similar to that shown in Fig. 8 is used quite widely.

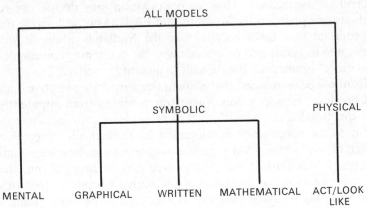

FIG. 8. A general classification of models.

Notice from the definition that the models we are studying are purposeful. Physical models for example do not include therefore *objects d'art* which may adorn the chief executive's office. This category will, however, include all those models which range from purely "acting like" through to purely "looking like." One example of the former is the representation of ventilation flow through tunnels by current flowing through an electrical circuit. Another example of this type is the combination of strings and pulleys weighted accorded to the volume of sales through a series of depots, which is used to find the centre of gravity of the system and hence suggest an "optimum location" for a central warehouse. An example of a physical model which "looks like" but does not act like (at least in the sense of internal operation) is the model of an aeroplane in a wind tunnel. Models of traffic flow have been used to demonstrate queues at road intersections and models of localities have assisted planners in designing layout. The physical model is however of only limited interest to the businessman because of the difficulties of simulating at all realistically the complexity of the systems involved.

Mental models of a situation are constructed automatically by the manager when confronted by the need to make a decision. Sometimes this form suffices, particularly when human behaviour is a predominant factor, as would be the case in deciding what qualities would be required in a foreman to be appointed in a section beset with labour troubles. On the other hand, despite its infinitely adaptive thought processes the human brain is simply incapable of storing and operating upon numerous calculations and then combining the results to form an appropriate decision base. Take the investment of £100 at 7 per cent compound annual interest. The computational procedure is elementary but how many persons could determine the principal at the end of five years without resorting to pen and paper?

For decision making in situations of even limited complexity it is therefore necessary for the manager to resort to some means of describing, storing, and analysing aspects of the problem. Written reports may be described as symbolic models but have obvious limitations in respect of the depth of analysis which may be achieved. A second class of symbolic model is the graph, where "graph" is used in its widest sense to indicate some form of draughtsmanship. Taking first the traditional understanding of the graph as a means of plotting and studying bivariate data, it is often the case that a "message" which is concealed by tabular presentation is made apparent by the process of graphing. A forecaster studying the relationship between two variables such as sales and time, or national consumption expenditure and disposable income would as a matter of course study the "scatter diagram" produced by a graphical plot. Useful as a graph of this type is, however, it is only of value on a very limited front. A graphical model of a much broader nature may indicate the flow of information within an organisation. It would be almost impossible to represent this other than by some form of arrow diagram. Another and very important use of arrows is in *network analysis*, by which means the sequencing of an organisation's activities may be indicated. This technique will be discussed at some length in Chapter 5.

By this time the reader will have realised that he has been using models for decision making throughout his life and hence the jump to the next stage, the mathematical model, should not, conceptually, be too difficult.

THE MATHEMATICAL MODEL*—INTERPRETATION AND CONSTRUCTION

To persons unfamiliar with the symbolism and procedures of mathematics and statistics, a mathematical model conveys as little as though the situation were written up in a foreign language. Although in many models it is the case that mathematical constants and operators appear which would be unfamiliar to the non-mathematician, there are other models which in fact use symbolism purely as a form of shorthand. For example, consider the following two equations:

I. $$c = 50 + .8d$$
II. $$q = 75p^{-.4}e^{.03t}$$

Where in I:

c = consumers' expenditure in a national economy
d = disposable income after taxes

and in II:

q = number of an item sold
p = selling price of the item
t = year number (0 for 1970).

---

* The usual approach adopted in presenting the mathematical model is at the outset to classify dichotomously, for example:

Optimising *v*. Descriptive,
etc.

This approach will not be adopted here, as it is suggested that this leads to a fragmented appreciation which hinders understanding of the overall methodology. Having worked through the general principles and problems of mathematical model building, we will then classify them in order to summarise and discuss the ideas which have been developed.

c and q are termed "dependent variables" whereas d, p, and t are termed "independent variables."

Given these definitions, few people would find difficulty in understanding equation I. It would for example be understood that if the disposable income were 1000 units then consumers' expenditure would be:

$$c = 50 + (.8)(1000) = 850 \text{ units}$$

and if d were increased to 2000 units then c would become 1650. It would then be noted that doubling the disposable income from 1000 to 2000 units would not result in a doubling of consumers' expenditure. All of this and more would be gleaned from the simple equation I. On turning to equation II, the non-mathematician would find difficulty in interpretation even though the implications of the relationship would be of great value in making pricing decisions. In the first case, e is not defined; it is in fact a constant frequently used in mathematics approximating to 2.718. Again p and c are raised to a power, in the latter instance including t. To a person understanding the form of such expressions it is appreciated that if for example the price p is doubled then the quantity q sold will fall by 40 per cent (economists describe the exponent of p as the price elasticity of demand). Additionally there is an autonomous increase in the quantity sold of .03 or 3 per cent per annum. Obviously then some understanding of mathematical symbolism and procedures is necessary if models are to be understood. To this end, Appendix I lists and explains various commonly used symbols, relationships and procedures which will enable mathematical models to be interpreted more easily.

A very important point may be raised at this stage; the above equations have been interpreted in terms of the symbolism used, but what in fact determines the *structure* of the equation? How is it that national consumers' expenditure is determined by disposable income? Why should the money in a man's pocket determine *exactly* his purchases? What about his previous patterns of spending and his future expectations? Why should the passage of time imply in the absence of price changes that demand for an item should increase at a constant rate per annum? It is obvious that an attempt is made to *predict* c and q in equations I and II. Equations I and II represent *assumed functional relationships* and are often described as *normative*, that is what "ought to be" or perhaps more realistically "might be." Some of the procedures involved in establishing normative relationships are discussed in this Chapter and Chapter 3. Another type of relationship may be recognised. Take the national economic indicators of a closed economy with national income y, consumers' expenditure c, government expenditure g, and investment expenditure i, then c may be represented as follows:

III. $c = y - g - i$

Equation III is an *identity* or positive relationship indicating that consumers' expenditure is *the same as* national income less the total of government and investment expenditure. An example of the difference between an identity and a normative relationship is apparent from studying the determinants of an organisation's profits, z. These may be described as the increase in assets over a given time period, when we have the identity

$$z = a_{t+1} - a_t$$

where a_{t+1} and a_t are assets at the end and beginning of time period t. Alternatively, z may be assumed to be determined by national income y, rate of inflation f, and mean temperature b, relative to a given period. In this case z is some function of y, f, and b written

$$z = f(y, f, b)$$

Many models include both identities and normative relationships. At present however models which have been developed to aid decision making within organisations (the "micro" level) are largely composed of identities in the sense that it is the actual processes such as accounting relationships which are modelled. The model (normally computerised) enables the consequences of differing inputs and outputs to be determined within hours or minutes, as compared with weeks of manual clerical effort. The major use of the more normative model has been at national or industry level (the "macro" level) to assess in particular, the implications of government decisions. The tendency is for macro models to extend downwards to industry level through linked sub-models, whereas organisational models are seeking to link with macro models, at the same time incorporating more normative elements.

As opposed to interpretation, the construction of mathematical models is a very different matter. It will be remembered that as far as decision making is concerned the model must be purposeful. It will in fact in many instances be used to aid the selection of the "best" alternative in respect of a particular goal or objective. The complexity of the model, never greater than the largest system it will embrace, will therefore depend on the size of the system and the importance of the decision. The model builder will construct a model which on the one hand may contain as little as one equation or inequation but on the other hand may involve thousands of such relationships. Whatever the sophistication, a first attempt at model building will lead to the following two major realisations:

1. That although a particular variable in a given equation will be either dependent or independent this does not imply that it may not fulfil the alternative role in another equation.
2. That there may be considerable difficulty in deciding how a dependent variable may be determined efficiently by other variables both in terms of the number of independent variables and, if applicable, the functional relationship involved.

Logically statement 2 is the starting point in model building and is absolutely basic to the whole process. However statement 1 will be dealt with first as conceptually it poses little difficulty and serves as a useful lead into the discussion of the second major point. Consumers' expenditure in an economy was described above by the relationship:

$$c = 50 + .8d$$

Within the scope of this model therefore d is an independent variable and c a dependent variable. Again the direct costs k, of producing an item will depend on the labour and material costs incurred and the model (an identity) is:

$$k = l + m$$

where l = labour costs
                 m = material costs

k is a dependent variable and l and m are independent variables.

Consideration of the system of which these models are only part suggest that further relationships may be modelled. For example in an economy not involved in international trade, national income y, is determined as the sum of consumers', government, and investment expenditure and may be expressed by the following equation:

$$y = c + g + i$$

where g and i are government and investment expenditure respectively. In this case, c is an independent variable. Readers may be

embarking on a train of thought at this stage on the lines perhaps
that "If y depends on c which depends on d, then what does d depend
on?" We shall return to this shortly. Extending the second example,
contribution to overheads z will depend on sales income s and
direct costs k. Thus:

$$z = s - k$$

and the train of thought suggests that the process is tending towards
a set of equations which interact in consequence of the occurrence of
variables which are both dependent and independent in different
parts of the model. Statement 2 above highlights the real problems
facing model builders; some answer is required to the questions:

(a) How many independent variables should be used to
"explain" a dependent variable?

(b) What is the form of the relationship between the dependent
and the independent variables?

(c) What values will the independent variables assume in the
future?

Quite apparently there is both an art and a science in model
building. For a system of any complexity in respect of which environmental factors need to be taken into account it is almost certain
that models of the same situation but constructed separately will
differ. This is mainly due to the model necessarily being less complex
than the real life situation which it seeks to describe. The model
builder in fact aims to construct a model of the simplest form which
will be accepted by the decision maker as the basis for studying
alternatives and making realistic decisions.

The natural starting point is the goal or objective under consideration. This may be the achievement of a certain level of profitability or cost. The factors contributing to the objective then need to
be listed. In the case of company profitability, these may be written
into an identity and will involve the various categories of income
and expenditure. As suggested above, identities may then be used
to describe the sales part of income as being determined by the
quantities sold multiplied by the various selling prices. Similarly
production costs may be determined by quantities produced multiplied by unit costs. These processes will enable a structural model
to be built and profitability arising from different levels of sales
and production costs to be estimated. The model builder may wish
to take the process a stage further. For example, sales income may

be determined in terms of selling price, total market, and market share. Note that this is the end of the line as far as identities are concerned. What is now required is a means of predicting total market and market share by the establishment of normative relationships. Perhaps some day it will be possible to estimate with understanding and precision such things as total markets for a product. At present, however, one must resort to a concept such as the *black box* which is depicted in Fig. 9. This recognises the complexity and apparent

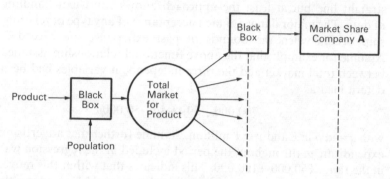

FIG. 9. Total and company market for a product "explained" by the black box.

unpredictability of the world and the people within it. It is for example accepted that both total market and the market shares for a product depend on marketing effort, selling price, customer attitudes, economic and natural environment factors, and so on. The model builder seeks to draw certain conclusions from this complexity. One might be that sales income increases as marketing effort increases. Another is that if many customers like the product they will continue to buy it. Or, as G.N.P. increases, then so apparently does demand for the product. Recognising that it is quite impossible to predict the *exact* size of the market the model builder aims to achieve a high degree of statistical association between total market and the independent variables which he finally includes. Hopefully many model builders resort at this stage to an attempt to establish a linear relationship between the dependent and independent variables. For example, total sales s, in £ may be predicted by G.N.P., advertising expenditure, and selling price as

$$s = c_1 + c_2 y + c_3 a + c_4 p$$

where c_1, c_2, c_3, and c_4 are constants, y is G.N.P., a is advertising expenditure and p is selling price.

Given time series of the variables and using a technique known as multiple regression (see Chapter 3) it is *always* possible to estimate some values for the constants. It is also possible to compute the "significance" of the independent variables, and this enables a recalculation of the regression after eliminating variables which are not significant. There has been a degree of blanket criticism of the way in which many model builders are prone to search for linear relationships. Certainly there is nothing sacrosanct about the straight line but at least the approach allows consistent handling of data. The major danger of tacit acceptance of any type of relationship occurs when the bounds of past experience are exceeded. Assume for example that the above functional relationship assumed between total market and the three independent variables had been determined as

$$s = 700,000 + 50y + 4a - 50,000p$$

with a and p in £ and y in £ million. Assume further that advertising expenditure a, throughout the period included in the regression was in the range £50,000–£100,000. This indicates that within this range, for y and p constant, advertising expenditure could be responsible for a total market variation of £200,000. The danger lies in the assumption that if for example advertising expenditure were increased to £200,000 the increase of £100,000 beyond the upper

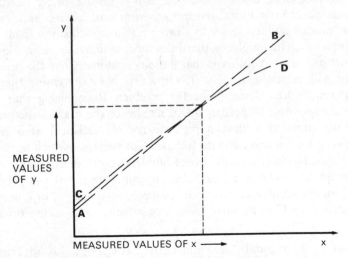

FIG. 10. Extrapolation of different functions.

bound included in the regression would increase total market by £400,000, other factors being constant. This may well be dubious speculation. The model builder would probably wish to represent advertising expenditure in such a way that successive increments in this area would produce less than proportionate increases in sales. This step, although feasible if advertising were the only independent variable, renders scientific estimation of the constants extremely difficult if there are a number of non-linear relationships. To emphasise further the distinction between the artistic and the scientific approach to model building and usage, consider the relationship between two variables x and y indicated in Fig. 10. Assume that within the limits of the measured values a straight line gives a good statistical fit. Any extension of this relationship will then be given by a point on the line AB. The scientific approach will therefore involve fitting mathematically the straight line AB and extrapolating as required. The model builder may however "feel"* that a straight line fit is inappropriate and eventually applies the curved function CD which within the measured region gives as good a fit perhaps as the straight line AB. Extrapolation of CD will lead to predictions of y which will differ considerably from those arising from the extrapolation of AB, a difference which will increase as x increases.

A CLASSIFICATION OF MATHEMATICAL MODELS

By this stage the reader will it is to be hoped have gained an understanding of some of the reasoning behind the construction of a mathematical model. The intention is now to summarise the major properties of models and discuss these on the basis of the following classification:

1. Positive *v.* normative. *assumptions made outside v within* *model.*
2. Structural *v.* predictive.
3. Probabilistic *v.* deterministic.
4. Static *v.* dynamic.
5. Optimising *v.* descriptive.

The first four classifications refer more to the type of model rather than the way in which it is used, whereas the converse applies to the fifth classification.

* For reasons which will be discussed in Chapter 4.

Positive v. *Normative* — includes the "might" happen.

As mentioned earlier one must distinguish between a positive statement represented by an identity and a normative statement represented by some relationship other than an identity. Using earlier examples:

$$y = c + i + g \text{ is a positive relationship}$$
$$c = 50 + .8d \text{ is a normative relationship}$$

For a model of any size, as, for example, one representing a company or system the usual starting equation is an identity which is then broken down into further identities until what might be described as the "boundary" is reached. The boundary exists either because the model is sufficiently comprehensive or alternatively because a variable such as demand cannot be determined *precisely* in terms of other variables. At this point, it is necessary, if it is wished to extend the boundary of the model, to search for statistical relationships which enable demand to be predicted. The resulting expressions which suggest how such a variable might or ought to be predicted are the normative components of the model. It has been mentioned that some multi-equation models contain positive and normative elements. At macro (for example, national) level, where aggregation is extreme, normative elements are usually essential if the model is not to become unwieldy. In these circumstances, model builders have free rein in their attempts to establish normative relationships which appear to explain better the subject of the model. On the other hand, at the micro end of the scale where the variables included in the model are much more precisely detailed (production cost of an item, number of skilled men available) it is frequently found that *no* normative elements are included. Decision makers accept that uncertainty exists but prefer to deal with this subjectively rather than bring in, via normative relationships, variables such as gross national product which they feel are too remote. The future will however see the greater use of normative elements in micro models as managerial decision makers gain confidence in their use and as information becomes more accurate and readily available. Further, linking of micro and macro models using both positive and normative relationships will occur as boundaries are extended.

Structural v. *Predictive*

In the process of building a model by seeking to explain more and more variables of significance, the system becomes increasingly represented by the equations developed. As an aid to understanding how the organisation functions this process is of itself of value to management. It is however usually the case that one variable in particular is of interest. This may be return on equity, total cost, manpower required, etc. and it is in general by no means clear from the structural equations how this may be predicted. The discussion which follows indicates how a predictive model may be derived from its structural form.

The author developed recently as an aid to the understanding of macroeconomic principles a model of the United Kingdom economy. The demand side of the model contains eight equations as follows:

I. $C = 200 + 0.889D$
II. $D = Y - T - E$
III. $T = -1300 + RY$
IV. $E = 0.12Y$
V. $I = 0.17Y + 0.5K$
VI. $Y = C + I + G + X - M$
VII. $X = 1.016X_{-1} + (4 - F_{-1})20$
VIII. $M = 0.4C_{-1} + (F_{-1} - 3)20$

Where
C = Consumers' Expenditure
D = Disposable Income
Y = Gross National Product
T = Net Taxes
E = Earnings Retained by Business
R = Marginal Net Tax Rate
I = Investment Expenditure
K = Change in Money Supply
G = Government Expenditure
X = Export of Goods and Services
M = Imports of Goods and Services
F = Rate of Inflation (at annual per cent rate)

Figures are in £ million and the time period used is the quarter. The subscript, -1, is used to specify the previous quarter.

Equations II and VI are identities whereas the remainder of the equations are normative. It will be noted that the variables, C, D, Y, T, E, X and M are dependent or independent according to the equation in which they are involved. Further it will be seen that this part of the model is wholly linear.

The prime purpose of constructing the model was to enable students of economics to assess the effect of the major government policy decisions. These were seen as marginal net tax rate, money supply, and government expenditure and occur in equations III, V and VI. Assuming that interest is centred on G.N.P. it is difficult to assess the effect on this of joint or individual changes in the policy variables. In order to do this it is necessary to combine equations and eliminate variables until G.N.P., Y, is expressed in terms of the policy variables only. The result of pursuing this procedure is the following predictive model for Y:

$$Y = \frac{1496 + 0.5K + G + 1.016X_{-1} - 0.4C_{-1} - 40F_{-1}}{0.048 + .889R}$$

For any quarter, figures for the previous quarter's exports, consumers' expenditure and rate of inflation will be available and thus the predicted value of Y will depend on governmental decisions in respect of K, G, and R. The predictive model however is of little value in describing how the economy works, and it is now apparent why the managerial decision makers must have some appreciation of the procedures used in its derivation. Managers cannot be expected to make decisions of a planning nature with confidence unless they are satisfied that the underlying structure of the model is sound. There must therefore be a continuing dialogue between the manager and the model builder during the construction of the structural model.

Probabilistic v. Deterministic
It has been stated that increasingly management is resorting to the probabilistic approach to problems of uncertainty. In the context of model building, this implies that both the input and output will be in the form of probability distributions. It is not intended at this stage to discuss at length the advantages and disadvantages of using probabilistic rather than deterministic estimates; this will be considered in Chapter 7. The aim here is to indicate the practical implications of incorporating probability distributions into models. The structure of the model is unaffected, what is required is a means of handling the probabilities. Direct analysis in the conventional sense is in general ruled out. Instead, many "runs" of the model are made to yield an output (*e.g.* net present value, internal rate of return) itself in the form of a probability distribution. Because of the numerous calculations involved a computer is essential, and the costs of using the model in a probabilistic manner are of course much greater than if the model were purely deterministic. Special

programming routines have however been developed to facilitate the handling of probability distributions. The opportunity is often made available for *either* single figure or probabilistic estimates of input variables to be manipulated. Assume for example that the most likely value of market share for the following year was assumed to be 14 per cent whereas the probabilistic view of market share was represented by the following distribution:

Zero probability less than 10 per cent
0.25 probability less than 11 per cent
0.50 probability less than 13 per cent
0.75 probability less than 14 per cent
1.00 probability less than 15 per cent

In either case the data could be entered into the same programme line, on say, line 240. In a particular programming language:

```
240 DATA    ,14, 1
```

would imply a market share of 14 per cent on a single figure basis whereas

```
240 DATA     ,105,,15,,177,;35,,132,,55,,140,,75,,147,,95
```

is a probabilistic input using five equally spaced points (.15,.35, etc.) taken from the accumulated probability distribution. When the programme was run each of these five points would be sampled randomly and equiprobably, with the result that market shares as low as 10.5 per cent and as high as 14.7 per cent would be incorporated in the calculations. Providing that at least one of the input variables is probabilistic, the output will be in the form of a probability distribution which must then be interpreted appropriately.

It should be stressed that the limitations of direct analysis apply to most probabilistic multi-equation models. Probabilities have been included in a type of mathematical programming termed linear programming (see Chapter 8) and a number of well known analytical procedures involving probabilities have been developed in such areas as inventory control and queueing theory. Further, one aid to decision making, the decision tree (*see* Chapter 6), would have made little impact if probabilistic outcomes had not been recognised.

Probabilities are playing an increasing role in the making of logical decisions. They achieve the very useful effect of causing the manager to be directly involved at both ends of the decision cycle (in addition, it is to be hoped, to during the cycle). He will contribute or agree the input probability distribution for variables included in the model and will also be the only person who will be able to make the ultimate decision based on the output distribution. Further implications of probabilistic and deterministic models will be examined in some detail in the Chapters which follow.

Static v. Dynamic

The distinguishing feature in this dichotomy is the internally generated time dependence of certain variables. It is important to appreciate that the time dependence is generated within the dynamic model. In taking decisions of a planning nature within an organisation, explicit recognition must be given to future uncertainty. Thus whatever type of model is used as a basis for decision making, values ascribed to variables will vary over time. However in many models these values are externally generated, and predictions may be made at will for any period in the short or long term provided the decision maker is confident that structurally the model is still relevant. However in some cases in model building a variable is best "explained" by including as an independent variable either an earlier value of itself or another variable. In that case, the model cannot be used statically for any future period but must be used dynamically, generating period by period values until the desired point in time is reached. As an example, assume that sales are to be predicted normatively. It is assumed that within realistic limits price changes will be matched by those of competitors and thus the effect of these on sales will not be significant. Two alternatives are considered:

1. Sales s, depend solely on advertising expenditure a.
2. Sales depend on advertising expenditure and additionally sales during the previous period.

Corresponding to these alternatives two normative equations are assumed to have been obtained (in £000):

I. $s = 4200 + a^{0.5}$
II. $s = 450 + 0.5a^{0.5} + 0.8s_{-1}$

where the subscript -1 refers to the previous period. If sales during the previous period were £5,000,000 then for an advertising expenditure of £250,000:

I. gives $s = 4200 + 500 = 4700$
II. gives $s = 450 + 250 + 4000 = 4700$ also

However, equation I is a static model and provided the decision maker has confidence that the relationship will continue to hold, the effect of an advertising expenditure of £500,000 four periods ahead may be estimated directly. On the other hand, as equation II is dynamic *all* advertising expenditures during the four periods would have to be taken into account and final sales determined step by step.

It will be noted that the econometric model of the United Kingdom referred to earlier in this Chapter is dynamic, in consequence of the external trade components.

It is important to appreciate that models which span a period of time and hence do not give an instantaneous static impression do not qualify for the description "dynamic" unless they include "lagged" variables of the type indicated above. Corporate planning and project evaluation frequently involve models covering many years, but it is quite common to estimate such variables as expenditures and revenues for five–ten years ahead external to the model and then use them as inputs; such models are static.

Optimising v. Descriptive
This dichotomy is due in part to the nature of the model and in part to the way in which the model may be used to provide a basis for decision making. The aim is of course to achieve the most favourable outcome possible, that is to optimise. Thus it would seem desirable that all models should qualify for the description "optimising." But what is it that we are attempting to optimise? Further, given that we are able to define precisely what it is that we wish to optimise are we able in a mathematical sense to achieve an analytical solution? The following discussion examines these questions, concentrating again on decision making at higher levels within organisations.

1. *The objectives*
Corporate objectives may at first sight be deceptively simple; increase sales by 10 per cent per year, maximise earnings per share, redevelop an area of a city during the next five years, etc. Inevitably, however, there will exist implicitly or explicitly constraints and requirements which must be satisfied. For example, it may be that a certain level of net investment is desired, that the ratio of debt to equity shall not exceed a certain figure. In the case of city redevelopment, there is a range of evaluation criteria relating to design

standards, preservation of old buildings and other socio-economic considerations which defies realistic quantification. What is the objective in the macro-economic exercise of the preceding section? Is this to maximise G.N.P.? What is the effect of this policy on inflation, and balance of payments? What weight should be given to prime corporate objectives and to subsidiary objectives? It is in fact realistic in some cases to set up an *objective function*, appropriately quantified so that a unique optimum (or by coincidence optima), may be determined. And if objective functions are established these must accurately represent the attitudes of the persons responsible for the corporate activity of the organisation.

The United Kingdom macroeconomic model may be used to demonstrate the purpose and effect of the objective function. It was suggested that the objectives were to maximise national welfare, this depending on G.N.P., unemployment, inflation, and balance of payments. Obviously there will be debate as to tolerable levels of the components of the objective function. How for example is inflation F, weighted against unemployment U? Decisions in this case would be a mixture of the subjective and the objective. A welfare function W, actually used was:

$$W = 2Y^{.5} - (15(U-2))^2 - 2F^2 - (X-M+40)/4$$

The determination of unemployment and inflation is not indicated in this Chapter, but both depend on the ratio between G.N.P. and potential output. As G.N.P. is increased relative to potential output, unemployment is decreased and inflation is increased. The balance of payments term accepts a deficit in visible trade of £40,000,000 and is influenced adversely by inflation. Apart from the latter term the objective function is non-linear, and its form derives solely from the primarily subjective attitudes of the author.

By introducing the objective function, the model has been converted from being purely *descriptive* to a form for which optimisation is possible.

2. *The problem of optimisation*
Given that we can set up an objective function of acceptable realism, why is optimisation not then straightforward? A major practical reason in many cases is that some of the variables are outside the control of the decision maker. Consider, for example, the predictive model for G.N.P. given above. It is implied that the United Kingdom government is totally able to determine G.N.P.

by manipulating K, G, and R. But apart from validity considerations concerning the structure of the model, it is a fact that external factors such as world trade will also affect G.N.P. It must be accepted that world trade to all intents and purposes is an *uncontrollable variable* determined outside the economy (that it was not treated in this way was due to the desire to make the model "self contained"). Similar uncontrollable variables are encountered in most decision making situations, for example total markets, competitors' marketing effort, future wage rates, etc. The presence of such variables in models makes optimisation impossible unless assumptions are made. The general mathematical model of a decision process is in fact frequently expressed* in the form

$$U = f(X, Y),$$

the aim being to maximise utility U subject to the controllable variables X and uncontrollable variables Y.

In some cases, it is realistic to assume values for the uncontrollable variables and also to set up a realistic objective function. It may then be possible to use the analytical methods of optimisation described in Chapter 8.

The techniques of optimisation have been used for many years to solve problems of stock control, replacement, queues, etc. (the familiar techniques of operational research). But these approaches, taken in the context of the total organisation or major system components of it, are generally cases of sub-optimisation. As soon as multi-equation models are developed, even assuming that the problems of uncontrollable variables and objective functions are overcome (except in the special case of mathematical programming), analytical optimisation frequently becomes impossible. For example, in the case of the econometric model, because of non-linear components the optimum value of G.N.P. over a period of time could not be determined by direct analysis. However the objective of optimising G.N.P. remains, and this is where the literature sometimes becomes confused. If optimisation by direct analysis is not possible then the whole model is often described as being "descriptive," despite the fact that other means may exist of determining the optimum. Basically in these circumstances single figure estimates of the uncontrollable variables are made, following which

---

* *See* R. L. ACKOFF AND M. W. SASIENI, *Fundamentals of Operations Research*, John Wiley & Sons, Inc., New York, 1968, Chapter 4, p. 94.

the effect of adopting different values of the controllable variables are assessed. In the case of *hill climbing* * (*see* Chapter 8) an optimum (possibly "local") is consistently approached, whereas if the input values are arbitrarily set by the decision maker there is no guarantee of convergence on the optimum and the search for the optimum may be a lengthy and costly procedure. The *process* of using a model in this way is known as "simulation," which is the subject of Chapter 7. A model is said to be descriptive if the decision maker finds it unrealistic or impossible to quantify evaluation criteria and hence establish an objective function. Descriptive models do, however, enable the consequences of ascribing values to variables (both controllable and uncontrollable) to be determined. As a result they are often referred to as "What-if?" models. For example, "*What* would be the effect on profitability *if* selling price were increased by 10 per cent?"

THE ROLE OF THE COMPUTER IN MODEL BUILDING AND USAGE

With the exception of a few highly aggregated models an electronic computer is a prerequisite for corporate and planning models. The need for a computer implies that in addition to the model builders, specialist staff are required to programme the model into the computer. The modeller and the programmer may be the same individual but whether they be one person or two there exists the problem of communication with the decision maker. The significance of this behavioural aspect will be examined further in later Chapters.

The technological path followed by computer manufacturers has had some influence on the nature of the first generation of corporate models. In general, the major manufacturers have concentrated on developing larger and faster computers and related software designed to operate in the batch mode. The programming languages employed have been in the main the traditional all-purpose type (*e.g.* Fortran), in other words the computation has been carried out as near to or as remote from higher management as other types of computation (payroll, stock control, invoicing, and so on). Certain other companies have developed systems for on-line computing using languages particularly suited to the "conversational" mode. In the latter circumstances, something of a dialogue may be

---

* *See* G. G. STEPHENSON, "A Hierarchy of Models for Planning in a Division of I.C.I.," Operational Research Quarterly, Vol. 21, No. 2, June 1970, pp. 230–233.

set up between the computer and a user linked to it through a tele-type unit and telephone lines, with the output possibly presented on a cathode ray tube.

During the last few years the so-called "time-sharing companies" have experienced a rapid rate of growth. Many organisations are coming to realise that there is some advantage in having a senior planner (or in some cases the decision makers themselves) able to gain direct access to the corporate or planning model stored within a time-sharing computer. Recognising this fact, the major manu-facturers of batch-mode computers are now developing systems which enable these to be used also on a time-sharing basis. When this has been achieved with a high level of efficiency, and assuming that computers of a sufficient size are held, this arrangement is likely to be the most satisfactory for medium and large sized organisa-tions. For although existing facilities offered by the time-sharing companies are ideal for smaller models (say, a hundred equations or thereabouts) capacity limitations preclude the manipulation of optimisation or probabilistic simulation models of thousands of equations.

Simultaneously with the development of computer hardware considerable advances are being made in improving the effectiveness of software, most particularly for time-sharing use. Planning within an organisation is a highly flexible process and planners do not themselves operate most efficiently within a rigid framework. Various programming languages are therefore being developed which facilitate modifications to both the model and the forms of input and output. Such names as Foresight, Oracle, FAPS (Finan-cial Analysis and Planning Systems), S.P.E. (Strategy Planning and Evaluation), and Prosper are being encountered. The planning and decision making avenues opened up by these developments in computer hardware and software will be examined further in Chapter 9.

GENERAL COMMENTS AND SUMMARY

At the beginning of the Chapter it was stressed that a decision did not involve only that moment of time at which a particular course of action was finally specified, but related to the whole process leading to the final event. For most effective decision making management should both be involved in and appreciative of the methods of analysis used. (It is the aim of the Chapters which follow to satisfy the latter requirement.) Some space was devoted to examining the environment of decision making, giving particular consideration to the ways in which the demand for decisions to be taken could arise. Mention was made of the fact that most decisions taken at a high level within organisations are of a planning nature and must therefore involve risk and uncertainty. It was suggested that for the most effective overall use of its resources, an organisation should support planning activity aimed at the attainment of objectives and goals arising from a process in which a conscious attempt is made to select the "best" courses of action at corporate level. The difficulty of determining what the "best" or "optimum" objectives may be, quite apart from establishing the best ways of achieving them, was recognised. It was noted in particular that objectives may be a mix of the quantifiable and the non-quantifiable, in which case the latter could only exist in the form of constraints rather than be part of an objective function as defined later in the Chapter.

It was then claimed that the model (and in particular the mathematical model) had a fundamental role to play in providing a basis for logical decision making. After presenting some of the concepts involved in constructing models, the latter were then examined according to certain aspects of their structure. An important distinction was held to be that distinguishing a normative model from a positive model. Whereas positive models are simply relationships which actually exist in real life expressed mathematically, normative models are relationships which attempt to explain the manner in which one variable may be determined by one or more other variables. In the first instance, a decision maker should be aware of the existence of normative relationships within models which he uses to aid his decision making. In the second place, use by him of normative models requires something of an act of faith, as the best of relationships appropriate to historical data may be inefficient in the future. Thus an extra region of uncertainty is added to the one which surrounds the values which are estimated for variables outside the control of the decision maker.

The quantitative aids which are described in the Chapters which follow are those which have been found to be of most value in relation to high level decision making during recent years. It is however important to appreciate that resort need not necessarily be made to ready-made models or techniques. Purpose built problem solving procedures, because of their relevance, are often likely to provide managers with a more effective basis for decision making.

Nevertheless as understanding of the behaviour of organisations increases it is inevitable that the body of hypothesis and theory will grow. A book by Horowitz* gives a first class exposition of the possible relevance of the classical and more recent theory of the firm to managerial problem solving at the tactical level of operation. In this book, models based on the supply and demand functions, production functions and so on of microeconomic theory are considered along with more recently developed models of operational research which have been shown to be effective at the tactical level of operations. It cannot be claimed in any sense that some of the theories of microeconomics have general application, but Horowitz performs the most useful task of bringing together quantitative analysis which has hitherto received quite separate treatment, and demonstrated a possible synergetic effect in doing so.

The final section of the Chapter indicated that for corporate decisions requiring a substantial basis of quantitative analysis a computing facility is imperative for the evaluation of models. In addition to problems of communication between the decision maker and the model builder, there may also exist a similar problem in respect of the computing activity. The advent of time-sharing and readily comprehensible languages which facilitate computation on-line and in real time will enable senior managers to first overcome any "mystique" which surrounds the computer, and secondly if they desire actually to use models to evaluate the consequences of decisions which they might wish to take. The availability of visual display units may prove to be of considerable value here.

---

* See IRA HOROWITZ, *Decision Making and the Theory of the Firm*, Holt, Rinehart and Winston, Inc., New York, 1970.

Chapter Three

BASIC MATHEMATICS AND STATISTICS

INTRODUCTION

The purpose of this Chapter is to present and develop (where necessary) the mathematical and statistical relationships, properties and procedures which are used elsewhere in the book. Readers who have advanced knowledge of mathematics and statistics need of course make no reference to this section. The author is however conscious of the fact that very many practising managers would make no claim to expertise in this area and that many students of management who aim to become practising managers take courses in mathematics and statistics which are too remote from possible applications in an organisational environment. An objective of this book is not that readers should acquire mathematical skills, but that they should gain at the minimum an appreciation of the manner in which quantitative formulations and solutions may be established. If the content of this Chapter appears to be fragmentary, then this is due to the fact that only material directly related to the developments in other Chapters is included; the author can see little point in digressing. If the erstwhile non-numerate reader concludes that the quantitative approach with its particular symbolism and language is not quite as formidable as had been imagined and develops a desire for further study, then a number of excellent books are available.*

In large part the mystique which surrounds mathematics, even at elementary levels, is due to the symbolism and notation which it employs. The effect of a departure from the written word in a passage can be catastrophic. The thread of the argument may be broken and a valuable insight lost. How often will a non-numerate manager omit to read an article (even though it might be included

---

* See JUDITH ATHERTON, MICHAEL J. C. MARTIN, AND GERAINT ROBERTS, *Mathematics for Management Science*, Holt, Rinehart & Winston, London, 1972, for basic mathematics and YA-LUN CHOU, *Statistical Analysis*, Holt, Rinehart & Winston, New York, 1969.

in his own professional journal) if at first glance it is seen to contain more than diagrams and words? With this in mind it is thought to be appropriate to present in Appendix I the equivalent in English of the mathematical and statistical notation used in this book. And it is recommended that a few minutes are spent reading through the list. It will be appreciated that in some cases the symbols used are simply shorthand (for example, "equals" and "the sum of"), whereas in other cases an "operation" is implied (for example, change brought about by differentiation). Mathematics could in fact be conducted in a spoken language and indeed some reformulation in this direction is required in order to programme analysis for evaluation by a computer (thus we might find

```
SQRT
```

indicating that a square root should be taken).

Another conceptual hurdle which arises frequently is the general as opposed to the numeric representation of a relationship. Ask a non-mathematician to reduce to its simplest form:

$$\text{I.} \qquad \frac{1}{n-1} - \frac{1}{n}$$

and some difficulty may be experienced. And yet the same person will find little difficulty in evaluating:

$$\frac{1}{3} - \frac{1}{4} \quad \text{as} \quad \frac{1}{12}$$

I is in fact the general model for subtracting two simple fractions when the denominators differ by one and will simplify to:

$$\frac{n-(n-1)}{n(n-1)} = \frac{1}{n(n-1)}$$

The remainder of this Chapter will be divided into two main sections. The first will deal with the necessary mathematics and the second with statistics. An attempt will be made to demonstrate that the latter is particularly appropriate to higher level planning decisions in organisations, due to the estimates, forecasts, and generalisations which are necessary.

REQUIRED MATHEMATICS

Linear Equations and Inequalities
Many decisions require the evaluation of relationships. It is known that sales revenue is related to the number of items sold and the

selling price, that tax revenue is related to income levels and working population and so on. Suppose that the rateable value of a local authority was £20,000,000 and that a rate income of £12,000,000 was required. The necessary rate R is then obtained as the solution of the *equation*:

I. $$20R = 12$$

It should be noted that it is not customary to include units (here £ m) in the equation if these apply to both sides. There is only one value of R (the solution) for which the relationship will hold, namely 60 pence. We say that the equation is *linear* or of the *first order*. The general purpose of writing relationships in the form of equations is to obtain a solution. But consider now the first relationship mentioned in this section, that between sales revenue S, items sold N, and price P. We now have an equation in three variables:

II. $$S = NP$$

with S the dependent variable and N and P independent variables. In order to obtain a solution for S, it is necessary to reduce equation II to the form of equation I and this can only be done by ascribing values to N and P. In a mathematical sense, the number of solutions possible for S is unlimited. If more than one unknown or variable is part of the analysis it may be possible to solve for them if more information is available through further relationships. In general to solve for n variables n linear equations are required (these are often described as "simultaneous" equations).

An understanding of how to solve simultaneous equations is of use in appreciating the concepts of linear programming which are discussed in Chapter 8. In that Chapter the following equations in two unknowns appear:

III. $$2S+3D = 450$$
IV. $$S+2D = 250$$

Probably the easiest way of obtaining a solution for S and D is to combine the equations to eliminate one variable, to arrive at a single equation in one unknown. Using the property that the relationship still holds if both sides of the equation are multiplied by the same number we multiply equation IV by 2 to produce:

V. $$2S+4D = 500$$

The next step is to subtract term for term equation III from equation

V to produce a single equation, which gives the value of D directly as 50. By substituting this value in either of the equations III and IV the value of S is determined as 150. The computations involved in solving the many simultaneous equations which arise from a practical linear programming application become very heavy, but are easily handled by an electronic computer.

Reference was also made in the heading of this section to linear inequalities. Their inclusion is of relevance on account of constraints which are present in most resource allocation problems and which may be formally incorporated within a linear programme. Inequalities describe the range of possibilities which are of the nature "greater than," "not greater than," "less than or equal to"; these are included in Appendix I. Manipulation of inequalities can be a little confusing but they can (as is the case in linear programming) be converted into equalities. For example, the inequalities of the form "less than or equal to" which are encountered in Chapter 8 and which may be written:

$$a \leqslant b$$

may be written $a+s = b$ where $s \geqslant 0$. Here it will suffice to take a different view of the inequality. By plotting a linear relationship on a graph a straight line will be produced. What is the graphical representation of a linear inequality? Consider a car assembly plant which can during a month assemble 2000 of model A or 1000 of model B. It would not be realistic to describe the production mix by the equation:

VII. $\qquad A+2B = 2000$

as in practice other limiting factors may exist. It may for example be the case that only 1500 engines are available monthly for model A and 800 for model B. In other words the solution of equation VII which is $A = 2000$ if all production is concentrated on model A, is not feasible. Assembly capacity should therefore be seen as a constraint to be considered along with all other constraints and is re-written as:

VIII. $\qquad A+2B \leqslant 2000$

As only two variables are involved, graphical representation of equation VII and inequality VIII is possible and is shown in Fig. 11. Considering equation VII alone, any point on the line XY is a feasible mix (*e.g.* point Z where $A = 1600$ and $B = 200$). But as

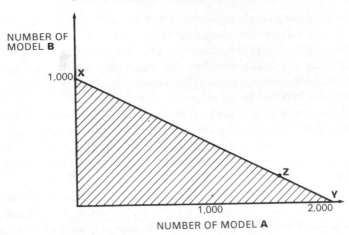

FIG. 11. Graphical representation of an inequality.

far as inequality VIII is concerned, any point in the shaded region is feasible (including the lines which bound the feasible region). The inequality permits zero assembly of A and B (a feasible but impractical mix) in addition to the very numerous non-zero mixes.

Higher Order Relationships
Linear equations are manipulated more easily than any other type of relationship, and the arithmetic involved in deriving solutions is in consequence at a minimum. In practical models of organisations the number of relationships may be very high, and it is of considerable advantage if it is possible to express these in linear terms. There is however no particular reason why linearity should apply rather than any other form of relationship. In fact, in a number of instances, the straight line could well be a less than satisfactory description of an organisation's performance. This may be demonstrated by considering the profits of a company for three successive years:

    1969 £1,000,000
    1970 £2,000,000
    1971 £3,000,000

During the period profits increase linearly, that is in a constant increment of £1,000,000. The growth rates (on a previous year basis) are, however, not linear. The 1970 rate was 100 per cent (£1,000,000 increase related to a base of £1,000,000) whereas in 1971 this fell to 50 per cent. For a constant growth rate, required profits in 1971 would have been £4,000,000.

In practice it is often found that linearity cannot be assumed and that higher powers or exponents are involved. A linear equation contains constants and terms in x only. A second order equation contains terms in x^2 (that is two xs multiplied together), a third order equation contains terms in x^3, and so on. Apart from the problem of estimating the nature of a higher order relationship (this receives some attention in Chapter 4) a major disadvantage is the computational difficulty of determining the various solutions. The order of the equation determines the number of solutions which exist, thus a quadratic (second order) possesses two, a cubic three, and a quartic four. There is no need, for an understanding of this book, to be familiar with analytical solution procedures for higher order equations, but it is felt that there may be some advantage in being able to appreciate the form of relationships of this type; this is best achieved by graphing.

Assume that the following relationship has been estimated between gross profit g, and the weekly quantity of an item manufactured and sold, q:

$$g = 200q - 0.05q^3 - 2000 \text{ where } g \text{ is in } £$$

The relationship is of the third order and although certain conclusions may be reached analytically a graph of gross profit against quantity may assist interpretation. The graph can be established by determining the values of the dependent variable g corresponding to a number of values of the independent variable q. A list of values is as follows:

q	$200q$		$0.05q^3$		2000	=	g
0	0	−	0	−	2000	=	−2000
10	2000	−	50	−	2000	=	−50
20	4000	−	400	−	2000	=	1600
30	6000	−	1350	−	2000	=	2650
40	8000	−	3200	−	2000	=	2800
50	10,000	−	6250	−	2000	=	1750
60	12,000	−	10,800	−	2000	=	−800

It is customary to use the vertical scale of a graph for the dependent variable and the horizontal scale for the independent variable.

Figure 12 shows in graphical form the relationship between gross profit and quantity manufactured and sold. The graph demonstrates much more clearly than the equation how gross profit varies

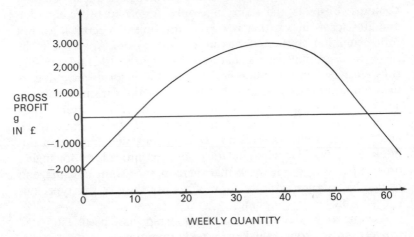

FIG. 12. The graphical representation of the non-linear relationship
$$g = 200q - 0.05q^3 - 2000.$$

with quantity. It can be seen that a profit can only be made if quantity falls within the approximate range 10–57. Determination of the points at which the curve cuts the horizontal axis indicate two of the three solutions to the equation:

$$200q - 0.05q^3 - 2000 = 0$$

The third solution falls in the negative region of q when q is about -70 (meaningful in mathematical if not practical terms). Figure 12 also indicates that there is one value of q (approximately 36) which generates maximum gross profit. This relationship will be used in a section which follows to demonstrate how a maximum may be determined analytically.

Further Exponential Relationships

Non-linear equations considered so far have included exponents which are whole numbers and positive. At one or two points in the book reference is made to exponents which are fractional, and in the development of logarithms below it is necessary also to examine the implications of zero and negative exponents.

Take first the positive fractional exponent; this may appear in a relationship of the form:

$$y = x^{a/b} \quad \text{(which may be written } \sqrt[b]{x^a})$$

This means that y is obtained by raising x to the ath power and then finding the bth "root" of this (in this context a root of a number is a value which when multiplied by itself a certain number of times will give that number). The same answer will be obtained whether the root is taken first or second, but it will be appreciated that smaller numbers will usually be obtained by taking the root first. For example, assume it is required to evaluate:

$$y = 64^{\frac{2}{3}}$$

Actually 4 multiplied by itself 3 times gives 64, that is 4 is the "cube" root of 64. Therefore the relationship is reduced to:

$$y = 4^2 = 16$$

If 64 had first been squared, larger numbers would have been involved. A negative exponent may always be converted to a positive exponent by inverting. Thus:

$$y = x^{-a/b} = \frac{1}{x^{a/b}}$$

For example:

$$y = x^{-2} = \frac{1}{x^2}$$

Values on each side of an equals sign may be cross-multiplied. The last relationship gives:

$$\frac{x^{-2}}{1} = \frac{1}{x^2}$$

and by cross-multiplication:

$$(x^{-2})(x^2) = (1)(1) = 1$$

Now when exponential forms of the same base are multiplied together the exponents may be added, in which case:

$$(x^{-2})(x^2) = x^{-2+2} = x^0 = 1$$

This means that any number (fractional or whole, negative or positive) raised to the power zero is one. This property is widely used in mathematics.

Logarithms

Expressing numbers or variables in logarithmic form is of major value in facilitating computation and analysis. Use is made of the previously stated property that multiplication of exponential forms of the same base permits addition of the exponents. Taking logarithms requires that all numbers shall be expressed as an exponential form of a common base, following which multiplication is reduced to addition (and division to subtraction). Two bases are most widely used; 10 for computational work and the constant e which plays an important part in mathematical analysis. The base 10 is most appropriate in consequence of the decimal nature of our number system. More formally:

$$\text{if} \quad a = b^x \quad \text{then} \quad \log_b a = x$$

where x is now the logarithm of a to the base b. Tables of logarithms to both of the bases mentioned are freely available. From a table of logarithms to the base 10 it will be found that to 4 places of decimals the logarithm of 2 is .3010, that is:

$$\log_{10} 2 = .3010 \quad \text{or} \quad 2 = 10^{.3010}$$

The tables are usually constructed by determining the power to which 10 must be raised to yield values between 1.001 and 9.999 in increments of .001.

As an example of the procedure, assume that evaluation is required of:

$$\frac{0.02 \times 300}{1.5}$$

It can be seen by inspection that the answer is 4. The various numbers may however be written as powers of 10 in the range of 1.001–9.999 (that is logarithms taken from tables). But it will be noted that only one of the numbers falls within the range, *e.g.* 0.02 is 2 divided by 100 which may be re-written as 2 multiplied by 10^{-2}. From logarithm tables, the whole expression may now be represented in powers of 10 as:

$$\frac{(10^{-2} \times 10^{.3010}) \times (10^2 \times 10^{.4771})}{10^{.1761}}$$

or

$$\frac{(10^{\overline{2}.3010}) \times (10^{2.4771})}{10^{.1761}}$$

Note that the negative portion of the logarithm is indicated by placing the minus sign over the 2. The remaining part of that exponent is positive. This is the customary method of using logarithms, but precisely the same result would be achieved if in that particular part of the expression the exponent was expressed as -1.6990. By adding the two exponents in the numerator and subtracting the exponent in the denominator the expression is reduced to a single power of 10, namely:

$$10^{.6020}$$

From the tables .6020 is the logarithm of 4, which is thus the answer required.

As might be expected, this cumbersome procedure is streamlined in the practical use of logarithms. The base never enters into the calculations, which are performed using the exponents only. The purpose of the method of presentation employed here was to attempt to convey the underlying principles of logarithms.

There are a number of useful properties of logarithms, of which the following are (for any base) of relevance:

(i) $\log a + \log b = \log (ab)$
(ii) $\log a - \log b = \log (a/b)$
(iii) $\log a^n = n \log a$

(i) may be demonstrated by letting

$$\log_{10} a = y \quad \text{and} \quad \log_{10} b = z$$

when $a = 10^y$ and $b = 10^z$ and $ab = (10^y)(10^z) = 10^{y+z}$. Taking logarithms to the base 10

$$\log ab = y + z = \log a + \log b$$

The proof of (ii) is along similar lines and (iii) may be derived from (i) as for the addition of n terms in $\log a$:

$$n \log a = \log a + \log a + \ldots + \log a$$
$$= \log (a . a \ldots a) = \log a^n$$

Differentiation

At just one or two points in this book, reference is made to "differentiation" and the "derivative." In order that the reader may have some understanding of the process involved, a few comments are made here. It is not proposed to give any more than the briefest of details partly because as stated already differentiation appears only infrequently in these pages, but more importantly because of the limited role of this branch of mathematical analysis in decisions of a planning nature.

Differentiation is part of the *calculus*, the mathematics of change. It is of use in determining precisely through analysis of the rate of change of a function such things as maximum or minimum points. Thus if it is possible to establish functional relationships for profits and costs, suitable operating levels corresponding to optimum performance may be established.

In the simplest terms if y, the dependent variable, is some function of x, the independent variable, we have:

$$y = f(x)$$

For each value of x there will be a unique value of y. Further information about the function may be obtained by determining the "slope" of the function at any value of x. In particular, if a continuous function has a maximum or minimum then at this point the slope is zero. The slope is obtained by differentiation and is in fact termed the first derivative. It is written dy/dx, which indicates the instantaneous rate of change of y with respect to x. The method of obtaining derivatives need not concern us here and the only standard result needed is as follows:

If $y = ax^n$ then $\dfrac{dy}{dx} = nax^{n-1}$ where n may be positive, negative or fractional.

NOTE: The rate of change of a constant is zero and hence the derivative of a constant is zero.

Consider $y = x^2$ when $a = 1$ and $n = 2$, then dy/dx is $2x^{2-1} = 2x$.

Thus the slope at any value of x is $2x$ and will increase as x becomes larger, positively or negatively. This will be seen to be the case if the function is plotted on a graph. If a function contains more than one term differentiation is carried out on a term by term basis. The relationship between gross profit g and quantity produced q used earlier was:

$$g = 200q - 0.05q^3 - 2000$$

The graph of this function indicated that a maximum value existed for g and this may be determined precisely by calculating the value of q for which the slope dg/dq is zero. Differentiating term by term with respect to q:

$$\frac{dg}{dq} = 200 - 0.15q^2$$

For $\qquad \frac{dg}{dq} = 0, \qquad 0{\cdot}15q^2 = 200$

The practical solution for q must be the positive value (mathematically this may be shown to give the maximum) and is 36.5. Inserting the nearest whole number, 37, in the expression for gross profit, a maximum of £2867 is indicated.

The space devoted to this procedure in no way relates to the importance of the calculus in mathematics. But as whole books describe only the basic principles it will be evident that the inclusion of additional pages in this chapter would not permit of anything more than the most superficial treatment.

Series
This section will indicate how the sum of a number of terms which have a common form may be determined. Use will also be made of the summation notation Σ to demonstrate how economies in writing may be achieved.

The two most basic types of series are arithmetic progressions (A.P.) and geometric progressions (G.P.). In the former case there exists a constant difference between terms, in the latter case the relationship is a constant ratio.

An example of an A.P. is:

$$3, 6, 9, 12, 15, \ldots$$

when the common difference is three.

A G.P. with a common ratio of three is:

$$2, 6, 18, 54, 162, \ldots$$

The differences and ratios can be whole numbers or fractions, negative or positive. It is often necessary to consider the sums of progressions, and there are a number of rules which assist in their determination. The major problem is whether the series are convergent or divergent. In the former case, the sum of an unlimited number of terms will tend to a limiting figure, whereas in the latter case the sum is unbounded.

Taking first, series of a limited number of terms, an A.P. with common difference d will be:

$$a, a+d, a+2d, \ldots, a+(n-1)d$$

the general term is $a+(r-1)d$ where the range of r is 1 to n. It may be shown that the sum of n terms in summation notation is:

$$\sum_{r=1}^{n} (a+(r-1)d) = \frac{n}{2}(2a+(n-1)d)$$

Thus the sum of the first six terms of the above A.P. where $a = 3$ and $d = 3$ is:

$$\frac{6}{2}(6+5\times3) = 63$$

A limited term G.P. with common ratio k is:

$$a, ak, ak^2, \ldots, ak^{n-1}$$

Again it may be shown using the general term that the sum of n terms is:

$$\sum_{r=1}^{n} ak^{r-1} = \frac{a(k^n-1)}{k-1}$$

For the G.P. written above $a = 2$ and $k = 3$, and the sum of the first six terms is therefore:

$$\frac{2(3^6-1)}{2} = 728$$

If the number of terms is not limited but is infinite then the sum of an A.P. will diverge in a positive or negative direction. The case of the G.P. can, however, be more complex. One example which will be given will be that in which the common ratio k is positive and lies between zero and one. The expression for the sum of the general G.P. with a finite number of terms is:

$$\frac{a(k^n-1)}{k-1}$$

As n tends to infinity (∞) because k is fractional, k^n will tend to zero. The sum is therefore:

$$\sum_{r=1}^{n} ak^{r-1} = \frac{a(0-1)}{k-1} = \frac{-a}{k-1} = \frac{a}{1-k}$$

For example the sum of:

$$4, 2, \tfrac{1}{2}, \tfrac{1}{4}, \tfrac{1}{8}, \ldots$$

which is converging and for which $k = \tfrac{1}{2}$ is:

$$\frac{4}{1-\tfrac{1}{2}} = 8$$

Compounding and Discounting

It is often necessary to take account of the time value of money in decisions of a financial nature. The principle of compound interest is widely understood. A sum of £A invested at an annual interest rate R will grow to £$A(1+R)$ at the end of year 1, £$A(1+R)^2$ at the end of year 2 and £$A(1+R)^n$ at the end of year n. Discounting operates in the reverse direction, so that the present value of a certain sum anticipated in the future may be obtained. Thus £S anticipated at the end of the nth year from the present time will be evaluated as £$S/(1+I)^n$ where I is the discount rate. The *net present value* (N.P.V.) of a series of sums generated by an initial investment £A will thus be in £:

$$-A + S_1/(1+I) + S_2/(1+I)^2 + \ldots S_n/(1+I)^n$$

If it is wished to determine the discount rate at which the N.P.V. is zero, often referred to as the *internal rate of return*, I.R.R., then a solution is required to:

$$A = \sum_{i=1}^{n} S_i/(1+I)^i$$

There is no simple way of achieving the solution and a computer is generally necessary to cope with the extensive calculations of a "trial and error" nature which are involved.

As an example of a rather different type, involving compounding and the sum of series, consider the calculation of the annual sum P, needed to recover the cost of a single investment A, in plant or equipment after n years.

If A had been invested at the rate R it would be worth $A(1+R)^n$ after n years. Assume that the first payment P is made at the end of the first year and the final payment at the end of the nth year. The sum P at the end of year $(n-1)$ will grow to $P(1+R)$, the sum P at the end of year $(n-2)$ will grow to $P(1+R)^2$, and so on until finally the first payment P will grow to $P(1+R)^{n-1}$. The annual payment P is then obtained from the equation:

$$A(1+R)^n = \sum_{i=1}^{n} P(1+R)^{i-1}$$

The right hand side is a G.P. with common ratio $(1+R)$, and this leads to:

$$A(1+R)^n = P\left[\frac{(1+R)^n-1}{1+R-1}\right] = \left[\frac{P}{R}\ (1+R)^n-1\right]$$

and

$$P = \frac{RA(1+R)^n}{(1+R)^n-1}$$

For example, assume $A = £1$ and $R = 0.1$ and that it is desired to calculate the annual sum P due at the end of each of eight years. This is

$$P = \frac{(0.1)(1)(1.1)^8}{(1.1)^8-1} = £0.19$$

STATISTICS

Statistics involves the basing of conclusions on observations. The word has its root in the Latin *status* meaning state, and it was in fact the case that until recent times virtually all observations were made at the instigation of government. As planning has become increasingly formalised in organisations of all types, the need to record and analyse data has led to statistics becoming a vital part of the decision process.

A major dichotomy exists within statistics, which arises from the manner in which the conclusions are drawn from observations. In the first place, there are conclusions which are restricted to the data collected or are extended beyond the observations in a non-scientific manner; this is the area of *descriptive statistics*. In the second place *inferential statistics* or *statistical method* relates to conclusions which are inferred about some *population* on the basis of a *sample* of observations drawn from it. In neither case can any conclusions which extend beyond the bounds of the observations be guaranteed as correct. Descriptive statistics affords the opportunity for informed guesses. Inferential statistics takes advantage of the theory of *probability* to provide a basis for decision making which, given consistent attitudes towards uncertainty and utility, may be claimed to be logical.

Each branch of statistics will be examined separately and as inferential statistics requires certain of the results of descriptive statistics the latter will be presented first. It should be mentioned that the treatment will be non-rigorous. Statistics can be very difficult to comprehend, involving a high level of mathematics, and even persons with a strong quantitative background may experience much conceptual difficulty in understanding analyses of a probabilistic nature. If readers of the section on inferential statistics wonder how these conceptual difficulties arise they would be well advised to study the subject further—if only for intellectual stimulation!

DESCRIPTIVE STATISTICS

The prerequisite for any statistical analysis is the availability of appropriate data. It is possible that the required information exists already, alternatively it may be necessary to make directed observations. These observations may require the setting up of an experiment or the recording of information on a form or questionnaire. A good deal of skill is required in the design of forms and questionnaires as even when the responding population is "captive," in the sense that a reply may be mandatory, ambiguous questions can produce the "wrong" answers. Usually organisations are able to obtain accurate information about their own ongoing operations. The greatest skill is required in designing and conducting surveys or investigations in the organisational environment. In addition to *sampling error* which arises by chance there also exists the possibility of *non-sampling error* which is caused by an inefficient procedure. Brief reference will be made to these two types of error below.

Descriptive statistics is concerned with collection, presentation and interpretation of data. The importance of the efficient collection of data has been stressed and it will be assumed that the stage has been reached when suitable raw data are available. (In passing, it may be mentioned that organisations frequently possess data which contain valuable answers to questions which are never put.)

The Presentation of Data

To provide the basis for an example it is assumed that a large national supplier of office equipment wishes to draw some conclusions about the magnitude of business undertaken through its several thousand distributors. Records are maintained in a computer of the value of monthly transactions and a sample (methods of sampling are discussed later in the Chapter) of sixty is taken indicating in each case the total value of transactions during the previous half year. These values, in the order arising from the sampling procedure, are shown in Table III.

TABLE III: VALUE OF TRANSACTIONS THROUGH SIXTY DISTRIBUTORS
DURING A SIX MONTH PERIOD

£	£	£	£	£	£
743	2161	3007	6600	7733	3301
2864	2073	2289	2001	9721	6421
4412	2117	48	163	7212	2640
2018	5246	4313	342	7868	6127
3471	2651	45	3615	5912	0
1414	4613	17	3618	2770	9348
8760	8312	2994	1988	5030	4623
3980	5862	6403	4000	2415	131
5086	3490	2898	6421	6009	4648
3215	5050	3002	4116	4660	2333

It would be very difficult to draw conclusions based on this raw data. Some classification is required before it is presented to anyone wishing to use it to arrive at a decision. This is afforded by drawing up a table in which the data are grouped together, and a possible way of doing this is shown in Table IV.

TABLE IV: THE RAW DATA OF TABLE III PLACED IN GROUPS

Number of distributors	Value of transactions during the six month period £(000)
10	0 below 2
23	2 below 4
14	4 below 6
9	6 below 8
4	8 below 10

This is much more comprehensive, but at the same time it will be appreciated that some of the original information has been lost.

In this instance, possibly the most significant omission is the fact that business through several distributors amounted to virtually nothing. It will also be apparent that care must be taken in selecting the most appropriate group interval. The fewer the number of groups then the more of the original information is lost. In the extreme case the whole of the data in Table III could be presented as a group of sixty within the range of £0–£10,000.

The method of defining group intervals in Table IV ensured that no ambiguity existed in allocating individual values to groups. The transaction valued at £4000 quite clearly falls in the group of £4000–£6000. It will be seen below that in order to take the analysis a stage further it is necessary to specify a single representative value for a group; this is usually the mid point. Strictly, the range of values in the group mentioned is £4000–£5999 and the mid point is thus £4999.5. In this case, little is lost by assuming a mid point of £5000.

Often tabulation is the extent of use of statistics, decision makers reading what they can into the classified data. If it is desired to make an impact on the reader, recourse is often made to pictorial or graphical presentation. Examples of pictorial presentation are pie charts and pictograms with which most people are familiar. Scaled axes are also used, particularly for various forms of bar charts. Here, details are given of one method of graphical presentation known as the *histogram*. Examination of Fig. 13 should enable the principle of the histogram to be clearly understood. The data of Table IV is used again, the *frequency* of each group determining

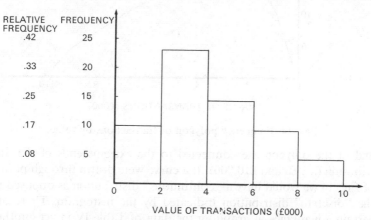

FIG. 13. Histogram of transactions by value.

the height of the bar corresponding to the number of distributors in each range of values.

It will be noted that both of the axes are scaled, although it is not necessary that both scales be identical. Now it may be easier to draw further conclusions about the nature of distributors; the effects of contracts and discounts, for example. The use of frequency on the vertical scale may lead to some difficulty if it is desired to compare one histogram with another as different sized samples may be involved. To overcome this, *relative frequency* may be used, in which case the proportion of total frequency is determined. This is shown as an additional vertical scale in Fig. 13 with relative frequency given to two decimal places.

The stepped nature of the histogram arises because of the manner in which the data are grouped. As an alternative to the histogram a *frequency polygon* may be constructed from the data. In this the frequency or relative frequency is plotted against the mid point of each group and the points graphed joined by straight lines. This is done in Fig. 14, when to complete the polygon the points at each

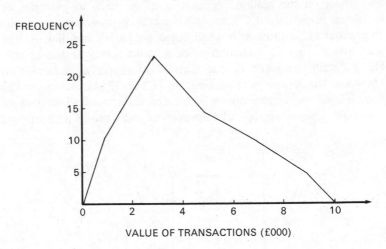

FIG. 14. Frequency polygon of transactions by value.

end of the polygon are connected to the extreme ends of the distribution (*i.e.* £0 and £10,000). If a curve were drawn through points of Fig. 14 we would have a "continuous" distribution as opposed to the "discrete" distribution indicated by the histogram. There are certain advantages in graphing the data of Table IV in yet another form, in this case, cumulatively. Cumulative frequency distributions are usually of the "less than" or "equal to or greater than" type. Fig. 15 indicates how the data of Table IV may be graphed according

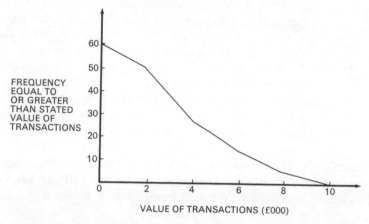

FIG. 15. Cumulative frequency distribution of transactions by value.

to the "equal to or greater than" type of distribution. An advantage of plotting cumulatively is that the full range of the distribution is taken into account and group central values are not required.

Analysis and Interpretation of Data

It has been implied already that the degree of analysis undertaken in the area of descriptive statistics is limited, and interpretation is to some extent superficial in nature. As conclusions are frequently based on sample results it is advantageous to be able to undertake comparisons between samples themselves or between a sample

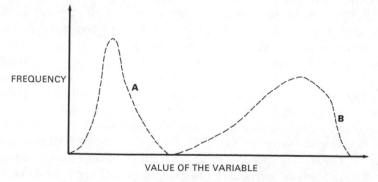

FIG. 16. Comparison between distributions.

and the population from which it is assumed to have been drawn. It may be for example that in order to study trends it is wished to make a comparison between the sample results of Table IV and the results of a sample taken the previous year. A visual comparison may be made using data which are tabulated or are graphed as a histogram or frequency polygon. But attempts to compare the whole of the distributions may lead to difficulties of interpretation. Statistics affords the opportunity to describe distributions by consolidated measures. Referring to Fig. 16 two distributions A and B are shown as continuous curves. It is immediately apparent that A and B are quite dissimilar. Descriptively the values of B are larger and more dispersed, and while both distributions are non-symmetrical B is "skewed" to the left and A to the right. Single figure measures are available which indicate the location, dispersion and skewness of distribution. We shall examine the first two of these.

Measures of Location

Instinctively most people would think in terms of an "average" to describe the location of a distribution. Three types of average are often encountered the mean, the median, and the mode. The mode is the most frequently occurring value (sometimes described as the "most likely" value) and is the value of the variable corresponding to the highest point of a frequency distribution. The median is the value of the variable at the point where the area of a distribution is cut exactly in half. Thus in Fig. 16 the median will be to the right of the mode in distribution A and to the left in distribution B. The median is obtained easily from a cumulative frequency distribution if relative frequencies are used. It is the value corresponding to a relative frequency of 0.5 or 50 per cent.

Both the mode and median are unaffected by extreme values of the distribution and although this may be unimportant if a distribution is nearly symmetrical the measures will be less satisfactory if pronounced skewness or irregularities exist. The mean provides an opportunity to take account of all measured values and as will be seen later is of more value than a purely descriptive measure. The arithmetic mean (often referred to simply as the "average") gives equal weight to all observed values; for example, by totalling the values in Table III and by dividing by 60 it is found to be £3905. The procedure is basically the same for grouped frequency distributions but in this case a degree of approximation is involved. Thus referring to Table IV only five values of transaction are recognised and these are the mid points of each group. We have therefore:

10 at £1000 =	£10,000
23 at £3000 =	£69,000
14 at £5000 =	£70,000
9 at £7000 =	£63,000
4 at £9000 =	£36,000
	£248,000

Again dividing by 60 the mean is £4133 compared with £3905 when the mean was calculated on the basis of individual values. It is fairly evident that the difference between the means arises because of the number of transactions falling at the lower end of the first group.

Measure of Dispersion

The second stage of describing distributions by single measures is to add to the measure of location some measure which indicates the variability or dispersion. There are a number of alternatives, of which the *range* is easiest to determine. From Table III the range is seen to be £0–£9721 (£0–£9999 from Table IV). With distributions which are not concentrated near the mean it is difficult to assess the significance of the range. Is there a steady decline in frequency until the limiting values are reached or is an isolated value detached from the bulk of observations? In the latter case, the range would be unrepresentative and other measures have been proposed which use the difference in value between the limits of some central portion of the distribution.

If it is desired to take into account all the observations a different approach is required. In the first place it is necessary to establish some reference point from which deviation is measured; this is usually the mean. Two measures of this type appear in this book; the *mean deviation* and the *standard deviation*.

As its name implies, the mean deviation is the mean of the deviations from the mean. To demonstrate both this and the standard deviation the values 0, 2, 4, 6 and 8 are used. The mean of these five values is 4 and the deviations from the mean are successively -4, -2, 0, 2, and 4. It is apparent that these sum to 0 (implying the definition of the mean itself). An indication of the extent to which the values are dispersed may be obtained by ignoring the sign of the deviation and then averaging. This leads to the mean absolute deviation (M.A.D.) which is used in Chapter 4. In the example used above M.A.D. is 2.4.

The mathematician is not very happy about dropping signs and the M.A.D. is not widely used in statistical theory. One way to remove the troublesome minuses is to square them! This leads to a set of squared deviations 16, 4, 0, 4, 16 the mean of which is 8. This is in fact the *variance*, and is in squared units. To revert to the original units it is necessary to take the square root of the variance, which is the standard deviation referred to above and which is larger than the M.A.D. The standard deviation and the mean are the two main "parameters" of distributions and a great deal of inferential statistics may be undertaken once the values of each of these has been estimated. It is possible to derive further parameters for distributions, the third of which describes skewness, but these will not be pursued here.

This is as far as we need to go into the field of descriptive statistics. There is a good deal more which is normally included in this area including ratios, index numbers, analysis of time series, but with some knowledge of frequency distributions and their means and standard deviations it is now possible to progress to inferential statistics.

INFERENTIAL STATISTICS

This branch of statistics differs from descriptive statistics both in the manner in which information is collected and in the method of interpretation which is used. Frequently inferences are to be made about the population from which a sample is drawn and unless the sampling procedure is conducted in a particular manner (to be described below) any conclusions made are likely to be erroneous. If the sampling procedure is acceptable then inferential statistics provides a means whereby analysis and consistent action becomes possible. As uncertainty exists about the population from which a sample is drawn estimation and probabilistic interpretation are involved. Probability is fundamental to inferential statistics and some space must be devoted to describing in outline relevant aspects.

Probability and Probability Distributions
A great deal has been written, much of it philosophical, about the nature and meaning of probability. The concept is readily under-

stood if consideration is being given to the possible outcome of an experiment when there is a long history available of actual outcomes of the experiment (the *relative frequency* approach). Or it may be the case that the likelihood of all possible alternative outcomes may be applied instinctively. Thus few people will have had experience of rolling an eight sided die and yet the chance of the die resting on any one side would be put unhesitatingly at one in eight (the *classical* approach).

In the former case a reasonable quantified interpretation of probability may be obtained by letting the number of times that a particular outcome has arisen from n experiments be x. Then x/n is the relative frequency and the probability of the outcome occurring may be written:

$$\text{Limit of } \frac{x}{n} \text{ as } n \text{ tends to infinity}$$

This immediately sets the scale as ranging from zero to one, implying impossibility to certainty.

Unfortunately, decisions concerning the future are often taken on the basis of little or no experience and this raises the very controversial question as to whether probability is, in these circumstances, meaningful. This book is mainly concerned with high level planning decisions and reference is made to probability in the majority of Chapters. Almost invariably it must be accepted that the probability used is *subjective* in nature. Two important issues are raised, the first being the unresolvable difference which may exist between the probability ascribed to a particular outcome by various individuals. Secondly there is the problem of actually arriving at a probability.

The first reaction of an individual to a request to put a specific probability on an outcome may be that this is unrealistic. It is however possible to consolidate the attitudes which may be held, and which arise from experience, expertise or hunch, into a numerical value of probability. Take the extreme case of the weather. The response to a request to place a probability on it raining a week next Thursday may well be that the request is absurd. Now suppose that an opportunity to win £100 is proposed. This may be gained in one of two ways; by finding at the end of the day in question that there has been no rain or picking out a black ball from a bag containing a mixture of black and white balls. Assume that initially the bag contains 100 white balls and no black balls. Everyone would choose to wait in the hope that it would not rain. Now replace a white ball by a black ball, so that there would be a one in a hundred chance of drawing at random a black ball. Again, the vast majority would choose to wait in their attempt to win £100. By following this procedure a point is reached at which there is indifference between selecting from the bag and waiting. If for example the bag contains fifteen black balls and eighty-five white balls at this stage, then a probability of .85 has been placed on it raining during the day in question. Admittedly if the indifference level had been approached in the other direction it is unlikely that the same probability would have been indicated, but it is very likely that it would have been of the same order. The purpose of this example is to indicate that if pressed decision makers will in situations in which they have minimum experience be prepared to think around the implications and quantify their attitude towards uncertainty.

Expectation

To readers unfamiliar with statistical terminology the word "expectation" may create some confusion. For it is often the case that an "expected value" cannot in fact materialise! For our purposes the expected value can be equated with the arithmetic mean and it is well known that this may also not accord with real life (*e.g.* 2.3 children per family). It may be difficult for a manager to reconcile feasible alternatives which he has listed and to which he has applied probabilities with a single value which although described as expectation is infeasible.

The calculation of expected value is quite simple. How much for example would repeated participation in the following game with a die be worth (ignoring questions of utility)?

(*a*) If numbers 1, 2, 3 or 4 are thrown: Win 6p
(*b*) If numbers 5 or 6 are thrown: Lose 10p

The probability of a 1, 2, 3 or 4 is two-thirds and the probability of a 5 or 6 is one-third. The expected value is then:

$$(\tfrac{2}{3})(6) + (\tfrac{1}{3})(-10) = \tfrac{2}{3}\text{p}$$

The game can only produce a win of 10p or a loss of 6p but the expected value is $\tfrac{2}{3}$p. Although this is not the face value of a coin it would tell a possible participant that if he were able to play the game many times for payment of $\tfrac{1}{2}$p each time he would *expect* to win. Conversely if he payed 1p per game he would *expect* to lose.

The mean of a probability distribution which may for a discrete distribution be written

$$\sum xP(x)$$

for all x, where $P(x)$ is the probability of a particular value of x, may be taken as being synonymous with expected value.

The Multiplication and Addition Theorems

There are two theorems of probability which are the basis for much analysis. These are the *addition theorem* and the *multiplication theorem* and they are demonstrated by reference to two events A and B where $P(A)$ indicates the probability of event A occurring and $P(B)$ the probability of event B.

The addition theorem:

$$P\begin{pmatrix} A \text{ or } B \\ \text{or both} \end{pmatrix} = P(A) + P(B) - P(A \text{ and } B)$$

The multiplication theorem:

$$P(A \text{ and } B) = P(A)P(B|A) \quad \text{where} \quad P(B|A) \quad \text{is}$$
read as the probability of B *given A*.

Two problems involving a pack of cards are now considered.

1. In the first place the probability is required of drawing at random a heart or a queen. It is known that the probability of a heart $P(A)$ is one in four and the probability of a queen $P(B)$ is one in thirteen.

Then by the addition theorem:

$$P(A \text{ or } B) = 1/4 + 1/13 - P(A \text{ and } B)$$

The probability of A and B (both a heart and a queen) is one in fifty-two. The required probability is therefore:

$$1/4 + 1/13 - 1/52 = 16/52 = 4/13$$

Note how the final term of the addition theorem is needed to avoid double counting when events are not "mutually exclusive."

2. The second problem is the determination of the probability of drawing a red card $P(A)$ and then without replacing the first card another red card $P(B)$. The complicating factor

here is the fact that the first card need not necessarily be red. By the multiplication theorem

$$P(A \text{ and } B) = (\tfrac{1}{2}) P(B|A)$$

As half the cards in the pack are red $P(A)$ is one half. The probability of drawing a second red card given that the first was red is now reduced to twenty-five chances in fifty-one. The required probability is therefore:

$$(\tfrac{1}{2})(25/51) = 25/102$$

This is slightly smaller than the probability (one quarter) of drawing two red cards in succession if the first is replaced. The multiplication theorem leads to an interesting result, as the right side may be written with A and B reversed. Thus:

$$P(B)P(A|B) = P(A)P(B|A)$$

When the relationship is expressed in the form:

$$P(A|B) = \frac{P(A)P(B|A)}{P(B)}$$

it is known as Bayes' Theorem. This will be shown in Chapter 6 to be of value in enabling the consequences of certain courses of action to be analysed *prior* to a search being undertaken for further information about the outcomes.

The Normal Probability Distribution

The addition, multiplication, and Bayes' theorems require that outcomes are viewed as discrete in nature. This leads to a tendency to restrict the number of alternatives recognised, for example to "high" demand and "low" demand which may be unduly restrictive. It is sometimes preferable to use observations to construct distributions which show more detail. By using a probability scale (note that this is identical with the *relative* frequency scale which is often described as "experimental probability") the histograms and frequency polygons of the last section may be viewed as *probability distributions*. The existence of certain types of probability distribution is vital to inferential statistics, although at this point it will not be apparent why this should be so. The particular distribution with which we shall be concerned is the normal distribution to which many real life variables do in fact approximate.

The main features of the normal distribution will be examined before its role in inferential statistics is studied. As shown in Fig. 17 it is symmetrical and bell-shaped. It is uniquely defined by its

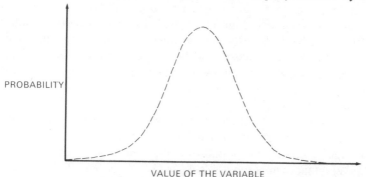

FIG. 17. The normal distribution.

mean and standard deviation, the latter determining whether the distribution is peaked or flat. The distance between the mean and the value of the variable where the distribution changes curvature (the point of inflection) is exactly one standard deviation.

Taking the whole of the area under the curve to be equal to unity, tables are available* which indicate the proportion of area under the curve between the mean and a certain number of standard deviations. For example the area between the mean and one standard deviation each side of the mean is .6826. This increases to .9544 at two standard deviations and .9973 at three standard deviations. As an example of how areas under the normal curve may be used, take the case of the height of an English male selected at random. Assume that the mean height is 5 ft 9 in. and the standard deviation of height is 2.5 in. Then the probability that the height of a man selected at random will fall outside the range 5 ft 6.5 in.–5 ft 11.5 in. is about 1 in 3 (1 − .6826), the probability that it will fall outside the range 5 ft 4 in. to 6 ft 2 in. is about 1 in 20 (1 − .9544), and there is a probability of about 1 in 400 that it will fall outside the range 5 ft 1.5 in. to 6 ft 3.5 in.

Sampling and Estimation
Much of inferential statistics is concerned with the estimation of population parameters (mean and standard deviation usually)

* See D. V. LINDLEY AND J. C. P. MILLER, *Cambridge Elementary Statistical Tables*, Cambridge University Press, 1968.

from sample observations. Broadly, the mean and standard deviation of a sample may be used as *point estimates* of the population parameters. Reference was made earlier to non-sampling error and sampling error. Non-sampling error implies all types of error which by proper design and conduct of the sampling procedure would be eliminated. This includes simple mistakes, but more importantly bias. An example of bias would be the acceptance of the first set of responses to a mailed survey as being representative of the total population mailed. It is well known that people with a particular interest are more likely to reply than people with little interest. Sampling error is of a quite different nature. Assume that a random sample of fifty men is selected with the purpose of estimating the average height of the population. It is possible (although highly unlikely) that each of the men selected would be 5 ft tall. It is obvious that the estimated mean of the population as 5 ft would be greatly in error. Sampling error is therefore due to chance.

The term "random" sample has been used. The question naturally follows as to how randomness is obtained. The most usual source is the random number table, a page of which is contained in Appendix II. Strictly, a random number lies within the range zero to one whereas a random digit is one of the whole numbers zero to nine. The probability of any random digit occurring is one in ten which implies that the distribution of random digits is rectangular. If it is possible to recognise individual members of a population then the random selection is achieved by numbering each individual and selecting from them using sequences of random numbers. For example assume that it is wished to draw a random sample from one hundred houses numbered 1–100. One way would be to use two adjoining columns of random digits. The first two columns of Appendix II would indicate selection of numbers 20, 74, 94, etc. It would be necessary to allocate the two digits 00 to house number 1 and proceed in this manner until the point is reached when number 100 is represented by the random digits 99. The random numbers 20, 74, and 94 would therefore select house numbers 21, 75, and 95.

There are many methods of obtaining samples,* some of which do not meet the requirements needed for the use of inferential statistics. Our assumption in this chapter is that any sample referred to is truly random, enabling statistical inferences to be drawn.

---

* *See* J. NETER AND N. WASSERMAN, *Fundamental Statistics for Business and Economics*, Allyn and Bacon, Inc., Boston, 1964, Chapter 11.

A fundamental theorem of statistics, the *central limit theorem*, may be expressed as follows:

"Regardless of the nature of the parent population (mean μ and standard deviation σ) the means of samples drawn from this population are distributed normally with a mean of μ and standard deviation of $\sigma/\sqrt{n}$"

(the latter is usually described as the *standard error*).

For the central limit theorem to apply, the sample size, n, must be sufficiently large (say, in excess of thirty) but the effect may be demonstrated by considering samples of just ten successive random digits taken from a random number table. By finding the average of many such groups of ten and building up a frequency distribution of means it will be evident that the majority of means cluster around the value of 4.5, as indicated in Fig. 18.

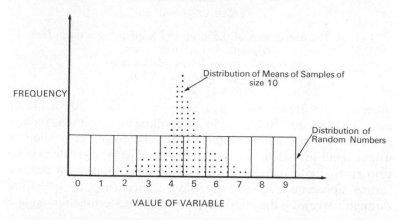

FIG. 18. The distribution of means of a sample of random numbers.

The central limit theorem enables point estimates of the population mean μ to be supplemented by *interval estimates*. If the sample size is n and the sample mean is $\bar{x}$, then by constructing an interval of several standard deviations' width around $\bar{x}$ the probability that μ is contained within the interval may be calculated. It is however necessary to estimate also the population standard deviation, and providing the sample is large there is little error in using the sample standard deviation, s, as an estimate of the population standard deviation σ.

Figure 19 indicates the outcome of taking samples of size n from a population. Remember that the location of μ is not known, it could only be determined by repetitive sampling. In practice, many

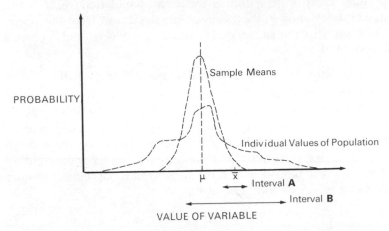

FIG. 19. The distribution of the mean of a sample size n taken from a population of arbitrary form.
(a) An imprecise linear relationship.
(b) A precise linear relationship.

inferences are drawn from single samples and the mean of one of these is assumed to be located at $\bar{x}$. It will be apparent that for any given sample size narrow intervals may be constructed about $\bar{x}$ with a small probability of containing μ, or wide intervals may be constructed with a high probability of containing μ. It will be further apparent that the only way of increasing the precision through narrowing the interval whilst at the same time retaining a high probability of containing μ is to increase the sample size. A *confidence interval* may be written formally as:

$$\bar{x} \pm zs/\sqrt{n}$$

The probability required will determine the number of standard deviations, z. For a confidence interval of 95 per cent a z value of 1.96 is specified. The $\sqrt{n}$ factor in the denominator explains why sample sizes in, say, public opinion polls, rarely exceed 2000. At this size $s/\sqrt{n}$ is usually very small and in order to halve the interval the sample size would need to be quadrupled to 8000. In other words, there are diminishing marginal returns in terms of precision for increasing sample size.

Much of inferential statistics is concerned with treating sample results for *significance*. Included are tests on sample means (*e.g.* quality control), sample proportions (*e.g.* effects of promotions), regression and correlation coefficients (*see below*) and so on. For these tests to be carried out it is necessary to make use of a number of statistical distributions. Strictly, the normal distribution of sample means (and proportions) is only applicable in the case of large samples. In practice the normal distribution is often assumed to hold for small sample statistics. Thus confidence intervals are constructed for forecasts based on a limited number of observations. Provided that approaches of this nature are accepted as being a rough guide only in the handling of variability, a useful supplement to single figure estimates is obtained.

Regression and Correlation

These two statistical techniques fulfil a major role in the fields of forecasting and general mathematical model building.

REGRESSION: A method of establishing a mathematical relationship between a dependent variable and one or more independent variables, in order that the value of the dependent variable for any set of values of the independent variables may be predicted.

CORRELATION: A mathematical procedure for establishing the strength of the statistical relationship between a dependent variable and a number of independent variables.

Regression and correlation are most easily studied when only one dependent and one independent variable are involved and when the relationship is assumed to be linear. Except in the physical sciences, relationships between variables are rarely precise. Whether based on the total population or sample results the graphical relationship between two variables is therefore of the form of Fig. 20 (*a*) rather than that of Fig. 20 (*b*). The relationship between x and y in the latter case is obviously linear and it is assumed that the relationship $y = mx + c$ is common to both cases, (that is the constants m and c are identical). Regression analysis (*see below*) has enabled a "best" straight line to be fitted in Fig. 20 (*a*) but it is apparent that there can be no *precise* forecast of y from x in this case. Some method of handling this imprecision is required. In the first instance, the strength of relationship between the two variables may be indicated by a *correlation coefficient*. This will be seen to be a dimensionless number which describes the strength but not the nature of the relationship. Alternatively, the regression analysis may be used to provide interval rather than point forecasts of the dependent variable (the width of the interval is zero in the case of the relationship indicated in Fig. 20 (*b*)). As regression and correlation are widely used in the areas mentioned at the beginning of this section, and as we have sufficient mathematics for the purpose, it is felt to be worthwhile to develop one or two results so that an apprecia-

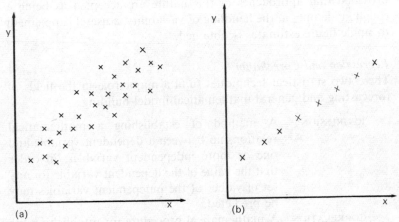

(a)   (b)

FIG. 20. Relationships between two variables *x* and *y*.

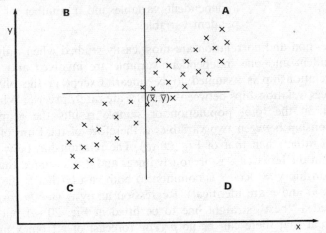

FIG. 21. New axes drawn through the means of the *x* and *y* values.

tion of this important branch of statistics may be gained. Figure 21 will be used to study both regression and correlation. In this, two additional axes have been drawn through the mean values of x and y which are a series of observations. The origin of the new axes will have "co-ordinates" $(\bar{x}, \bar{y})$ and any point (x_i, y_i) may now be written

$$X_i = x_i - \bar{x} \qquad \text{and} \qquad Y_i = y_i - \bar{y}.$$

It is now required to determine the "best" line through $(\bar{x}, \bar{y})$ and also the correlation coefficient between x and y.

Calculation of the Best Line

As the line passes through the new origin the equation of the best line may be written:

$$\hat{Y} = mX,$$

where $\hat{Y}$ are the values of the dependent variable which would be predicted from values of the independent variable X. The forecast values $\hat{Y}$ will differ from the observed values Y, that is the "forecast error" will be:

$$Y - \hat{Y} = Y - mX$$

Some will be positive and some negative, by squaring they are all made positive. The criterion used for fitting the line is that the sum of the squared errors or deviations shall be minimised. This has led to the frequently encountered description "least squares," which may be used in establishing both linear and non-linear relationships. Mathematically, we have therefore for n observations:

$$E = \sum_{i=1}^{n} (Y_i - mX_i)^2 \quad \text{to be minimised.}$$

The value of m which determines the best line is required, and this may be obtained by equating the first derivative of E to zero:

$$\frac{dE}{dm} = -2m \sum_{i=1}^{n} X_i(Y_i - mX_i) = 0$$

Thus $$\sum_{i=1}^{n} X_i(Y_i - mX_i) = 0$$

and $$\sum_{i=1}^{n} X_i Y_i = m \sum_{i=1} X_i^2$$

Dropping the subscripts, the required value for m, the regression coefficient is:

$$m = \frac{\sum XY}{\sum X^2}$$

Consider the following paired observations of x and y:

x	y
1	3
2	2
3	5
4	6
5	7
6	4
7	8
Totals 28	35

giving $\bar{x} = 4$ and $\bar{y} = 5$.

We need X, Y, XY, X^2, and these are as follows:

X	Y	XY	X^2
−3	−2	6	9
−2	−3	6	4
−1	0	0	1
0	1	0	0
1	2	2	1
2	−1	1	4
3	3	6	9
Totals 0	0	21	28

That is $\sum XY = 21$ and $\sum X^2 = 28$

hence: $m = \dfrac{\sum XY}{\sum X^2} = \dfrac{21}{28} = .75$

and the best line is thus $Y = .75X$.

As $Y = y - \bar{y} = y - 5$ and $X = x - \bar{y} = x - 4$ then in terms of x and y $(y - 5) = .75(x - 4)$ and finally $y = .75x + 2$. The values of y forecast by the regression may now be compared with the observed values from which the regression was derived.

Observed x	Observed y	Forecast y ($y = .75x+2$)	Forecast error (Observed y − Forecast y)
1	3	2.75	.25
2	2	3.50	−1.50
3	5	4.25	.75
4	6	5.00	1.00
5	7	5.75	1.25
6	4	6.50	−2.5
7	8	7.25	.75

It will be shown in Chapter 4 how the variability of forecast errors (as expressed by their standard deviation) may be used to construct confidence intervals around point forecasts.

Regression analysis also enables the standard error of the regression coefficient m to be determined. For it should be remembered that m is calculated from a sample of size n. For greater precision, a larger sample may be used but m is still only an estimate of the true regression coefficient and sampling error cannot be excluded. Interval estimates of m (which is the slope of the line) may be made and the implications of these are also discussed in Chapter 4.

Correlation

It was mentioned that the strength of association between variables may be measured by the coefficient of correlation. Actually, more meaning may be attached to the square of this coefficient, termed the *coefficient of determination*. From Fig. 20 it will be apparent that there is a greater degree of association between x and y in case (*b*) than in case (*a*). In other words, the more a graphical plot approximates to a straight line (or a particular curve) the greater the correlation. This fact may be used to present a descriptive interpretation of the correlation coefficient. By reference now to Fig. 21, it will be seen that relocation of the axes will cause the paired observations to fall into one of the four quadrants A, B, C and D. It is customary to express X as being positive in A and D and negative in B and C, whereas Y is negative in C and D. Thus for:

points in A XY is positive
points in B XY is negative
points in C XY is positive
points in D XY is negative

Therefore the sum of XY will serve as a measure of association between x and y. For if most points fall in A and C $\sum XY$ will be large and positive, if most fall in B and D $\sum XY$ will be large and negative whereas if little relationship exists the points will be scattered through A, B, C, and D and $\sum XY$ will be small.

$\sum XY$ will however increase as the number of observations increases and it is also affected by the units of x and y. Standardisation is achieved by dividing $\sum XY$ by the standard deviation of x and y and then taking the average. The coefficient of correlation r is then obtained as:

$$r = \frac{\sum XY}{n s_x s_y}$$

Referring to the data for which the regression coefficient was calculated, $\sum XY = 21$, $n = 7$ and it may be shown that both $s_x = 2$ and $s_y = 2$ hence:

$$r = \frac{21}{(7)(2)(2)} = .75$$

which because coincidentally the standard deviations are the same is also the value of the regression coefficient.

Although this is not immediately apparent, r lies in a range from -1 to $+1$. Further, there exists a relationship between r and the regression coefficient m, which may be written

$$\frac{r}{m} = \frac{s_x}{s_y}$$

The coefficient of determination, r^2, was mentioned. If the coefficient of correlation between x and y has been obtained as 0.8, then the coefficient of determination is 0.64. This indicates that the regression of y on x accounts for 64 per cent of the variance of y; the remaining 36 per cent being statistically unexplained.

As with the regression coefficient, the significance of the correlation coefficient may be determined. With large samples of observations even small coefficients may be significant, whereas large coefficients may have little significance if the sample is small. Even if relationships between variables appear realistic, decision makers should always be able to satisfy themselves that estimated parameters are statistically significant before using models based on analysis of this nature.

Multiple Regression and Correlation

The discussion so far has centred on the relationship between one dependent variable and one independent variable. When analysing time series, only one independent variable (time itself) is usually involved. Prediction of a variable in this way may however be considered too restrictive due to the exclusion of independent variables which are thought to be determining factors. It is frequently possible to draw up a list of variables which seem to be of significance in determining what value a dependent variable shall take. For example in Chapter 2 G.N.P., advertising expenditure and selling price were used in one relationship to predict sales. It is possible that other variables such as climate, population, interest rates, and so on could also be determinants of sales. The causal relationships between the dependent variable and each of the independent variables will vary in strength. For example, the impact of climate on sales may be immediate and obvious whereas the influence of change in interest rates may be more difficult to explain. This approach is complicated by the fact that various sets of the independent variables may show high measures of correlation within themselves, either directly or through other sets which are not included in the list of independent variables. Thus G.N.P. and population are in most countries increasing. In part, the increase in G.N.P. will be due to population increase and it may be that the ratio of *per capita* G.N.P. may be more attractive as an independent variable than population and G.N.P. separately. It will be evident that the compilation of a list of independent variables for the purpose of multiple regression will involve subjectivity and will demand a degree of "creativity" on the part of the analyst. Not least of his problems will be the difficulty of establishing relationships which are acceptably linear or may easily be transformed to meet this requirement.

The brief examination of regression analysis based on one independent variable suggests that the method of least squares is relevant to multiple regression and in practical analyses an electronic computer is almost a prerequisite. The availability of computer packages is of great benefit to the analyst, as different sets of independent variables may be used and coefficients of multiple correlation and determination calculated. The significance of the partial regression coefficients may also be obtained, and this will indicate which independent variables have the greatest influence on the dependent variable.

A possible relationship between sales s, G.N.P. y, advertising expenditure a, and selling price p, was mentioned above, and the equation used in Chapter 2 was:

$$s = c_1 + c_2 y + c_3 a + c_4 p$$

where c_1, c_2, c_3, and c_4 are the partial regression coefficients. Ignoring units, an actual relationship generated by a computer may be:

$$s = 73.2 + .02y + 1.41a - .67p$$

with a coefficient of multiple correlation of .86. Further, it may be indicated that the partial regression coefficient of .02 for G.N.P. is not significant, in which case the multiple regression can be recomputed with only the two independent variables, advertising and price. This procedure is sometimes referred to as the *step-wise elimination* of variables. A new relationship will now be generated, for example, as:

$$s = 86.5 + 1.59a - .83p$$

with a coefficient of multiple correlation of .91.

A useful output feature of computer packages of this type is a so-called *correlation matrix*, which indicates the correlation coefficient for association between all possible pairs of variables (including the dependent one).

Multiple regression and correlation analysis can therefore be a powerful tool in establishing predictive relationships of the normative form which may be used directly for forecasting purposes or as a structural component of a model. As with all relationships which are constructed on the basis of historical data, however, judgment must be exercised in extending their use beyond the limits of the observation used in the analysis.

Chapter Four

FORECASTING VARIABLES FOR PLANNING DECISIONS

INTRODUCTION

In Chapter 2, the general model of a decision process was expressed as:

$$U = f(x, y)$$

where U is utility, x the set of controllable variables and y the set of uncontrollable variables. It may be that the decision is viewed as involving no uncontrollable variables, for example a distribution system operating within a constant environment of supply and demand. In this case, the general model will be:

$$U = f(x).$$

The first of the expressions may be said to imply a *planning* decision, whereas the second involves a *design* decision. Strictly, "controllable variable" is a blanket term to include variables which are observable and hence measurable or which may be the subject of a policy decision on the part of the decision maker. It will be appreciated that a spectrum of variables will exist between completely controllable (for example, tomorrow's selling price) and completely uncontrollable (for example, the severity of the next winter). The degree of uncertainty will dictate whether a variable can be classified as controllable or whether it should be classified as uncontrollable, in which case estimation will be required. This Chapter is concerned with procedures by the use of which a basis is provided for ascribing logical values to uncontrollable variables.

How may a value ascribed to a variable qualify for the description "logical"? Brown* suggests that:

"The best estimates of the future will be based upon an analysis and projection of past results viewed throughout in the light of

---

* *See* R. G. BROWN, *Smoothing, Forecasting and Prediction of Discrete Time Series*, Prentice-Hall, Inc., Englewood Cliffs, N.J., 1963, p. 2.

experience of the processes involved and of new circumstances anticipated."

Brown also makes a distinction between a "forecast" and a "prediction." Although these words are often seen as being synonymous, it is of value to study the implications of the two alternatives which he defines as follows:

FORECAST: An estimate of a future result based purely on a projection of a series of past results.

PREDICTION: A forecast modified to allow for any changes in the relevant factors which it is known, or experience suggests, will take place.

The value of these definitions arises from the distinction which they make between on the one hand, a mechanical procedure and on the other hand, a procedure which involves a contribution from the decision maker. The involvement of the decision maker will depend on the "importance" of the variable. Most managers are prepared to accept routine forecasting of demand for stock items, only being involved by exception when certain limits are exceeded. They would, however, study very carefully a forecast of wage rates for five years ahead before incorporating the value in a decision model.

A criticism of Brown's definitions is that certain estimating procedures would appear to be excluded. For example, in the case of a new product, "past results" will not exist. Again, there are other estimating procedures which although subjective may be termed logical because they are seen as being the most appropriate approach. These will include a field sales force consensus of estimated demand for a high valued speciality product, the method adopted in certain high technology companies when senior officials play the roles of their opposite numbers in companies which are seen as prospective customers in order to evaluate design and cost features and the so-called "Delphi" technique* for technological forecasting. It is therefore preferable to extend a definition of a prediction so that it includes any estimating procedure involving explicit managerial judgment on the understanding that the procedure is accepted as being the most appropriate.

---

* See B. C. TWISS, *Managing Technological Innovation*, Longmans Ltd., London, 1974, pp. 84–87.

In this chapter we shall be concerned with forecasting methods as defined above, as there frequently is some relationship between the value which a variable will assume in the future and the value which it has held in the past. Further, if we take into account some of the statistical method outlined in Chapter 3 it will be appreciated that a forecast can only be an estimate, and a measure of the uncertainty involved may be obtained by applying confidence limits. Thus a forecast may be presented in two forms:

1. As a point estimate.
2. As an interval estimate.

As probabilities are implicit in confidence intervals, the two forms may be seen as providing the basis for the inputs of deterministic and probabilistic models respectively. Interval estimates are obtained by considering the *forecast errors* which have arisen. A forecast error for any point in time is the actual value which occurs less the forecast value. If the forecasting method is efficient, then the mean forecast error over a number of periods should be zero. If this is not the case, the forecast is said to be *biased*. A major aim is to achieve an unbiased forecast. This does not mean of course that forecast errors will be eliminated but that they will occur randomly and will be described by a probability distribution. Further, if the forecasting method is to be of value the forecast errors will not be large (the usual criterion, as forecast errors are both positive and negative, is that the sum of their squares shall be minimised).

It is important to appreciate precisely what is being forecast. This presents no problem in respect of the point estimate, as this is assumed to be the *best* estimate of the variable at some time in the future. In the case of the interval estimate, however, care must be taken to distinguish between a confidence interval for the *mean* and a confidence interval for *individual values*. The distinction should be apparent from the discussion which follows.

A time series used for a forecast may be considered as a sample from a large population and hence sampling error will arise. If N points of a series are used and the standard deviation of individual values is σ then the standard error of the estimate will be $\sigma/\sqrt{N}$. If the point estimate is F (and the errors are assumed to be distributed normally) the interval estimate will be

$$F \pm z\sigma/\sqrt{N}$$

where z, the standard normal variate, will be determined by the level of confidence adopted. For example, assume for a series without a trend* that

$$F = 2000, \quad \sigma = 400, \quad N = 64 \quad \text{and} \quad z = 1.96$$

for 95 per cent confidence, then the interval estimate will be:

$$2000 \pm \frac{(1.96)(400)}{8} = 2000 \pm 98$$

This does not imply that (at the 95 per cent level of confidence) the actual value will generally lie between approximately 1900 and 2100 but only that the *mean* forecast will be contained by this range. In order to consider individual values, it is necessary to take into account variation of these individual values.

The variance of individual forecast values is obtained by summing the variance of the individual values and the variance of the estimate (which is the square of the standard error) and is therefore:

$$\sigma^2 + \frac{\sigma^2}{N}$$

and the standard deviation of the individual forecast is the square root of this namely:

$$\sigma\sqrt{1 + 1/N}$$

The interval estimate for individual values will be:

$$F \pm z\sigma\sqrt{1 + 1/N}$$

which in the above case is

$$2000 \pm (1.96)(400)\sqrt{65/64} = 2000 \pm 790$$

At the 95 per cent level therefore individual values are forecast within the range 1210–2790, which at the same time is very imprecise and yet more "realistic."

Many forecasts are based on much fewer than sixty-four historical observations. This will obviously increase the uncertainty surrounding the forecast. If only a small number of historical observations of a variable which is not distributed normally are available or in the case of a larger number of historical observations

---

* Some writers use the convention that every time series possesses a trend, positive, negative or zero. In this book trend is only used in the non-zero sense. A time series without trend is often described as being "stationary."

(say, above thirty) which do not occur randomly then interval estimates made in the above manner are, in theory, not justified. In practice such calculations are often undertaken to give an indication of the uncertainty involved.

Before a forecast is generated it is important that historical data shall be examined for homogeneity. Attention must be given to the following factors:

1. The units of measurement: for example, output recorded partly in long tons and partly in metric tons.
2. Distribution policy: could at some point have changed from regional to national, home to export.
3. Demand: gain or loss of major customers; demand affected by limitations of supply.
4. Value of sales: major price changes; devaluation; inflation.
5. Labour relations: strikes, absence, wage agreements.
6. Natural causes: weather, disasters.

All of these factors could create major disturbances in the time series. If the disturbances are of short duration (the "impulse" effect) then the actual figures involved should be ignored in forecasting. If the series are permanently shifted to a new level (the "ramp" effect) then either the earlier portion of the time series should be weighted to achieve homogeneity or the forecast should be based on the latter part of the series only.

Needless to state, the decision maker will take into account anticipated changes of the type mentioned in 1–6 above, in considering whether the forecast is acceptable or whether it should be modified to become a "prediction."

Before considering in some detail the various methods of forecasting it is necessary to give some thought to the timing of the forecast. It is customary to refer to short, medium, and long term forecasting. Sometimes, but not invariably, the futurity of the forecast is indicated. For example short term may relate to a horizon of six months, medium term to one of from six months to five years and long term to one beyond five years. It is of course necessary in planning to specify the point in time to which plans relate, but strictly the futurity of a forecast must take some account of the forecasting time period involved. If this period were a day then ninety days or three months ahead would be long term. In the case of a longer time period such as a year the problem does not arise, as the forecast can be made to relate to a quarter or other fraction of a year. It is necessary, therefore, in describing a particular forecast as short, medium, or long term, to take account of the number of forecasting periods ahead for which the forecast is made.

A CLASSIFICATION OF FORECASTING METHODS

To forecast, past results are used to provide estimates of a variable in the future. This does not necessarily imply that "past results" refers only to a time series of the variable under consideration. We have already encountered the normative relationship in model building and therefore can appreciate that an efficient method of forecasting a variable may be on the basis of multivariate analysis. Multivariate analysis (which was described in outline in Chapter 3) is a major component of the field of *econometric* forecasting, in which sophisticated statistical analysis is employed in an attempt to establish efficient predictive relationships between economic variables. In these relationships, time may or may not be included as an independent variable. Nevertheless, it eventually becomes necessary to forecast those variables (for example, population and G.N.P.) which may be independent and qualify for the description "uncontrollable" in a functional relationship. The following classification is confined to those forecasting methods which utilise time series of a variable and by use of which uncontrollable variables may be quantified in models used in planning decisions:

1. *The Classical Approach:* in which the time series is broken down into a number of constituent parts which are then forecast individually.
2. *Tracking Methods:* in which forms of averaging are employed to smooth the time series and hence facilitate forecasting.
3. *Non-linear Trend Curves:* in which non-linear functions are fitted to the time series, usually to take account of long term growth or decay factors.

THE CLASSICAL APPROACH TO FORECASTING

This postulates that the component effects of an actual value A, are trend T, seasonal S, cyclic C, together with an irregular effect, e. Most importance in forecasting by this method is given to trend and, for periods less than a year, seasonal effects. The structural determination of A varies, but the most widely used model is of the following multiplicative form:

$$A = TSC + e.$$

A forecast is obtained by estimating T and multiplying this value by estimates of S and C, both of which on average are unity.

Trend

Traditionally, linear regression has been employed. There is however no reason why in the long term a straight line should adequately describe a time series. It was mentioned in Chapter 3 that a rising straight line implies a decreasing rate of growth and often other rates of growth are more appropriate. By a simple transformation, linear regression may be applied to the particular case of constant growth rates. For example, if a series is growing on average at the rate of r per cent per annum then A may be approximated by

$$A = K(1 + r/100)^t$$

where K is a constant and t is the number of years. Taking logarithms:

$$\log A = \log K + t \log(1 + r/100)$$

This relationship indicates that if the logarithms of A instead of actual values of A are plotted against time, the points should lie about a straight line. Thus if in addition to plotting the time series on ordinary graph paper the same series is plotted on semi-logarithmic graph paper (vertical scale logarithmic, horizontal scale arithmetic), it will be apparent whether it is realistic to use linear regression.

TABLE V: U.K. PRODUCTION OF NUCLEAR ELECTRICITY

Year (t)	Production (A) GWh
1956	58
1957	409
1958	304
1959	1201
1960	2079
1961	2395
1962	3660
1963	6472
1964	8349
1965	15,822
1966	21,011
1967	24,228

As an example of the use of the logarithmic transformation, consider the United Kingdom production of nuclear electricity given in Table V.

Using linear regression first on the actual values in Table V and secondly on their logarithms, two equations each including time as the independent variable may be determined (many computer programmes are available for this purpose). These are:

I. $$A = -6700 + 2133t$$
II. $$\log A = 1.99 + 0.22t$$

where year 1956 = 1.

The goodness of fit of these lines as measured by the coefficient of determination is 81 per cent for the arithmetic data, and 94 per cent for the logarithmic data. Equation I indicates a constant yearly increase of 2133 GWh (an overestimate during the early years and an underestimate during the later years). Equation II requires the coefficient of t to be written in logarithmic form ($\log 1.66 = 0.22$), when the estimate of growth rate is seen to be as high as 66 per cent per annum. Although equation II is a better fit during the period under consideration, the high rate of growth rapidly brings into question its suitability for the purpose of forecasting. Table VI indicates some evaluations of the two regression equations.

TABLE VI: AN EXAMPLE OF FITTING A STRAIGHT LINE TO ARITHMETIC AND LOGARITHMIC DATA

Year	Actual production GWh	Estimated production GWh (equation I)	Estimated production GWh (equation II)
1965	15,822	14,631	14,562
1966	21,011	16,765	24,009
1967	24,228	18,898	39,585
1968	27,195	21,031	65,264
1990	?	67,961	3,900,000

The actual production of nuclear electricity during 1968 was 27,195 GWh and it is evident that both equations provided a poor forecast. The danger of forecasting with continuing high constant growth rates will be apparent from the forecasts for 1990. The extrapolated value arising from equation I is feasible, albeit unlikely, but the corresponding value from equation II is impossible. Therefore, if the method of fitting curves to forecast trend is to be employed it is necessary to search for some function which in addition to pro-

viding a good fit through historical data is realistic in the future
(this will be pursued in the section on non-linear trend curves later
in this Chapter).

It is necessary to study the extrapolation of linear regressions a
little more closely. Earlier in this section the use of a time series to
forecast was likened to taking a sample from a population. The
point was made that because of sampling error uncertainty would
exist in estimating both mean and individual forecasts. This was
demonstrated by reference to a time series possessing no trend.
What is the effect of sampling error if a trend exists?

In the linear regression $y = mx + c$, m, the slope or trend, and c
are only estimates of what may be termed the "true" m and c. Except
by coincidence as the time series is extended m and c will change. If
the aim were to predict y from x by *interpolation* (time not being the
dependent variable) little error would be involved, providing a strong
relationship existed between x and y and a sizeable sample had been
taken. In forecasting, however, *extrapolation* is necessarily involved
and in this case (statistical) uncertainty will increase the longer the
forecast. Considering only m and its standard error, it is possible
to construct confidence limits for m which pass through the mean
values of y and t at E and which because we are dealing with slope
will diverge. It is apparent from Fig. 22 that for a given level of confidence the interval surrounding F will become wider as the forecast

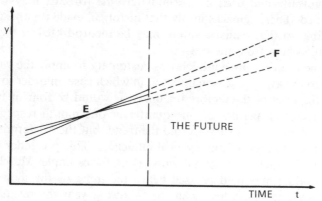

FIG. 22. The effect of uncertainty in slope, m.

is extended. When the standard error of c is taken into account,
broadening still further the confidence interval, and it is remembered
that only the *mean* forecast is being estimated, the high degree of

uncertainty involved is emphasised. And all of this ignores the major assumption, namely that a straight line fit will adequately describe the time series in the future. Thus forecasting on the basis of trend (whether linear or not), particularly in the long term, should be treated with great caution. If the variable (uncontrollable) is a sensitive component of a model developed for a major planning decision, any forecast of it should be subjected to all tests of credibility. In these circumstances, it is unwise to rely purely on forecasting and unreasonable, if the forecast eventually turns out to be a bad one, to blame the statistical analysis used.

Seasonal Factors

It may at first sight appear surprising that the tilt of the earth's axis is of much significance in forecasting methods. It is of course because of this tilt that the seasons occur, with their influence on weather, animal and vegetable cycles. These effects are so pronounced (for example, sales of particular types of clothing and foods, varying leisure pursuits, unemployment, efficiency of open-air work) that other determining factors may well be submerged. A prerequisite of the seasonal factor (at least in the opinion of the author) is that it should be capable of explanation. This then endows it with powerful properties which if taken into account enable the forecast to be upgraded. On the other hand, if seasonal factors are calculated mechanically and used indiscriminately the forecast may well be degraded. These remarks imply that historical evidence or data are desirable so that realistic values may be incorporated in the forecasting system from the outset.

In the multiplicative model, it is customary to apply the value of unity to the average seasonal factor, in which case, in order to avoid bias, the total of the factors for one year would be four or twelve, for forecasting periods of one quarter or one month respectively. Seasonal effects will vary around the trend, but their determination must take account of any cyclical influences. This precludes taking a ratio of actual A, to a trend value T, as, for example, March sales of a product may be depressed below the trend by the state of the economy one year whereas in the following year the reverse may apply. A useful method is to take a ratio of A to a smoothed value of the variable. The process of smoothing anticipates one of the methods of tracking, namely the moving average, which is considered in more depth later in this Chapter.

The simplest form of moving average requires the summation of a number of consecutive terms of a time series and dividing the sum by the number of terms included. The resulting average is then located at the mid point of the terms involved. Successively, a new term is added and the oldest term is dropped, with the result that the average advances by one term at a time. If only a few terms are included in the moving average smoothing will not be pronounced, whereas oscillations will tend to disappear as the number of terms included is increased.

It was mentioned that cyclic oscillations (in particular those relating to the state of the economy) could affect the determination of seasonal effects. As many cyclic oscillations possess a periodicity of several years they may be tracked by using a simple moving average covering a shorter duration. It is important that the most appropriate period is selected for the moving average. As seasonal effects occur repetitively within one year, the period required is (for monthly data) twelve months, by the use of which some cyclical but all seasonal influence will be smoothed out. By taking the ratio of A to a twelve month moving average centred on A, an estimate of seasonal effect is obtained.

Because of the general assumption that actual values are located at the mid point of a time period, a minor difficulty arises in respect of the precise location of a twelve month moving average. If the period January–December is taken, the average will be centred between June and July and there will be bias if either the month of June or July is divided by this average. A half month shift is required and this is achieved by constructing a special form of a thirteen month moving average. The construction is as follows:

JAN. +	FEB. +	– – – –	+ DEC.
	FEB. +		+ DEC. + JAN.

JAN. + 2 FEB. +   – – – –   + 2 DEC. + JAN.

A twelve month time series commencing in February is therefore added to one commencing in January. Each of the months from February to December will carry double weight, whereas the month of January will carry the values which arise in successive years. The bias arising from using separate Januaries will in general be insignificant. If the total is divided by twenty-four a weighted thirteen month moving average centred on July will result. The ratio of A to the weighted average will now be a measure of the seasonal effect. The procedure is demonstrated in Table VII.

TABLE VII: DETERMINATION OF SEASONAL EFFECTS

1	2	3	4	5	6
			Sum of successive		Seasonal effects
		Twelve-month	twelve-month	Column 4	column 2
Month	Actual	total	totals	$\div 24$	$\div$ column 5
JAN.	560				
FEB.	480				
MARCH	600				
APRIL	620				
MAY	680				
JUNE	620	7040			
JULY	580	7030	14,070	586	0.99
AUG.	560	7050	14,080	587	0.95
SEPT.	600	7030	14,080	587	1.02
OCT.	·640	7050	14,080	587	1.09
NOV.	580		14,080	587	
DEC.	520				
JAN.	550				
FEB.	500				
MARCH	580				
APRIL	640				

Column 6 of Table VII deliberately incorporates the description seasonal "effects," as these must be studied in order to assess whether it is appropriate to incorporate them in the forecasting system as seasonal "factors." The decision may to some extent be intuitive, particularly if limited data are available. If it is possible to determine seasonal effects over several years, then the decision may be better founded. For example consider the four cases in Table VIII in which seasonal effects have been determined by the procedure demonstrated in Table VII. Each case demonstrates different properties.

TABLE VIII: INTERPRETING SEASONAL FACTORS

Case	Seasonal effects for years:					Seasonal factor
	1	2	3	4	5	
A	0.8	0.9	0.9	1.0	1.1	1.1 or 1.2
B	0.7	0.8	0.7	0.9	0.9	0.8
C	1.3	1.2	1.3	0.7	1.3	1.3
D	0.7	1.2	1.0	0.6	1.3	?

In case A because the seasonal effect appears to be increasing it would probably be unrealistic to employ the mean of 0.94. A more realistic decision would be to adopt the last value determined, 1.1, or if the rising trend is thought likely to continue, a factor of 1.2.

In case B the seasonal effects may reasonably be averaged and used with confidence if the below average effect can be explained. A seasonal factor of 0.80 may be thought to be appropriate in this case.

In case C the comments made in respect of case B would have applied except for year 4 when the seasonal effect was 0.7. If this effect could have been explained by a strike or bad weather it would be sensible to ignore the 0.7 and average the four values remaining. If no explanation could be given for the low figure, then a recurrence of this effect could not be discounted. It would then be advisable to treat case C as D, which follows.

Case D is typical of many seasonal effects which are computed in practice. The decision whether or not to use seasonal factors at all hinges largely on whether a pronounced seasonal effect is evident for one or more months. If this is so it would not be sensible to ignore the evidence. In these circumstances, the balance remaining from twelve after taking account of seasonal effects where they exist would be divided equally among the remaining months. For example, for three months of the year the total of seasonal factors may be six. This would imply that the remaining nine months should be treated as if the seasonal effect were less than average, and would indicate seasonal factors of twelve less six divided by nine, that is 0.67.

Once seasonal factors are adopted it is important that they should be reviewed annually and modified if necessary. Some forecasting schemes include procedures for automatically updating seasonal factors. This practice is not to be recommended unless controls are incorporated.

Seasonal factors have been discussed at some length as they should be considered when forecasting for time periods less than one year whatever method is used. If seasonal effects are evident, the general procedure is to deseasonalise and forecast, following which the forecast is reseasonalised.

Cyclical Effects

Oscillations other than those which may be explained seasonally are described as cyclical. These are often apparent in time series of some length particularly in respect of those variables which are affected by the state of the economy. Studies of trade cycles suggesting periodicities of seven or eleven years were undertaken many years ago, but with the increasing involvement of government along Keynesian lines theories of a natural cyclical movement of the economy have receded. Considerable attempts are however being made to predict turning points (peaks and troughs), as obviously these have profound implications for many major decisions. If trend and seasonal effects are not pronounced the outcome of a decision may well be determined by the cyclic variation of the economy. However until means of forecasting cyclical effects with some efficiency become available this aspect is better incorporated in the conversion of a forecast to a prediction along the lines indicated at the beginning of this section.

The classical representation of actual value A is sometimes transformed to:

$$\frac{A}{TS} = C + e$$

where A divided by TS is described as a "normalised" value. If the normalised values are smoothed by a moving average and graphed, cyclical effects will, if present, stand out clearly.

Referring to Fig. 23 it is apparent that in the future the cyclical effect could follow any path such as A, B, or C and that the assumption of any one of these could, except in the short term, create large forecast errors.

A danger which exists in determining historical cyclical move-

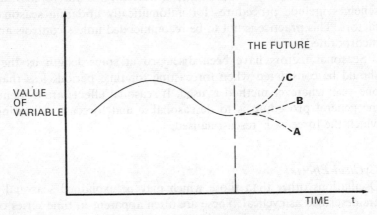

FIG. 23. The cyclical effect.

ments is that the application of a moving average to random terms will itself generate a cyclical effect. Thus for example in the above expression for normalised variables, if C is zero the presence of e may result in an apparent cyclical component if a smoothing process is employed.

Summary of the Classical Approach

The idea of breaking down an actual value into several components is attractive. Certainly trend, seasonal, and cyclical effects may be recognised retrospectively. The treatment of trend is limited by dependence on the straight line, and, although by use of the logarithmic transformation the method is extended to cover constant growth rates, neither the latter nor the more usual assumption of linear trend of actual values can be expected to continue unchanged. An exception should perhaps be made for variables which are related to population growth and which are not subject to substitution effects, in which case a constant growth rate may not be unrealistic. As demonstrated in Fig. 10, it is often possible to fit a number of different functions with much apparent precision, the straight line being just one of these. The various functions will however produce widely differing forecasts.

The minimum requirement if the classical approach is to be employed with any confidence is the existence of a stable forecasting base including an appropriate number of terms. If, as is often the case, a straight line is fitted to a time series of six or seven values, the combined effect of the standard error of the regression coefficient, together with uncertainty as to whether a straight line is a valid assumption and the difficulty of forecasting cyclical effects will produce a forecast of little value. A superior prediction may in fact be possible by subjective judgment. At least a dozen values are normally required to reduce the statistical errors to an acceptable level. Having accepted the validity of the approach, forecasts may be short, medium, or long term, with the confidence intervals and hence uncertainty increasing through time.

TRACKING METHODS

A plot of a time series will in general indicate much variability. If trend and oscillatory effects (seasonal or cyclical) do exist, they may well be obscured by the degree of apparently random fluctuations. Tracking methods enable the major portion of the random fluctuations to be smoothed out, revealing the underlying move-ments. The basic outcome of the tracking method is therefore an "average" path through the time series which can be studied by the forecaster and used to support a prediction or alternatively a mechanistic forecast. Provided the fluctuations which occur in a time series approximate to random, the consequence of averaging a number of successive terms will be to reduce the effect of the fluctuations. The averaging of the actual values of a variable over four periods could be represented by:

$$\frac{A_t + A_{t-1} + A_{t-2} + A_{t-3}}{4}$$

or $\qquad 0.25A_t + 0.25A_{t-1} + 0.25A_{t-2} + 0.25A_{t-3}$,

where the subscripts of A refer to the particular time period. It will be seen that only a fraction (one quarter) of each actual value is taken. This fraction is referred to as a "weight." Tracking methods require consideration to be given to the number of terms to be included in the average and the weights to be given to each term. The literature* abounds with different methods of tracking time series, but each is basically a moving average. A broad classification of tracking methods may be made according to whether the num-ber of terms which they include are limited or unlimited.

Number of Terms Limited

Moving averages may be applied to a time series by successively fitting to a number of points by least squares, say, a cubic function. The outcome is a limited term moving average in which weights may vary symmetrically about the middle term. Usually, however, the weights are applied arbitrarily. The simplest form of arbitrary moving average allocates equal weights to each term, as in the above case of the four term average. Writing F_t as the forecast made at the end of period t for period $t+1$ then:

$$F_t = 0.25A_t + 0.25A_{t-1} + 0.25A_{t-2} + 0.25A_{t-3}$$

This forecast will be unbiased in the absence of trend.

It is usual, as mentioned earlier, for all "actuals" to be assumed to be centred within the period to which they refer. Thus F_t is in

* *See*, for example, R. G. BROWN, *Smoothing Forecasting and Prediction of Discrete Time Series*, Prentice-Hall Inc., Englewood Cliffs, N.J., 1963.

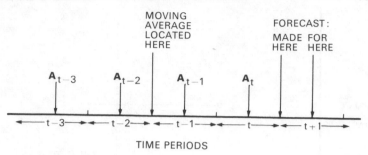

FIG. 24. The forecasting procedure.

theory a forecast for A_{t+1} centred half a period ahead in $t+1$. The procedure is demonstrated in Fig. 24. Also shown in Fig. 24 is the location of the average, which is between periods $t-2$ and $t-1$. The age of the average related to the location of the most recent actual, A_t, is seen to be one and a half periods. In general, for moving averages with equal weights and including N terms:

$$\text{Age of average} = \frac{N-1}{2}$$

An odd number of terms is often used, as the average then coincides with an actual value.

Correction for Trend

To consider the implications of trend, refer to Fig. 25. The actual values of the time series from period $t-3$ to period t are shown as crosses. The average, depicted by a circle is, as before, located between periods $t-2$ and $t-1$. If the average is used as the forecast for period $t+1$ it is evident that for a rising trend the forecast error $(A_{t+1}-F_t)$ will be positive. Furthermore, if the same procedure were repeated at the end of period $t+1$ the forecast error would again be positive. Thus if no modification is made for trend the forecast will be consistently biased. The modification may be accomplished easily by making an addition to the forecast each period. For example, a measure of the trend per period may be obtained by averaging A_{t-2} and A_{t-3} and subtracting this from the average of A_t and A_{t-1}. Dividing the difference of the two averages by two periods (the difference in time between them) will give the required trend. As the four term moving average is one and a half periods old it is necessary to add two and a half trends to F_t to give

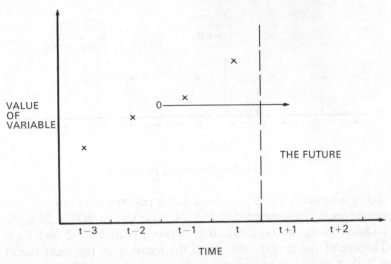

FIG. 25. The effect of trend.

F_t^1 the forecast modified for trend for period $t+1$. This is represented symbolically by:

$$(A_t + A_{t-1} + A_{t-2} + A_{t-3})/4 + \tfrac{5}{2}(\tfrac{1}{2}(\tfrac{1}{2}(A_t + A_{t-1}) - \tfrac{1}{2}(A_{t-2} + A_{t-3})))$$

which reduces to:

$$0.875A_t + 0.875A_{t-1} - 0.375A_{t-2} - 0.375A_{t-3}$$

If the values of A_{t-3}, A_{t-2}, A_{t-1}, A_t were two, four, six and eight substitution in the trend modified formula would show F_t^1 as ten which follows the rising trend of two per period. In order to forecast further than one period ahead then correspondingly more than two and a half trends must be added to F_t. For example, four periods ahead would require the addition of five and a half trends. This is of course extrapolating linearly and as oscillatory movements are usually present in time series the danger of failing to predict turning points increases as the futurity of the forecast increases.

The number of terms actually included in the moving average is a matter for judgment. The greater the number of terms the smoother will be the series of averages but at the same time care must be taken that cyclical effects are not obscured. A further point is that for moving averages containing many terms the age of the average will be appreciable. For example the age of a thirteen term moving average is six periods and circumstances surrounding the series may well have altered during that time. In order to reduce the age of the average but still include an appreciable number of terms, more weight could be given to recent values of the variable (quite apart from any treatment of trend). The allocation of weights would be very arbitrary, however, and if this approach is to be adopted it is best undertaken by the method involving an unlimited number of terms.

Number of Terms Unlimited

To readers unfamiliar with this approach, a moving average of an unlimited number of terms may seem an unlikely concept. The basis of the approach is that the forecast for a given period takes some account of the forecast for the previous period. Thus a recursive relationship is implied through all forecasts. The relationship between two forecasts may be expressed verbally as "This month's forecast is determined by last month's forecast modified by a proportion of the forecast error," or symbolically as:

III. $$F_t = F_{t-1} + \propto (A_t - F_{t-1})$$

The proportion $\propto$ by which the forecast error is multiplied is known as the *smoothing constant*, and will usually lie in the range 0–1 (an exception to this will be mentioned below). It will be appreciated that by forecasting in this way reference to the latest period only is required. In order to see how a forecast of this nature is based on a true average it is necessary to rewrite equation III as:

IV. $$F_t = \propto A_t + (1 - \propto) F_{t-1}$$

and as $F_{t-1} = \propto A_{t-1} + (1 - \propto) F_{t-2}$, equation IV may be rewritten:

V. $$F_t = \propto A_t + \propto (1 - \propto) A_{t-1} + \propto (1 - \propto)^2 A_{t-2} + \propto (1 - \propto) A_{t-3} + \ldots$$

It is now apparent why this approach involves an unlimited number of terms. The actual values carry weights which, for $0 < \propto < 1$, decrease in theory to zero at an infinite number of terms. The weights progressively include higher exponents of $1 - \propto$ and, because of this feature, the descriptions "exponentially weighted moving average (E.W.M.A.)" or more commonly "exponential smoothing" are used.

The weights $\propto$, $\propto (1 - \propto)$, $\propto (1 - \propto)^2$, etc. form an infinite converging geometric progression, and their sum is therefore the ratio of the first term to the complement of the common ratio $(1 - \alpha)$:

$$\frac{\alpha}{1 - (1 - \alpha)} = 1$$

The sum of the weights being unity, the series qualifies to be described as an "average."

The age of the average so produced is not immediately apparent. In order to determine this it is necessary to consider the age of each term individually and the weight attached to it. Taking the age of the most recent value of the variable as zero, the next most recent as one and so on, then the age of the average is:

$$0 . \alpha + 1 . \alpha(1 - \alpha) + 2 . \alpha(1 - \alpha)^2 + \ldots$$

This for $0 < \alpha < 1$ is an infinite converging series, the sum of which gives:

$$\frac{1 - \alpha}{\alpha} = \text{age of average.}$$

This property is of use as a means of demonstrating how by changing the value of the smoothing constant α this tracking method may be given widely differing properties. For example:

if $\alpha = 1$,   age of average $= 0$,
and if $\alpha = 0$,   age of average $= \infty$.

Referring to equation III, α values of one and zero give $F_t = A_t$ and $F_t = F_{t-1}$ respectively. The former of these relationships implies zero age and a completely sensitive forecast in which the forecast for the next period is this period's actual value. In the latter case the implication is that the forecast never changes, and hence is completely insensitive to actual values. The average may then in a sense be considered as infinitely old.

By assuming values of α between zero and one the age of the average will be changed. $\alpha = 0.5$ gives an age of only one period and hence a very sensitive forecast (equivalent to one based on a three term simple moving average). In practical forecasting systems, $\alpha = 0.1$ or 0.2 is more usual, giving ages of nine and four periods respectively. The selection of the "best" value of α is important, and will be considered below.

Correction for Trend
As in the case of the simple moving average, a biased forecast may result if an allowance for trend is not included. In consequence

of the popularity of tracking methods, particularly for short term forecasting, much has been written on alternative approaches involving trend correction. A comparison is made in a monograph on short term forecasting* between the methods suggested by Holt, Brown, and Box and Jenkins. Holt and Brown treat trend explicitly but in a different manner. In the former case a "most recent" estimate of trend is made, whereas Brown's estimate relates to the location in time of the smoothed average, namely $(1-\alpha)/\alpha$ periods ago. Modification for trend is made linearly in each case. The major problem in Holt's approach is that to suppress highly fluctuating estimates of current trend it is necessary to use a very small smoothing constant (0–0.03 is mentioned) and it is even suggested that trend may be estimated at intervals of six to twelve months. In Brown's approach, trend updating is included routinely, but here the problem is that trend is extrapolated over the age of the average and into the future on a linear path. It is suggested in the monograph that Brown's approach is less general than Holt's but this presumes that in the former case the same value of smoothing constant is used to update the average and the trend; this of course need not be so. In this section, an approach based on Brown's will be developed. This is simple in concept and has been found to be effective in practice.

First an estimate is made of trend. F_t, it will be remembered, takes account of all actual values to date but is based on an average of age $(1-\alpha)/\alpha$ periods. The estimate of trend taken is:

$$F_t - F_{t-1}.$$

Although based on averages, the estimate of trend will in many instances be subject to fluctuation and more acceptable is an "average" trend T, obtained by the smoothing process:

$$T_t = \alpha(F_t - F_{t-1}) + (1-\alpha)T_{t-1}$$

Forecast with trend $F_{t,k}^1$, k periods ahead is now:

VI. $$F_{t,k}^1 = F_t + \left[\frac{1-\alpha}{\alpha} + k\right]T_t$$

Note that if the forecast is for one period ahead, then $k = 1$ and

$$F_{t,1}^1 = F_t + T_t/\alpha$$

---

* See G. A. COUTIE et al., Short-term Forecasting, Oliver and Boyd Ltd., Edinburgh, 1964, pp. 8–11.

In addition to forecasting for a particular period, it is often desirable to make a forecast of total demand *during* a number of periods. If demand during the following n periods is required, this will be

$$\sum_{k=1}^{n} F_{t,k}^{1}$$

which from equation VI is:

$$\left[n \ F_t + \frac{T_t}{\propto} + T_t \cdot \frac{(n-1)}{2} \right]$$

The procedure so far. is summarised under columns 1–7 of Table IX. Note that if the period used is less than one year, seasonal effects may be evident. If this is the case, additional columns will be required so that column 2 (Actual) may be deseasonalised and columns 6 and 7 (Forecasts) may be reseasonalised. As seasonal factors will differ from period to period, an average of these will be required to reseasonalise forecasts for several periods taken together. Table IX will be used later in this section to illustrate the computational procedures involved.

Forecast Errors and Interval Estimates
The forecast generated in columns 6 or 7 of Table IX, being a single figure, gives no indication of the efficiency of the routine. To what extent may future actuals differ from the point forecast and is the forecast unbiased? In order to answer these questions it is necessary to study the forecast errors $(A_t - F_{t-1})$. These it will be seen are generated in column 8 of Table IX. Ideally, the forecast errors will be small and distributed at random about a mean of zero. It is often found that their distribution approximates quite well to the normal distribution, and this enables confidence intervals to be constructed. If the forecast errors are large and the normal distribution is not a good fit (as demonstrated by plotting on normal probability graph paper) it is advisable to study the distribution of the ratios A_t/F_{t-1}. If, as is sometimes the case, a cumulative plot of the ratios on log-normal probability graph paper approximates to a straight line the ratios may be assumed to be distributed lognormally and again confidence limits may be constructed.

In practice, changes over time combined with the nature of the tracking approach to forecasting often result in forecast errors which may not be random, and will vary about an average which is

TABLE IX: FORECASTING ON THE BASIS OF EXPONENTIAL SMOOTHING—SMOOTHING CONSTANT 0.1 THROUGHOUT

1	2	3	4	5	6	7	8	9	10	11
Period	Actual	Current average (forecast without trend)	Estimate of trend	Smoothed trend	Forecast for next period	Forecast during next three periods	Forecast error	M.A.D. of forecast error	Standard deviation of forecast error	95 per cent interval for next period
		(0.1) Col. 2 + (0.9) Old Col. 3	Col. 3 − Old Col. 3	(0.1) Col. 4 + (0.9) Old Col. 5	Col. 3 + (10) Col. 5	(3) Col. 3 + (33) Col. 5	Col. 2 − Old Col. 6	(0.1) Col. 8 + (0.9) Old Col. 9	(1.25) Col. 9	Col. 6 ± 1.96 Col. 10
1	775	325*	+50*	+50*	825*	2625				
2	837	376	+51	+50	876	2778	+12	24*	30*	817 935
3	890	427	+51	+50	927	2931	+14	23	29	870 884
4	937	478	+51	+50	978	3084	+10	22	28	923 1033
5	972	527	+49	+50	1027	3231	−6	20	25	978 1076
6	998	574	+47	+50	1074	3372	−29	21	26	1023 1125
7	1010	618	+44	+49	1108	3474	−64	25	31	1047 1169
8	1020	658	+40	+48	1138	3558	−88	31	39	1062 1214
9	1025	695	+37	+47	1165	3636	−113	39	49	1069 1261
10	1148	740	+45	+47	1210	3771	−17	37	46	1120 1300
11	1140	780	+40	+46	1240	3858	−70	40	50	1142 1338*
12	1185	821	+41	+46	1281	3981	−55	42	53	1177 1385

* Starting estimates.

non-zero and unstable. If this is so, there is little point in attempting precise estimation of the parameters (in particular standard deviation) of the distribution of forecasting errors. Brown* suggests a simple method of estimating standard deviation based on its relationship with mean absolute deviation (M.A.D.) for a normal distribution when very nearly:

$$\text{Standard Deviation} = 1.25 \text{ M.A.D.}$$

The M.A.D. of forecast errors may be estimated readily from all previous forecast errors by employing the updating smoothing procedure:

$$\text{New M.A.D.} = \alpha(\text{Current Forecast Error}) + (1-\alpha)(\text{Old M.A.D.})$$

Although not in the form developed in Chapter 3, M.A.D. defined in this manner is an average but with more weight given to the recent forecast errors.

Having obtained by these means an estimate of the standard deviation of forecast errors and on the assumption that these are distributed normally interval estimates at any required level of confidence may be constructed. All of this procedure is undertaken in columns 9, 10, and 11 of Table IX. An additional column would be necessary if an interval estimate for demand during a number of forecast periods were required.

Value of the Smoothing Constant

It will be appreciated that exponential smoothing is used on three separate occasions in Table IX, that is in respect of current average, smoothed trend, and M.A.D. of forecast error. The values to be given to the smoothing constant in each case may only be assessed in relation to the general objectives which are:

(*a*) To minimise over time some function of forecast error.
(*b*) To provide point and interval forecasts which are not subject to excessive fluctuations.

Objective (*b*) is satisfied without difficulty. Large perturbations do occur from time to time and it is important if they are not ignored that their effect should be spread. A smoothing constant of 0.1 or 0.2 is therefore appropriate. Usually objective (*a*) is to minimise

---

* See R. G. BROWN, *Smoothing, Forecasting, and Prediction of Discrete Time Series*, Prentice-Hall, Inc., Englewood Cliffs, N.J., 1963, p. 283.

the square root of the mean of the square of the forecast errors (R.M.S.). This approach takes more account of large forecast errors than would one involving the minimisation of M.A.D. If an extensive historical base exists for forecasting then trials with permutations of $\propto$ from 0.1 to 0.5 or higher may be undertaken on the historical data to suggest appropriate values of the smoothing constant. Obviously the computations are heavy and should, if possible, be undertaken by a computer. If there is no historical base, values for $\propto$ need to be assumed and may require modification as data become available. As a practical guideline in these circumstances it is sometimes found that if $\propto = 0.1$ is used in updating current average (age = nine periods) a higher value of 0·2 or 0·5 is preferable for updating trend.

Advantage may be taken in certain instances of the reduction in age of the data which arises from higher values of the smoothing constant. A value of $\propto = 0.5$ may for example be appropriate through periods of unusual circumstances such as strikes, bad weather, and the installation of the forecasting system itself. The value of $\propto$ may then be reduced to the original level when the unusual circumstances are some two or three periods in the past.

Reference was made to values of the smoothing constant $\propto$ not lying within the range zero to one. In fact if the value of $\propto$ lies between one and two then the coefficients of the terms of equation V above are successively positive and negative. It may be shown that for example when $\propto$ is 1.5 the sum of the coefficients is again unity, indicating that the expression is an average. Forecasting using the expression of equation IV, with $\propto$, say, 1.5 and not requiring a correction for trend, is very convenient. If, however, a forecast for more than one period ahead is required, an additional procedure based on recent foreecasts is involved. If the various components of forecasts based on the procedure used in Table IX are collected together, positive and negative coefficients also result. It is a feature of forecasting methods of this type which have been designed to cope with non-stationary time series that terms of both signs are included. There have been a number of attempts to overcome the problem of finding the most appropriate value for the smoothing constant by developing systems in which the smoothing constant is updated as new values of the variable being forecast become available. Trigg and Leach* describe an efficient system of

---

* See D. W. TRIGG AND A. G. LEACH, "Exponential Smoothing with an Adaptive Response Rate," *Operational Research Quarterly*, Vol. 18, No. 1, 1967.

this type, but accept that the computer based mechanistic procedure which is involved may result in useful information not reaching the decision makers when significant changes occur.

Forecast Efficiency and Control

It is customary to measure the efficiency of a particular forecasting method by its ability to cope with the three changes from the stationary situation depicted in Fig. 26. As might be expected, there

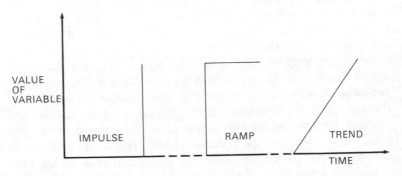

FIG. 26. "Tests" for forecasting methods.

is no one "best" system for all circumstances. The major problems in the test condition of Fig. 26 are to achieve rapid response but to avoid overreaction which may cause oscillations. Many claims have been made in the literature for short term forecasting systems of high efficiency. The method of smoothing incorporating trend correction and described in detail above is a fairly effective compromise.

It is important to appreciate also that except in the cases of time series which are stationary or follow a constant linear trend, the consequence of the usual practice of forecasting by linear extrapolation must on occasions give rise to sequences of errors which are both large and of the same sign. That is to say, the forecast will be at least temporarily biased. This will occur particularly when cyclic movements with turning points occur.

Forecast errors should, over time, approximate to zero. Whether randomness is evident or not, runs of errors of similar sign and occasional large errors will occur and any control system adopted must take account of this. Various approaches have been derived as control limits in forecasting including the *cumulative sum technique** and *tracking signals*. The former, which involves accumulating the forecast errors period by period, is very sensitive to a significant change from the average of zero.

Tracking signals have been suggested by Brown and Trigg and relate the accumulated sum of errors (in the case of Brown) and the smoothed error (in the case of Trigg) to M.A.D. A short paper by Batty† discusses these and other methods of monitoring forecasts.

Whatever control system is used, action will be indicated when the control limits have been exceeded. Following any action which is taken accumulated forecast errors will be reset to zero.

If the reason for the out-of-control situation is known and the suitability of the forecasting system is not in question the "unusual" information may be discounted. If there is some doubt as to the efficiency of the forecasts, changes may be required in the value of the smoothing constants or a search for a new forecasting system may be necessary. In the latter context, however, given the fact that a number of fairly effective short term forecasting systems have been developed, there is perhaps too much emphasis on accurate fits to historical data. The main objective of a forecasting system is to provide a good forecast, and the extent to which mathematical and statistical procedures are employed should be in some balance with other types of analysis of, say, a financial and economic nature.

A Numerical Example of Exponential Smoothing

To summarise the discussion of tracking methods involving an unlimited number of terms, exponential smoothing incorporating a correction for trend is applied to the data included in Table IX which is seasonally unaffected. The procedure is demonstrated using values of the smoothing constant x, of 0.1 for all three smoothing processes. It is assumed that twelve periods of historical data are available and that the values of x adopted are a first attempt in developing the most appropriate system.

In order to develop the forecast it is necessary to assume starting values, and these are marked with an asterisk. As twelve periods of data are available there exists a basis for estimates of trend (columns

---

* *See* P. J. HARRISON AND O. L. DAVIES, "The use of cumulative sum (Cusum) techniques for the control of routine forecasts of product demand," *Operations Research*, Vol. 12, No. 2, 1964.

† *See* M. BATTY, "Monitoring an Exponential Smoothing Forecasting System," *Operational Research Quarterly*, Vol. 20, No. 3, 1969.

4 and 5) and standard deviation (column 10). On the assumption that the forecast for the second period is the first period actual plus one trend value, column 6 is determined, and by projecting backwards, current average (column 3) takes the value 325. Included in the table is an example of a forecast for the total of three periods (column 7). The calculations are based on the relationships developed above under the heading "Correction for trend."

By following the instruction at the head of each column, forecasts are generated to period 12. Of particular interest is column 8, in which forecast errors are listed. It will be noted that these become negative and large; in other words, the forecast is at least temporarily biased. This is explained by the initial estimate of trend, which is too high. Alternatively, the low value of smoothing constant used for trend made this respond only slowly to a decline in the rate of increase of the actuals (column 2). Apart from the possibility of using high values of α for the first few periods, it is evident that the forecast errors from period 6 onwards would have been reduced if α had been 0.2, 0.3, or even as high as 0.5. The reader may wish to undertake this exercise.

The reason for the temporary bias in the forecast becomes evident if the data are plotted as in Fig. 27. It is clear that with the exception

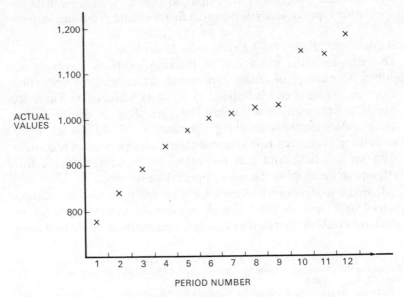

FIG. 27. The time series of actual data in Table IX.

of the discontinuity around period 10, there is a marked decrease in the rate of increase. By projecting linearly, future values were appreciably overestimated. This again emphasises that tracking methods are essentially short term. If, for example, a forecast had been made in period 2 for period 8 this would have amounted to 1126, over 100 in excess of the actual figure of 1020.

The figures used in this example will be referred to again during the following discussion on non-linear trend curves.

NON-LINEAR TREND CURVES

This approach to forecasting may be examined through the work of a group of staff employed by I.C.I. Ltd.* It is concerned mainly with demand for goods and services, that is variables which are mainly uncontrollable and which require a stable forecasting base of some length. It takes account of the fact that apart from certain staple services and items of diet which presumably will continue to be demanded as long as mankind exists, all other services and commodities offered by organisations will possess a life cycle. The cycle length may vary from a few months to several thousands of years and may be of the form shown in Fig. 28. Quite obviously variations

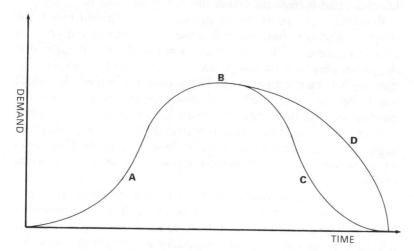

Fig. 28. The life cycle of a commodity or service.

* See J. V. CREGG et al., *Mathematical Trend Curves: An aid to Forecasting*, Oliver and Boyd Ltd., Edinburgh, 1964.

about the cycle may be very marked and a necessary requirement of the approach is that the underlying long term movement is not obscured by shorter term cycles and trends. Whereas the classical method is limited to growth which is assumed to be linear or at a constant rate this approach recognises that if a life cycle is likely to exist a straight line description is necessarily short term.

The general form of a life cycle shown in Fig. 28 demonstrates an initial period during which the values increase to a point of inflection (A) following which values continue to increase but at a decreasing rate (this part of the cycle is often described as an "S-curve"). From the peak value (B) a decline will take place following a path which will be determined by the factors causing the decline. In some cases, a point of inflection (C) may be reached due, say, to some traditional demand being maintained for a product or service (for example, bowler hats and roof thatching). On the other hand, substitution effects or changes in taste may induce a rapid reduction to zero through point D. Obviously other forms of life cycle exist. For example, there may be long term fluctuations rather than an approximation to a smooth curve. A decline from a peak may occur at a decreasing rate, and there may be long periods of stable values. Nevertheless, many time series conform with the first part of the life cycle, that is from the origin through point A to B.

Reference may be made to primary energy products for the purpose of illustration. Nuclear generated electrical output is at present presumed to lie below point A in Fig. 28. It is thought that the global supply of oil has passed through A and is therefore increasing but at a decreasing rate. Gas production in the U.K., which was in decline has entered a new phase superimposed on the old position and will (probably) follow again an S-curve. Coal production, at least in the U.K., has also been in decline although there is a suggestion that the long term trend is turning upwards. Time series based on mineral products provide examples of life cycles of great length.

The first step is to assess whether it is appropriate to forecast a time series by fitting a non-linear trend curve. A decision based on a plot of actual data may be difficult to make because of irregular effects. It is, therefore, usually necessary to smooth the data first using a simple moving average. In order to achieve a sufficient degree of smoothing five or more terms will, in general, be required to be included in the average. It is customary to use an odd number of terms, in which case the average will coincide in time with an actual value. It will be appreciated that if for example seven terms are used, this will mean that an average will not be available for three periods at each end of the series. And, as it is desired to establish a long term trend, it is evident that for an acceptable forecasting base a considerable history is required. These requirements limit the application of this approach only to variables which have been accurately recorded for a substantial time.

The second step is to decide which non-linear function fits the time series "adequately." There is an infinite variety of non-linear functions, many of which will fit the data extremely well. It will be recollected from Chapter 2 that although many models fit existing data very well, extrapolated results may vary considerably according to which model is used. The same comments apply to non-linear trend curves when for one set of data coefficients of determination approaching unity may be obtained for functions of different curvature. The approach suggested by the proponents of this forecasting method is that before selecting a trend curve arbitrarily, regression analysis should be used to provide estimates of *slope* over time. The slope estimates are then used to aid the selection of an appropriate trend curve, following which regression analysis is again used to obtain the best fit of the trend curve selected.

The Use of Slope in Curve Selection
The moving average used to smooth the time series is assumed to involve an odd number of terms. The number of terms may be expressed as $2n+1$, in which case the moving average centred at time t is:

$$(A_{t-n}+\ldots\ldots\ldots A_t+\ldots\ldots\ldots A_{t+n})/(2n+1).$$

If linear regression is used over the $2n+1$ periods, it may be shown that slope over this time is:

$$\frac{3(-nA_{t-n}-\ldots-A_{t-1}+A_{t+1}\ldots+nA_{t+n})}{n(n+1)(2n+1)}$$

For example, consider the six actual values, 10, 16, 21, 28, 30 and 35. The five term moving averages coincident with the actual values of 21 and 28 are 21 and 26 respectively. Slope estimates centred on the two actual values are, by substituting in the formula above, 4.1 and 4.7. Thus averages and slope estimates may be generated for any time series over any number of terms. But how may selection of an appropriate curve be facilitated? Use is made of the fact that a straight line is readily established by visual inspection and the procedure is to transform the estimates of slope by a number of functions of the moving average. If a straight line, over time, of "slope transforms" is produced by a ratio involving slope estimate and some function of moving average, then a particular curve is suggested as being an appropriate fit to the actual data.* A number of curves which may be an appropriate fit for part of a life cycle and excluding the straight line are summarised, together with their related transformations, in Table X. The procedure is to plot against time all of the slope transforms. If a plot approximates a straight line, then one curve is suggested. If no transform satisfies the requirement then none of the curves listed is an appropriate fit.

TABLE X : SELECTION OF A TREND CURVE BY A STUDY OF SLOPE TRANSFORMS

Transform	Approximated by a straight line which is:	Suggested curve is:
Slope itself	At an angle to horizontal	Parabola
Slope/Moving Average	Horizontal	Simple Exponential
Slope/Moving Average	At an angle to horizontal	Logarithmic Parabola
Logarithm of slope	Sloping downwards over time	Simple Modified Exponential
Logarithm of (Slope/ Moving Average)	Sloping downwards over time	Gompertz
Logarithm of ((Slope/ Moving Average)^2)	Sloping downwards over time	Logistic

Referring to Table X, the Simple Exponential ($A_t = ab^t$) has been encountered under the classical approach to forecasting. In this case, a constant and continuing rate of growth is implied. As at some time during the life cycle a limit is reached, it is useful to have curves which satisfy this condition and these are represented here

---

* For example, assume that variable A_t is related to time, t by the second order function, the parabola, then:

$$A_t = a + bt + ct^2$$

Differentiating with respect to t:

$$\frac{dA}{dt}t = b + 2ct$$

A_t is represented by the moving average at t and $\frac{dA}{dt}t$ by the slope computed over the period of the moving average. Thus if b and c are positive constants, slope will approximate to a straight line rising over time.

by the modified exponentials (Simple, Gompertz, and Logistic). The Gompertz and Logistic curves possess the additional property of a point of inflection and restrict the search if examination of slope of the smoothed data reveals a change of curvature.

The calculations involved in determining moving averages, slope estimates and slope transforms are heavy and are best done in a routine manner by a computer. The procedure is to input the time series and calculate slope transforms according to every type of trend curve which it is wished to investigate. The output will include a numerical listing under each transform which is then plotted and visually assessed for straight line properties.

Fitting the Non-linear Trend Curve
The third step in this method of forecasting is the fitting of the selected curve and the determination of point and, if required, interval forecasts. Assuming that a particular curve has been suggested by examination of the slope transforms it is now necessary to establish by regression analysis the parameters of the particular curve. Again, extensive calculations are involved and a complementary computer programme is desirable in which curve fitting routines and extrapolation are available for each function included in the slope transform programme.

Assume that study of the slope transforms suggest a Gompertz curve as being an appropriate fit, then using the data of Table IX the equation of the curve arising from regression analysis is:

$$\text{Log}\, A_t = 3.16 - 0.26(0.91)^t$$

Suppose that a forecast were required for period 21. This by substitution is 1319. If a straight line had been fitted to the data of Table IX, the resulting straight line would have been:

$$A_t = 808.63 + 33.84_t$$

and a forecast for period 21 on this basis would be 1485, which is significantly different from the Gompertz forecast. To complete the comparisons a forecast using the exponential smoothing procedure of Table IX for period 21 is obtained by adding eight trend values to the last forecast in the table to give 1649. Which of these forecasts, if any, would be selected by the decision maker would depend upon how credible they appeared to him. This is the point at which the transition from a forecast to a prediction (as defined at the beginning of the chapter) would in all probability occur.

GENERAL COMMENTS AND SUMMARY

Decisions of significance within organisations frequently require quantified bases. If the decision does not relate to the immediate future then forecasting and prediction is involved. Many decisions because of ignorance or lack of computational support use subjective and often crude methods. Whilst due regard must always be taken of opinion which is expert (not just authoritative) it is important to assess whether historical data will provide an analytical basis for estimating future values. In retrospect, it might be said that it is frequently the case that a sustained pattern of movement of a variable embraced both past and future. Unfortunately patterns of movement in many instances are neither regular nor prolonged and the large number of determinants of most variables make many "regular" patterns pure coincidence. The construction of models which explain *ex post* the values of dependent variables is often achieved efficiently. If estimation involves *interpolation* of the independent variable considerable confidence may be placed in estimates made using the model. If, as in the case of time series, the independent variable is time then interpolation is of little practical use. Forecasting involves looking forward and confidence in the forecast is only realistic if the forecasting model continues to apply. It is thus necessary to have confidence in the continuing applicability of the forecasting model. The classical approach and the approach based on non-linear trend curves assume such continuing applicability (although it is to be expected that the parameters of the models will be periodically updated). Tracking methods make no such assumption but simply aim to follow the time series as closely as possible, relying on most recent estimates of average and trend. Because of this, tracking methods are essentially short term, it being inadvisable to forecast more than one or two periods into the future. Trend curves are more suitable for longer term forecasting and certain non-linear functions may appropriately be used if a stable base of suitable length is available and continuation of the trend selected is considered likely.

Other short term forecasting systems have been developed in which data points are incorporated successively and yet which cannot strictly be described as tracking methods. A novel feature of the Box and Jenkins* technique is the development of models

---

* *See* G. E. P. BOX AND G. M. JENKINS, *Models for Prediction and Control*, Department of Systems Engineering, University of Lancaster, Technical Reports 1–11, 1966.

which relate, for example, the current value of a variable to weighted recent values of the variable through the process of auto-regression. Of considerable attraction is the Bayesian approach developed by Harrison and Stevens.* Basically this is an adaptive method, but one in which the extent to which account is taken of a new observation is based on its significance measured by the probability of such a new value occurring.

Seasonal effects should always be isolated in short term forecasting provided their existence may be explained. In this case, much more efficient forecasting will be achieved by following the process of deseasonalising, forecasting, and reseasonalising the forecast.

The difference between interval forecasts for the mean and individual results should be appreciated. By viewing the forecasting base as a sample then sampling error will exist, and to the variance of individual values must be added the estimated variance of the mean forecast itself. Whether forecasts of mean levels or individual values are made will depend to some extent on the relative importance of the variable being estimated. From the viewpoint of risk aversion, an organisation able to adopt a long-run attitude (averaging good with bad years) will be prepared to accept forecasts of mean levels whereas organisations to which one bad year may spell disaster will be more concerned with individual values.

The selection of the most suitable approach is facilitated by the availability of substantial and accurate historical data. There is no guarantee however of this "suitability" extending into the future. Any forecasting system used in a routine manner needs inbuilt control. In general, the control will not cause the system to adopt a more suitable form but will indicate that either modification or replacement by an alternative method is necessary.

Models of organisations are becoming increasingly sophisticated. At the level of planning decisions the purpose of such models is more usually to "examine" the future. If logical estimates of uncontrollable variables are not input to the models then whatever the degree of sophistication. of the model itself the output will be illogical. The forecasting methods described in this Chapter should give an insight into some of the difficulties which arise in estimating future values of variables of an uncontrollable nature.

---

* See P. J. HARRISON AND C. F. STEVENS, "A Bayesian Approach to Short-term Forecasting," *Operational Research Quarterly*, Vol. 22, No. 4, 1971.

Chapter Five

NETWORK ANALYSIS AND DECISION MAKING

INTRODUCTION

In Chapter 2, an organisation was likened to a large craft being piloted through time and space by its chief executive. To outsiders the net effect of organisational decision making and activity may suggest that the movement is somewhat ponderous. Very large organisations such as British Petroleum, Unilever, the National Coal Board and local authorities are seen to be operating, in total, within a few per cent of the previous year and the impression may be gained that this is due more to inertia than conscious effort. Whilst it is true that the internal structure of some organisations changes only very slowly through time, the superficial appearance of constancy may conceal fundamental internal restructuring. Companies may have been acquired, major projects started, new products or technology introduced and so on. In these circumstances static organisational models, except of the most general financial nature, are inappropriate and planning must take account of the dynamic effect of change. The consequences of the major variations mentioned above, such as the rationalisation of production, the tying up of resources, the introduction of new methods of financial management and control may span several years. And if logical planning decisions are to be taken at high levels some formal method is required of estimating as precisely as possible the state of the organisation at specific times in the future.

Furthermore, if corporate objectives are in any sense to be efficient it is essential that the potential effectiveness of the organisation's resources should be realised by appropriate allocation to activities. There is again something of the chicken and the egg situation here. Ideally, given the organisation and its environment, consideration of existing and potential resources should indicate realistic and quantified objectives. In fact, potential resources are frequently determined in part by the objectives which are set. Thus, as suggested earlier, objectives which are quantified are usually arbitrary to some degree. Despite the fact that the objectives themselves may not qualify to be described as optimal it remains desirable to search for the best way of attaining whatever objectives are set. The planning of total resources in the longer term to meet corporate objectives is an ultimate aim of management. In many organisations at the present time sub-corporate goals (implying projects in the case of non-cyclic activity or periodic milestones in the case of continuing or cyclic activity) are being planned and achieved through the use of the technique of *network analysis*. In some instances progress has been made by these means towards the co-ordinated planning of a number of sub-corporate goals. It will be suggested that network analysis, which originally was used very much to plan and control isolated one-off projects within organisations, is a potential tool whereby a total view may be taken of the application of resources over time. The technique will be shown to have value in assessing the alternative courses of action open to an organisation.

THE NETWORK: ORIGINS AND CONSTRUCTION

The main deficiency of the human brain is its inability to store and handle large quantities of sequenced information. Few people are able to assess the implications of even two moves ahead at chess without using the physical model of the chess board and the pieces. In such a gaming situation a person who is able to evaluate sequenced alternatives is a likely winner. In real life, however, such clear-cut gaming situations are not always apparent and the manager thinks more of achievement or non-achievement than of winning or losing. Particularly with objectives based on a non-cyclic sequence of activities there is often in retrospect little to indicate whether they have been achieved with efficiency or not. Despite the fact that there is general recognition of the great complexity of planning a major project, the lack of overall standards for purposes of comparison allows inefficient management to aim to meet its objectives without resorting to any logical aid to planning. In order to achieve goals with efficiency, some analytical aid is necessary. This has of course been recognised for many years and bar charts, in which the length of a bar is proportional to activity duration, have long been used for scheduling purposes. And it is certain that in an attempt to cope with complex interrelationships such means as the linking of bars to indicate a constrained sequence were employed in the past. However, for a project of any complexity efficient planning on these lines is impossible and acceptable completion has only been achieved by good fortune or excessive application of managerial effort.

One hears of various claims from both sides of the Atlantic for the invention of the graphical model known as the network. It is however no coincidence that it came to prominence shortly after large electronic computers became available, as it will be seen that extensive calculations are involved. Most of the current characteristics of the approach are due to one or other of two original developments. Critical Path Method (C.P.M.) was developed in the United States chemical company of duPont from about 1957 and Program Evaluation and Review Technique (PERT) was devised at the same time to aid the planning of the introduction of various weaponry (notably Polaris) in the United States forces. It is not surprising that the former method was primarily cost oriented, whereas in the latter instance the emphasis was on time. Over the years each approach has been modified and extended so that at the present time similarities between the two by far outweigh the differences. Users still refer to PERT and C.P.M.; perhaps network analysis is a preferable description. Claims have also been made for other techniques such as the *method of potentials* and the *precedence network* but differences between all methods which employ a network are not fundamental. One extension which will be discussed below is the method of estimating activity durations by using PERT.

The network is a unique arrangement of arrows, each arrow representing an activity or a constraint and commencing and ending at an *event*. PERT is more concerned with events such as the beginning or ending of an activity, C.P.M. emphasises the activities themselves. The following description of the components of the network are on the lines of C.P.M.

(a) An *activity* is represented by an unbroken arrow, the length of which (usually) is unrelated to the length of the activity. The nature of the activity is indicated against the arrow, or there is a coded reference.

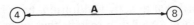

FIG. 29. An activity with start and end events.

(b) A circle at the commencement and end of an activity represents a moment in time described as an *event*. Each event is numbered so that activities may be coded uniquely. In Fig. 29 activity A is shown with its start event, 4 and its end event, 8.

(c) In order that each activity shall be coded uniquely and, additionally, that account is taken of all constraints and interrelationships it is necessary to introduce a *dummy* activity of zero duration. The use of the dummy activity (shown by the broken line) to achieve unique coding is demonstrated in Fig. 30.

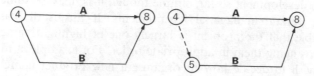

FIG. 30. The use of a dummy activity to achieve unique coding.
(a) Activities A and B not coded uniquely.
(b) Activities A and B coded uniquely by the introduction of dummy 4–5.

In Fig. 31 activity 9–11 is a dummy, the effect of which is to make the commencement of activity Y dependent on the completion of both activity W and activity X. Note the importance of the dummy 9–11 operating in the right direction. If the dummy were reversed (becoming 11–9) the interrelationships would be changed.

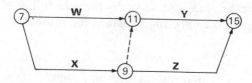

FIG. 31. The use of a dummy to indicate a constraint.

This short list completes all the basic procedures necessary for the drawing of a network employing deterministic activities* but quite obviously some skill is necessary in completing the logic of a complex project. Many managers find it useful to draw out a small network in order to try and highlight some of the problems likely to be

* The reference to deterministic activities here implies that all activities are planned to be undertaken. It will however be appreciated that alternative courses of action may be indicated as time passes. Reference will be made to so-called *probabilistic networks* in Chapter 9.

encountered during a project. The size of the network (in terms of activities) is not necessarily related to the importance of the project but more to the detailed level of the decisions which will be taken. A senior manager responsible for, say, a city redevelopment will wish to take account of the time required to construct a new bus station but he will not be concerned with the time allocated for painting it. In a network diagram referred to him the construction of the bus station may be represented by a single arrow. Painting will be one of many arrows representing the activities involved in constructing the bus station for which a separate and more detailed network may be drawn.

The development so far, simple though it is, may be sufficient to satisfy certain managerial requirements. If this is the case it is probable that the problem is largely one of highlighting activities and arranging them in appropriate order. For example, a manager may wish to decide how to organise a new product launch or to plan the preparation of final accounts when some tolerance may exist in respect of completion date. In these cases, the major resource is likely to be himself or those members of staff working closely with him. Valuable though the sequencing of activities in this way may be, deductions may become blurred when there are a number of paths through the network. It is therefore very desirable to supplement the ordering of activities by more specific scheduling. This will involve, in the first instance, an analysis involving activity durations which will indicate the time period during which an activity may take place and secondly the scheduling of an activity with due regard to competing demands for resources.

ANALYSIS OF THE NETWORK

To this point (that is the construction of the network logic) the effort has been of necessity manual, but hereafter a computer may take over. The decision to employ a computer will depend largely on the number of activities involved. Depending on staff availability over a hundred activities may be analysed manually, but a computer rapidly becomes desirable when this number is substantially exceeded.

Analysis requires an estimation of activity durations. For the time being it will be assumed that these are deterministic, although it will be appreciated that uncertainty exists in the estimation of activity durations. The implications of this uncertainty will be discussed under a separate heading below.

Once activity durations have been incorporated in the network, it is possible to calculate earliest and latest event times (E.E.T.s and L.E.T.s), which are defined as follows:

EARLIEST EVENT TIME: The earliest moment in time at which an event may occur, being determined by the path with greatest duration leading into that event.

LATEST EVENT TIME: The latest moment in time at which an event may occur without delaying project completion. L.E.T. is determined by the path with longest duration leading out of that event.

There are many ways of indicating E.E.T.s and L.E.T.s on networks, here E.E.T. will be written in a circle and L.E.T. in a square, both adjacent to the event.

Consider Fig. 32, in which a network has been analysed using the

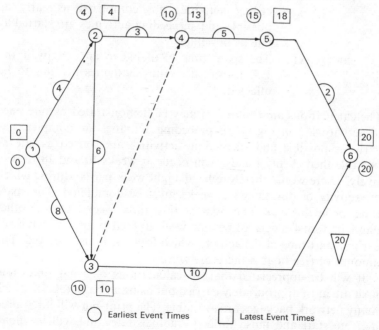

FIG. 32. A network analysed for E.E.T.s and L.E.T.s.

activity durations indicated (in weeks) in the semicircles adjacent to each arrow. The inverted triangle containing the number 20 indicates that the target is twenty weeks, and this determines the L.E.T. of the final event. Reconciliation of target time with the E.E.T. of the final event will be considered below. It will be appreciated that E.E.T.s are determined working from event 1 to event 6, whereas L.E.T.s are determined in the reverse direction; in each case, account is taken of longest paths leading to or from events.

Of immediate note is the fact that for some events E.E.T. and L.E.T. are the same whereas in other cases they differ. In the latter instance this suggests that events are not fixed in time but possess a certain quantified latitude. It is however dangerous to draw deductions solely from event times. For example events 1 and 3 are fixed in time but the same is not true of activity 1–3. The amount of spare time or *float* available to an activity is determined by reference to the E.E.T.s and L.E.T.s of both start and finish events together with the activity duration. The two types of float used most extensively are defined as follows:

TOTAL FLOAT: The spare time available to an activity if preceding activities are completed as early as possible and succeeding activities are started as late as possible.

FREE FLOAT: The spare time available to an activity if the E.E.T.s of succeeding activities are not to be affected.

The calculations are routine, as may be demonstrated by reference to activity 4–5 in Fig. 32. If preceding activities are completed as early as possible and succeeding activities are started as late as possible then events 4 and 5 will occur at weeks 10 and 18 respectively. There would therefore be an eight week period during which an activity of duration five weeks must be completed. The spare time, or in this case total float, is thus three weeks. On the other hand, if event 4 is delayed beyond week 10 then event 5, which is the earliest start time of the activity which follows, is also delayed. The amount of free float is therefore zero.

It will be appreciated that all calculations of event times and float are most appropriately carried out using a computer, for which many network packages are available. The print-out will if required indicate start and finish times by actual dates and will list float. Additionally, a bar chart is an option in most packages, in which case float is usually placed after the activity. Thus activity 4–5 of five weeks' duration (represented by crosses) and possessing three weeks of total float (represented by dashes) would appear in some print-outs as xxxxx–––. The question arises as to which float should be included in a bar diagram. The problem may be discussed by reference to Fig. 33, which is a bar chart indicating total float

ACTIVITY	DURATION	TOTAL FLOAT	FREE FLOAT	WEEK NUMBER																			
				1	2	3	4	5	6	7	8	9	10	11	12	13	14	15	16	17	18	19	20
1–2	4	0	0																				
1–3	8	2	2																				
2–4	3	6	3																				
2–3	6	0	0																				
4–5	5	3	0																				
3–6	10	0	0																				
5–6	2	3	3																				

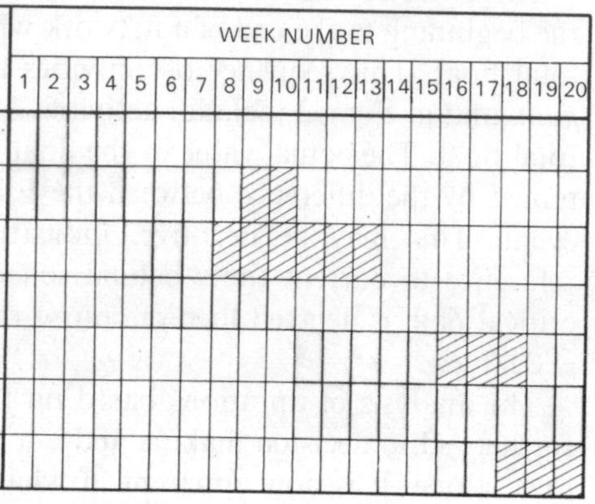

FIG. 33. Bar chart arising from analysis of the network shown in Fig. 32 and showing total float (hatched).

(hatched) attaching to each activity of the network in Fig. 32. It might be supposed that an activity may be undertaken anywhere within the period of float plus duration. To an extent this is true, but note must be taken of the effect of the consumption of float on succeeding activities. By definition, if free float is consumed subsequent activities are unaffected. Thus activity 1–3 may be completed as late as the end of week 10 without interaction. If activity 2–4 extends beyond week 10 then the earliest start times of activities 4–5 and 5–6 are affected, reducing the float available. The important point is that total float is *shared* among activities on an isolated path. This will be appreciated when it is realised that activities on an isolated path may be replaced by a single activity. For example if in Fig. 32 a single activity 4–6 replaced the two activities 4–5 and 5–6, it would possess a total (and free) float of three weeks. Care must therefore be taken in interpreting indicated float. Some computer outputs list total float only and it is necessary to trace paths on the network which share this float. If both total and free float are given, a more complete picture is presented. It is worth noting that a bar chart including total float only is to be preferred to one listing free float only. In the latter case some activities which are not in fact fixed in time would appear to be so (for example activity 4–5 in Fig. 32). For an isolated path of, say, six activities possessing total float, only the final activity would have free float. It is important for purposes of scheduling to show all activities with float.

There will be one (or coincidentally more) path(s) extending from the beginning to the end of a network which possesses the minimum total float. This sequence of activities is referred to as the *critical path*, and in Fig. 32 includes activities 1–2, 2–3, and 3–6, with zero total float. The actual value of the float on the critical path is determined by the difference between the E.E.T. and L.E.T. of the final event. This may be negative, indicating that the project is, by reference to current time, behind schedule. If any activity on the critical path is delayed then of course the completion of the project is delayed.

The analysis of durations based on the logic of the network is a further aid to decision making and is a more powerful tool than the logic alone. It is now apparent in what sequence and during what specific intervals of time activities must be undertaken in order to meet a timed goal. It may be that an activity refers to the actions of a single manager, such as the gaining of approval for some undertaking from his Board, the Unions, or a Government Department, in which case his own involvement may be small. But assuming that he has estimated with realism the times involved, the total interval indicated should enable him to assess progress and expedite it if necessary. It is however often necessary to take into account resource limitations, and to this end the specific estimate of float for each activity may be of considerable value.

THE ALLOCATION OF RESOURCES

At any moment in time an organisation possesses a certain stock of the factors of production, land, labour, and capital. The former is often invariable but changes in the stock of labour and capital throughout time are customary. As was mentioned earlier, the ideal but hopeful corporate objective is the allocation of resources to maximise some objective function determined in relation to the environment. The corporate plan may in fact suggest marked changes in resources by, for example, divestment, diversification, or acquisition. As soon as goals are set, however, it is necessary to estimate the type, quantity, deployment and duration of use of each individual type of resource so that the goals may be achieved in the most efficient manner. The background for decisions of this nature is one of high uncertainty, particularly if the production of goods or services is planned. For example what extra revenue would be obtained by bringing a product on the market six months earlier than had been planned originally? What would be the extra cost of obtaining production by this time? An erroneous forecast of demand would certainly affect the outcome and yet a prediction on these lines is unavoidable. Although the situation is one of considerable and changing complexity, network analysis can in many respects assist in making logical decisions by providing efficient estimates of the timing of events which are largely determined by the decision maker (for example, the availability of supply).

It is first necessary to indicate by reference to all activities the types of resource which will be required during a project. On the assumption that a supply of each will be available, it is then desirable to establish the extent of the availability and whether this will vary over time. The bar chart is now of great use in determining whether the supply of resources will meet the demand. The principle may be outlined by reference to Fig. 33. Assume that a particular resource is demanded as follows:

Activity	Resource requirement (units)
1–2	0
1–3	1
2–4	3
2–3	3
4–5	3
3–6	2
5–6	1

The peak demand for this resource if activities are started as early as possible will occur during weeks 5, 6 and 7, when seven units will be required. If however activity 2–4 is delayed as long as possible then the float available to this activity and activities 4–5 and 5–6 will disappear. But the result will be to decrease demand for the resource during weeks 5, 6 and 7 to four units and the peak demand (for five units) will now occur from weeks 11–20 inclusive. Obviously the total demand for the resource has not been reduced, but it has been smoothed* considerably. As a generalisation, the smaller the organisation or operating unit the greater the advantage of a smoothed demand for resources. In larger organisations where a number of projects may be in progress at any time, there is the possibility of resource switching. Alternatively, if it is anticipated that resources will not be required during a certain period there will be opportunities in the larger organisation to undertake such things as overhauls, special projects, training and so on.

It is rarely possible to achieve a totally smoothed demand for a particular resource throughout a project. The general trend in demand is an early peak followed by a gradual decline. Making certain assumptions about resource availability and an objective function it is possible to optimise allocation both within and between resources. The major query, however, surrounds the assumptions which are made. The approach and its potential will be examined in Chapter 9. The problem of a notional ceiling (related to normal operating time) on resource availability will be apparent from a plot of demand shown in Fig. 34 for a particular resource,

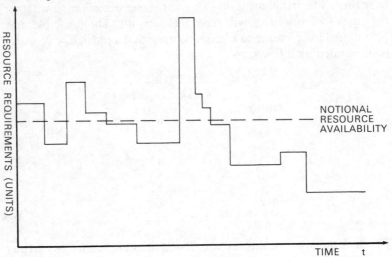

FIG. 34. Demand for a resource. Activities commenced as early as possible.

* The terminology used in the literature is not standard, but two situations may be recognised. In the first of these, the project duration is maintained and float is consumed in an attempt to reduce the variability of demand for a resource within the fixed time interval. This has been described as *resource smoothing*. In the second situation, a limitation of resource availability is recognised and the activities are scheduled in order to minimise the project duration. The description *resource levelling* has been given to this procedure.

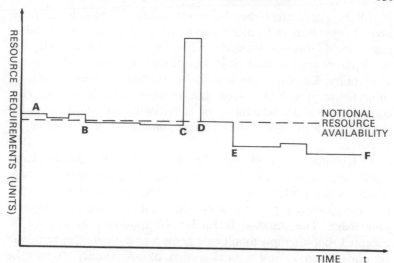

FIG. 35. Resource demand smoothed by re-scheduling.

assuming all activities are started as early as possible. By studying the bar charts for the project, rescheduling of activities should enable a certain degree of smoothing to be achieved. Assume that the outcome is as indicated in Fig. 35, when certain conclusions may be drawn:

1. Period A–B: Throughout this time the demand is somewhat in excess of supply. It might be preferable however to increase the resource availability by overtime or weekend operations rather than attempt to obtain extra resources.
2. Period B–C: Over this period demand equals or is slightly less than supply. It may be concluded that it would be desirable to make the resource available to the project throughout the interval. A small excess in supply could be a useful contingency measure.
3. Period C–D: Rescheduling has not eliminated this peak. A large organisation may be able to allocate an additional supply temporarily. If this is not possible, two alternatives exist: either a portion of the project is sub-contracted or the completion date is delayed.
4. Period E–F: A significant and fairly constant excess of resource availability exists over this period. Consideration may then be given to redeployment or even redundancy.

It will be appreciated that by rescheduling to smooth resources float is consumed and hence more activities will become critical or near critical; this will demand a higher level of control. It will also be apparent how difficult it is to optimise in respect of resource availability. Resources can usually be procured, dispensed with or subjected to greater utilisation, but we have been considering only one resource and rescheduling of activities to smooth demand for this may well influence adversely the smoothing of other types of resource.

If demands for available resources from other undertakings within the organisation are recognised, the combinatorial magnitude of the problem will be evident. Optimal solutions to such problems are not possible with the existing state of analytical knowledge. The situation is further compounded as it must be accepted that attempts to allocate resources in the longer term will be undertaken against a background of uncertainty. It may be thought by a manager that such allocations might just as well be made on an instinctive basis (as was customary in the past). However, sufficient experience has been gained to date to conclude that even if the "optimum" is only an ideal, *heuristic methods** will guarantee allocation of resources in a more efficient manner. Most large computer companies offer packages† which enable resources to be allocated within and between projects. The heuristic routines used differ considerably and because of the need for systematic rules some of the schedules when examined on an individual basis appear unnecessarily restrictive. Nevertheless, by comparing the results suggested with known optimal schedules using reference networks it has been found that near optimal situations have been reached. A feature of the computer packages available is their scope. Networks of several thousand activities and about a hundred different types of resource may be analysed in this way.

The problem of resource allocation is essentially one of scheduling. An optimal allocation of resources which is the aim of the procedure implies minimum variability in demand for (unlimited) resources if the project duration is fixed or minimum project duration if re-

* Heuristic methods are those which attempt to determine an optimum solution by trial and error methods based on judgment or analysis when the latter may not be employed to obtain the optimum directly.

† *See* GAIL THORNLEY, ed., *Critical Path Analysis in Practice*, Tavistock Publications, London, 1968, Appendix 3.

sources are limited. The problem of minimum cost will be examined in the section which follows.

ACTIVITY DURATIONS WHICH MAY BE VARIED OR ARE UNCERTAIN

The analysis to this point has involved fixed and deterministic activity times, although some implications of making estimates have been mentioned. It is necessary to consider both the trade-off between time and cost and the accumulated effect of uncertainty. As mentioned earlier, C.P.M. was developed in an environment which was highly cost sensitive and it was to be expected that special efforts would be made to establish the duration of a project which was associated with minimum cost, taking account of such factors as direct and indirect costs, penalty costs and the advantages of early completion. The PERT approach recognised that single figure durations could only be "best estimates" and that if planning decisions were to be realistic account need to be taken in a more formal manner of uncertainty. This was achieved by treating activity durations as random variables.

THE C.P.M. TIME-COST PROCEDURE

The C.P.M. approach recognises a relationship between the duration and variable cost of an activity.* It is reasonable to assume that this should take the form of Fig. 36. It is assumed that if there were no external constraints an activity would be completed in that time associated with the minimum cost of all resources. Note that this time, the point N in Fig. 36, the *normal time*, does not necessarily preclude the use of resources outside normal working hours, it is simply that time associated with minimum cost. An increase or reduction in the time taken will therefore involve additional cost. Reduced times are of more interest, and increased marginal costs in this direction would be expected. Point C indicates the minimum "reasonable" duration below which any further shortening is patently uneconomic, and is termed the *crash time*. The argument is therefore that any selected interval between normal and crash times is feasible and implies a specific cost. Further, a reasonable

* See A. BATTERSBY, *Network Analysis for Planning and Scheduling*, Macmillan & Co. Ltd., London, 1964, p. 67.

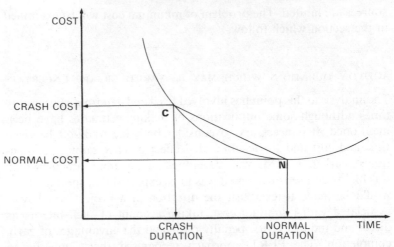

FIG. 36. The relationship between cost and time for a single activity.

approximation to the function is the chord CN which permits computation of the ratio:

$$\frac{\text{Crash Cost} - \text{Normal Cost}}{\text{Normal Time} - \text{Crash Time}}$$

The description *cost slope* is given to this ratio. If now it is possible to quantify such features as fixed costs and the cost of not completing by a certain date (penalty cost or loss of revenue, for example), then by manipulation of activity durations and costs a project

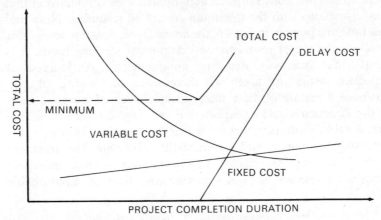

FIG. 37. Optimisation using normal and crash times.

duration may be suggested which differs from that which would arise if all activities were scheduled at normal duration. The procedure is indicated graphically in Fig. 37. Most computational effort is involved in generating the profile of total variable cost. Hand computation is feasible for networks of up to one hundred activities and computer procedures are available for larger networks providing the time-cost curves of all activities are of the form shown in Fig. 36. Reference is made in Chapter 9 to an analytical procedure for obtaining points on the variable cost curve which offers greater flexibility (but which is restricted at present to networks of about fifty activities). In many instances the target date would automatically be equated with the time when a penalty was first to be incurred, but it is worth noting that analysis may suggest completion of the project on some date before a penalty cost is involved. This would be determined by the comparative slopes of fixed and variable costs.

It is important to appreciate that the cost of an activity is a function of the time required. Resources have therefore been viewed in terms of total cost and the question of their availability has not been raised. If the total activities of an organisation are under consideration, unlimited resources may not usually be assumed. Thus this approach, for which the assumption of unlimited resources is required, will generally involve sub-optimisation (except perhaps in the very small organisation with limited activities).

Some account may be taken of uncertainty if it is assumed that the total *resource* necessary to achieve a specific activity time may be described by a probability distribution. Thus for example in order to complete an activity in ten weeks it may be felt that the probability distribution of a resource (which may be cash) could be described as in Table XI.

TABLE XI: THE PROBABILITY DISTRIBUTION OF A RESOURCE
TO MEET A SPECIFIC ACTIVITY TIME

Average resource level (units)	Probability
50	0.3
40	0.6
30	0.1

The advantage of this approach is that times may be viewed deterministically. However, the computations become more complex and problems of resource constraints may arise. The method will be discussed further as a means of selecting among major projects within an organisation in Chapter 9.

THE PERT APPROACH TOWARDS UNCERTAINTY

It must be accepted that even if resources of all kinds are apparently freely available, uncontrollable factors (the weather, deliveries, strikes) must from time to time influence activity durations. Uncertainty therefore applies both to the resources required and the duration of activities. Whilst the establishment of bivariate distributions are a possibility the analysis and its interpretation would become impossibly complex. Another approach is therefore to exclude explicit recognition of resource variability and to apply probability distributions to durations alone. This is the basis of the treatment of uncertainty by PERT.

For some activities involved in a project, there is a history of experience; in other instances activities are novel. In either case PERT requires that estimates of variability should be made. Practical experience will enable a probability distribution to be suggested, but if there has been no experience of a particular activity the distribution will be entirely subjective. However the computations involved in handling probability distributions in a project of any size would be prohibitive and a more simple approach is required. If it is assumed that the distribution of times is unimodal (and this need not necessarily be the case, particularly if an activity contains two or more sub-activities) then an infinite variety of shapes is possible. Three examples are given in Fig. 38, (a) which is symmetrical and narrow, (b) which is symmetrical and broad, and (c)

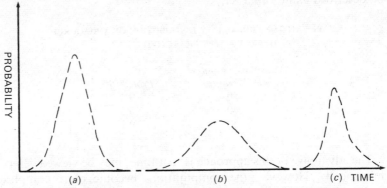

FIG. 38. Possible probability distributions of activity durations.

which is skewed to the right. The first of these may represent a simple routine activity, the second a more complex but still routine activity (involving mainly controllable variables) and the third an activity in which uncontrollable variables play a significant part. It is worth noting that as no activity duration may be less than zero the tendency (particularly if the activity is short) is for the distribution to be skewed to the right.

One distribution which satisfies the requirements of a single mode and a variety of shapes is the Beta distribution. It may be demonstrated* that for the Beta distribution the arithmetic mean is determined by the upper and lower limits and the most likely value (the mode). Further, the variance of the distribution is determined by the upper and lower limits only. Strictly, the precise shape of the Beta distribution employed is necessary to quantify the mean and variance, but for distributions which are neither very peaked or skewed approximations which are quite widely applicable may be used. Writing $E(t)$ for the mean or expected duration and $V(t)$ for the variance of a duration we have:

$$E(t) = \frac{O + 4M + P}{6}$$

$$V(t) = \frac{(P - O)^2}{36}$$

M, O, and P are the most likely, optimistic, and pessimistic estimates of the duration respectively. It is now apparent why PERT is often described as the "three-time estimate method." It is also apparent that subjective probability distributions need not be established explicitly. More recently, it has been suggested† that O and P are more realistically viewed as durations which have a certain probability of being exceeded (in either direction as appropriate). In effect, this implies the setting up of confidence limits (of the order of 90 per cent) and also leads to modification of the above expressions for expected times and variance of times. The procedure is, however, basically the same and the following analysis will be undertaken with the more customary expressions for $E(t)$ and $V(t)$.

* See A. BATTERSBY, *Network Analysis for Planning and Scheduling*, Macmillan & Co. Ltd., London, 1964, Appendix 1.
† See J. J. MODER AND C. R. PHILLIPS, *Project Management with C.P.M. and PERT*, 2nd edition, Van Nostrand, New York, 1970, pp. 282–6.

By reference to Fig. 39, the three-time estimates for O, M, and P are 2, 4, and 14 respectively and the E.E.T. for event 7 is zero.

Then, for event 11:

$$E(t) = \frac{2+16+14}{6} = 5.33$$

and

$$V(t) = \frac{(14-2)^2}{36} = 4$$

If the E.E.T. of event 11 had been calculated on the basis of the most likely time, this at 4 would have been significantly less than the 5.33 arising from the use of the expected time. Furthermore, the E.E.T. of 5.33 has associated with it a variance of 4; in other words, it may well be greater than 5.33 by an appreciable amount. By repeating the procedure for each activity, expected times and variances for successive events throughout the network may be determined by accumulating along any desired path. In order to reach conclusions about the overall duration of the project, it is necessary to trace each path leading into the final event. Some paths may be discounted because of the large quantity of float available, but it is important to appreciate that a path which, on the

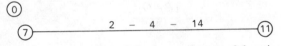

FIG. 39. An activity with three-time estimates of duration.

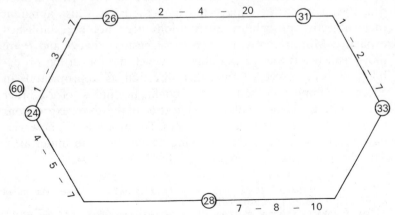

FIG. 40. Part of a network, indicating three-time activities.

basis of most likely times, had been established as critical may not be so using expected times and variances. To quantify the comparison it is necessary to introduce a further assumption, namely that the final event time is normally distributed. Most activities will be statistically independent, and provided the critical path contains, say, above a dozen activities this assumption is fair.

Figure 40 is part of a network and includes three-time estimates in weeks for five activities. It is assumed that by consideration of paths leading into event 24 the expected time, $E(t)$, of this event is determined as 72 weeks with a variance $V(t)$, of 8. The E.E.T. of event 24 calculated on the basis of most likely times is 60 weeks. Attention is focussed on event 33, for which, using *most likely times*, the E.E.T. would be $60+5+8 = 73$ weeks, with the lower path critical. What effect have the three-time estimates on event 33 and the criticality of the paths leading into it? Table XII provides the necessary calculation using the previously specified formulae for $E(t)$ and $V(t)$.

TABLE XII: CALCULATION OF $E(t)$ AND $V(t)$ FROM THREE-TIME ESTIMATES

Path	Activity	Three-time estimate			$E(t)$	$V(t)$
		O	M	P		
Upper	24–26	1	3	7	3.3	1
	26–31	2	4	20	6.3	9
	31–33	1	2	7	2.7	1
	Total		9		12.3	11
Lower	24–28	4	5	7	5.2	.25
	28–33	7	8	10	8.1	.25
	Total		13		13.3	.5

The effect on event 33 of the upper and lower paths is now:

Upper path: E.E.T. of event 33 $= 72+12.3 = 84.3$ weeks with a variance of $8+11 = 19$

Lower path: E.E.T. of event 33 $= 72+13.3 = 85.3$ weeks with a variance of $8+.5 = 8.5$

Note that each of these E.E.T.s is much greater than the E.E.T. of 73 weeks determined using most likely times. However, by the adoption of three-time estimates a two dimensional comparison is necessary in order to decide which of the two paths is critical and what conclusions may be drawn about the final event. We have expected times and, through variance, standard deviations and using the assumption of normally distributed times the comparison may be expressed graphically as in Fig. 41. The three-time estimates

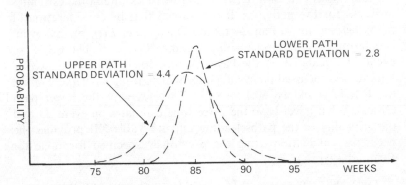

FIG. 41. Normal distribution of E.E.T. of event 33 of Fig. 40 according to the upper and lower paths.

for each activity implied a probabilistic input and consequently the output should be interpreted in probabilistic terms. It will be noted from above that there is only a 50 per cent chance of event 33 being completed within 85.3 weeks by reference to the lower path whereas the upper path duration at this level of probability would be 84.3 weeks. In other words, the lower path, as in the case of most likely times is critical. Fifty per cent probability levels are, however, not customary. More usually much higher levels are employed. For example, a manager may ask "within what duration is completion 98 per cent probable?" Ninety-eight per cent of the area under a normal curve falls to the left of 2.3 standard deviations above the mean. The durations indicated by each path at the 98 per cent level are therefore:

Upper path: $84.3 + (2.3)(4.4) = 94.4$ weeks
Lower path: $85.3 + (2.3)(2.8) = 91.7$ weeks

At this level of probability the upper path becomes critical and the reversal of criticality between the two paths becomes more. pronounced as the probability level is increased. Certainly the inferences differ markedly from those arising from a consideration of most likely times alone, when on this basis the lower path is critical by some four weeks. It is also of interest to note that the E.E.T. of 73 weeks arising from most likely times accumulated along the lower path is over four standard deviations below the expected time of 85.3 weeks. The probability of completing within 73 weeks is therefore negligible.

In practice, there may be many paths through a network, and assuming that E.E.T.s are calculated by the use of expected times it is necessary to examine near critical and critical paths. This will enable a more realistic estimate to be made of the time necessary for completion of the project. Examination of critical and near critical paths will enable deductions to be made and questions to be asked in respect of individual activities. For example activity 26–31 in the network of Fig. 40 is obviously highly significant. Why should the pessimistic time at 20 weeks be some four months in excess of the most likely time? The activity may refer to the procurement of some item of equipment from abroad or the signing of a new wage agreement. Even though, perhaps, approval has not yet been given for the project, could not preliminary and conditional negotiations commence which would result in a reduced variance on the activity? If variance is due to an uncontrollable variable such as the weather, are techniques available which will reduce the effect of extreme conditions? It is apparent that although the PERT approach to durations is a little more demanding than single figure estimates, the analysis will enable a fuller appreciation to be made of significant activities in the chain of events.

Having accepted a probabilistic approach to planning, there are implications with regard to control. Expected and latest completion dates compatible with the probability level used will be determined for individual activities. It would be unrealistic then to attempt to finish each activity by the expected date at the expense of extra resource committal. However the expected dates will be used in the construction of bar charts and by the use of resources at "normal" levels it will be accepted that some activities will be completed before and some after their expected time. The latest time will provide an upper action limit, and will be treated in the same manner as total float, being common to the path. Conceptually, the approach to uncertainty offered by PERT is very attractive. Nevertheless, rather than an increase in the use of probabilistic times the reverse has been the case during recent years. Consistent reasons for this have not been given. Certainly the explanation is not a computational one as very large networks can be handled by existing computer packages. Possibly the cause is rather more subtle. It is continually stressed that in order to extract maximum benefit from network analysis it should be used both as a planning and control tool. It is the author's experience that the use of probabilistic times is ideal for planning purposes and is in accord with the general approach to uncertainty which increasingly is favoured by management. Extension of the procedure to the control of activities becomes less attractive as estimates of variability which were carefully considered before the commencement of a project may become unrealistic as the time for the activity to be undertaken approaches. And as the activity progresses, at the most only one of the three estimates made originally can be correct. Therefore as each event is reached the probabilistic estimate of the final event will require recalculation, necessitating a great deal of repetitive computation.

GENERAL COMMENTS AND SUMMARY

It has been shown that the basic requirements needed to construct and analyse a network are very simple. Sufficient experience has been gained over the years by comparative studies and post-completion audits to generalise about the success of the technique. Experience has however mainly been gained in non-cyclic activities and although senior management have been involved according to the significance of the project, network analysis has not yet in general been seen as a tool which is an essential part of the high level planning process. This is despite the fact that it is in the planning part of a project that the technique has been universally acclaimed (organisational problems have often devalued network analysis as a control device).

The approach suffers from the same disadvantage as all quantitative analytical methods (except those which are mandatory, such as the preparation of financial statements), that they are non-essential to the actual decision. Organisational objectives will be achieved (providing the organisation remains in existence) whether or not the method of reaching them is based on appropriate analysis. The decision to build a multi-million pound production complex in a foreign country *could* be made without any estimate of the resources required and the returns anticipated. Naturally enlightened management would not consider taking a decision of this significance without appropriate quantitative analysis, and network analysis would seem to provide a highly relevant part of this.

As a planning tool for a single project, networks could claim to meet a major need as efficient estimates may be made of resource requirements and the timing of events. The difficulty arises in assessing the possible wider adoption of the technique in a multi-project situation, that is at a truly corporate level. Quite apart from uncertainty in relation to the total resources available to an organisation, there exists the analytical difficulty of allocating limited resources among competing projects in a manner which is optimal (the prospects for this will be examined further in Chapter 9). As the existence of variables which are uncontrollable may be recognised in nearly every planning situation, the quantity of resources needed to complete a particular activity cannot be stated with certainty nor, given unlimited resources, can there be any guarantee that an activity will be completed in the time estimated. One aspect of network analysis, namely the PERT approach to uncertain durations, has proved to be of value in some instances. Conceptually, this approach is more suited to the planning process than control and hence may come to be more favoured at higher levels in organisations. Present indications are however that because of the ability of network analysis computer based programmes to deal with an enormous amount of data, efforts will be made to treat problems of resource allocation over the whole organisation in relation to deterministic estimates of times (and resources). Uncertainty will then be taken into account by studying the sensitivity of conclusions to changes in certain times (and resource availabilities) which are thought to be most significant.

Chapter Six

DECISION TREES

INTRODUCTION

In the previous chapters discussion has centred on concepts and procedures which are fundamental to the making of logical decisions. It is now desirable to bring together these concepts and procedures in such a form that they are of practical value to the manager in deciding on a particular course of action. Whilst there will always be a place for the custom built problem solving procedure a number of identifiable and different approaches have emerged during the last two decades (in fact, the majority were developed during the 1950s). Such names as decision trees, linear programming and simulation will be known to many managers.

This chapter will be devoted to the decision tree* and developments based on it. It is seen as an appropriate lead into the study of major analytical techniques, as its relevance to all levels of management may be readily established. For any decision of complexity a means of presenting all relevant alternatives is required; this is particularly true if future decision points are anticipated. Any branching procedure is difficult to present sensibly in written or tabular form, and some form of "tree" is quickly suggested. In this way the logic of the problem may be shown graphically and this in itself can be of considerable value to the decision maker. Decision trees also enable uncertainty to be taken into account, as the various chance outcomes which follow a decision may be demonstrated. Immediately chance outcomes are incorporated, one is bound to approach the analysis in a probabilistic manner and to think in terms of utility and expected values as discussed in Chapters 1 and 3.

On the basis of these introductory remarks, it is possible to define the decision tree as follows:

---

* One of the earlier introductions to this topic was J. F. MAGEE, "Decision Trees for Decision Making," *Harvard Business Review*, July–August 1964, pp. 126–138.

DECISION TREE: A graphical representation of a series of decision points, alternative activities and (usually)
chance outcomes, arranged chronologically
and terminating in all of the final outcomes
which are thought to be both significant and
distinguishable prior to the first decision being
taken.

As implied, however, there is more to the decision tree than a
straightforward mechanistic calculation. Apart from the ability to
specify alternative sequences of decisions and chance events it can
be of considerable value in suggesting how uncertainty may be
quantified. If, for example, the quality of a decision can be improved
by further information which is obtainable, then it provides a
means of choosing a course of action intermediate between a decision to act immediately (hoping for the best!) and of waiting to see
(and by then having missed the boat!). In other words, it is possible
to estimate the value and cost of information, which itself is usually
not perfect. Additionally, the decision tree provides a means of
assessing the sensitivity of a decision to changes in estimates of
values, costs, and probabilities which have been used to reach that
decision. In the decision trees which are drawn out below, decision
points will be represented by an inverted triangle and chance events
by a circle. The simplest situation is one which is entirely deterministic and this will be used as an introduction.

For example, consider a company with plant which can produce
either product A or product B. The demand for product A exceeds
the productive capacity of the company and there is also export
potential. Demand for product B which has no export potential is
completely satisfied. Ignoring the time effect of money and the
scrap value of plant, annual contributions for products A and B
have been estimated for the next few years as £300,000 and £400,000
respectively. The life cycle of each product is estimated to be 6 years.
If, however, the productive capacity of the plant is increased (assume
for simplicity that the cost of increasing capacity is a direct cost of
£100,000 which is incurred at some time before the end of the second
year) the contribution from product A will increase to £400,000 per
year after 2 years if marketed at home and will rise to £500,000 per
year if in addition it is exported. The best alternative is readily
obtained by a simple calculation, but the steps involved may be seen
more clearly from the decision tree shown in Fig. 42. The figures

in the tree are total contributions calculated over the years involved. Each alternative is listed and in addition the alternative of dropping both products is added at the first decision point. It is sometimes proposed that the alternative "stop" should be included at each decision point. This should be done whenever there is a possibility that other alternatives may be less favourable. For example, if one were selecting from among zero change in asset position and possible decreases in asset position the former would be chosen. In the case of Fig. 42 a "stop" is not included at the second decision point, as each outcome indicates positive contribution and the decision to continue marketing has been indicated by the stated intention to increase capacity. When probabilities together with discounting are introduced it is however advisable to include explicitly the "stop" alternative at each decision point.

Even from this simple example, it is seen how the need to specify each alternative promotes rigorous analysis of the situation. For example the question may be asked as to why product A, even though in limited supply, should not be marketed at home and abroad immediately. This would add two further alternatives to the first decision, one being to export while extra capacity was being constructed and the second being to market at home and abroad throughout the six years without increasing capacity. For simplicity, these further alternatives have not been included here.

In a manner similar to network analysis therefore the "logic" of the problem is completed before estimates are incorporated. The procedure which is then adopted will be apparent from Fig. 42. The

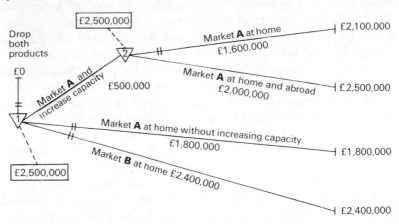

FIG. 42. The decision tree for two alternative products.

units (usually contribution or "equivalent" cash flows) are written against each alternative and are accumulated for each of the eventual outcomes. For example, considering the alternative of marketing A and at the same time increasing capacity, it will be seen that £500,000 is indicated. This is obtained from the contribution of £300,000 for two years less the cost of £100,000 incurred in increasing capacity. The final outcome of marketing A at home only will then be £500,000 plus £400,000 for four years, that is a total contribution of £2,100,000. For each decision there will be a favourable alternative, and the value of the best final outcome following the decision in question is shown in a square box attached to the decision triangle by a broken line. The selection of earlier alternatives is obtained by working backwards from the most future decisions and comparing at each step the value of the alternative courses of action. By reference first to decision 2 it will be noted that the more favourable of the two alternatives is that involving the decision to market at home and abroad. The decision to market at home only, which is estimated to be worth £2,100,000, is therefore blocked off and the value of decision 2 then becomes the value of marketing at home and abroad namely £2,500,000 over the six years. Four alternatives are shown at decision 1, with estimated values of £2,500,000, £2,400,000, £1,800,000 and £0, from which it is apparent that the decision to increase capacity on the assumption that product A will be marketed eventually at home and abroad is the most favourable.

Before proceeding to consider how uncertainty may be taken into account, an important opportunity afforded by decision trees will be considered. It is clear that any values included in the tree are estimates only and yet it is implied that the same confidence is placed in estimates for six years ahead as in those for earlier years. In the above example, the alternative selected is based on estimates involving export performance which has not been undertaken before and will not in fact commence for two years. Examination of the figures used reveal that if contribution arising from marketing product A at home and abroad fell by £50,000 per year, the total contribution from the alternative selected would fall to £2,300,000, and the most favourable alternative would now be the marketing of product B (at home). This "What-if?" type of question based on an apparently optimum solution is a form of sensitivity analysis which can be of the greatest value in achieving the decision finally taken. For it is quite wrong to suggest that the apparent "solution" which emerges from initial estimates should be implemented without further thought. A decision maker should never proceed with a decision if he feels that further consideration is desirable. Sensitivity analysis will be referred to extensively during this and the following Chapters.

Reference was made in the definition of a decision tree to "chance outcomes." These follow decision points and enable the decision maker to broaden the analysis to cope with uncertainty. A whole range of opportunities is afforded for the preparation of an appropriate basis for logical decision making and the various aspects will be considered under the following headings:

1. Selecting the alternative using expected values.
2. The value of perfect and imperfect information.
3. The effect of utility on the selection of the alternative.

There are of course limitations of the technique, and these will be discussed finally.

SELECTING THE ALTERNATIVE USING EXPECTED VALUES

In general, the future is uncertain: costs, receipts, the timing of events and so on. A major feature of decision trees is that it is possible to make decisions under conditions of uncertainty. These are not decisions which will guarantee a particular outcome but ones which, given realistic inputs, enable logical courses of action to be taken.

The addition to the components of the tree which is needed to take account of uncertainty is the chance event which indicates that matters outside the control of the decision makers may lead to one of a number of different outcomes. These outcomes are often referred to as "states of nature" and may in fact arise from climatic conditions as well as a host of other causes (customer attitudes, competitors' activities, wars, natural disasters, etc.). This adds a new dimension to decision making as simple cost/benefit comparisons are now not possible among alternatives. What is needed is some measure of the uncertainty which it is felt attaches to an alternative. This is provided by probability, which in very many decision situations facing managers must be determined in a manner which is largely subjective.

For each chance event it is necessary to recognise the outcomes which, in the terminology of Chapter 3, are mutually exclusive and exhaustive. The probabilities which are given to each outcome will then total one exactly. It is customary in the use of decision trees to confine the number of chance outcomes to two or three. This inevitably places some restriction on the decision maker as it may well be felt that the classification, for example, of demand into the three categories high, medium, and low, together with the allocation of appropriate probabilities, is too artificial. Nevertheless, if some such assumptions are not made the decision tree will rapidly become unwieldy. For example, consider a situation in which three alternative decisions are in each case followed by three chance outcomes, and that this cycle is repeated sequentially three times. Then the number of final outcomes is three raised to the sixth power, that is 729. Each of these would need to be evaluated in order to select the most appropriate alternative. It is therefore often found that when the number of alternatives is large there is a tendency to restrict the chance outcomes in each case to two. For example, in the above case of three cycles in sequence the number of final outcomes would then be reduced to six raised to the third power, that is 216. It will be appreciated that it is sensible to first establish all the apparently important "alternative–chance outcome" sequences and then to consider less significant sequences. Sometimes this process will lead to the discovery that an important sequence of events has been overlooked. For example, it might have been planned to follow "high demand" with the construction of a new plant and to satisfy the only other chance outcome of "low demand" from the existing plant. The introduction of a suitably quantified third chance outcome of "medium demand" may suggest that the existing plant is re-equipped with production machinery of higher capacity. And it may be that the latter alternative which previously had been overlooked is an important factor in the decision which is finally taken.

As an example of the chance event, refer again to Fig. 42. It has been noted that the decision to produce A and increase plant capacity was based on single figure estimates of contribution. Do the decision makers feel that such deterministic estimates are too restrictive and do they feel able to make realistic probabilistic estimates of demand? If so, what effect will this have on the decision which is taken? Suppose management decide to recognise the possibility of just two levels of demand, namely high and low, both at home and abroad from year 3 onwards. Then four chance outcomes in respect of the alternative under consideration are possible. These are shown in Table XIII, together with estimated annual contributions.

TABLE XIII: ESTIMATED ANNUAL CONTRIBUTIONS, FROM MARKETING
AT HOME AND ABROAD, YEARS 3–6 INCLUSIVE

	High demand abroad	Low demand abroad
High Demand Home	£500,000	£300,000
Low Demand Home	£200,000	−£50,000

Assume also that if capacity is not increased and as a result either A or B are marketed at home only, then the chance outcomes (restricted to two) with the estimated annual contributions from year 3 onwards are as follows:

Product A:	High Demand	£350,000
	Low Demand	£100,000
Product B:	High Demand	£500,000
	Low Demand	−£100,000

Similarly, estimated contributions arising from A if it is marketed at home only following an increase in production capacity are:

	High Demand	£450,000
	Low Demand	£0

It is assumed that contribution during the first two years may be estimated in a deterministic way with confidence, being £300,000 per year for product A and £400,000 per year for product B, as mentioned earlier. A further assumption is that for reasons of contractual obligations and company image once the decision has been taken to market a product from year 3 onwards this will apply to the end of the estimated product life even if a negative contribution occurs.

The probability placed on the demand for product A being at a high level from year 3 is 0.8 for the home market and 0.5 for the export market. It is concluded that the levels of demand at home and abroad will be independent of each other. The probability placed on high demand (in the home market) for product B is also 0.8. Figure 43 now includes the extra information arising from the introduction of chance events. It will be noted that assuming that one or other product is marketed, and including the alternative of stopping at each subsequent decision, there are now thirteen final

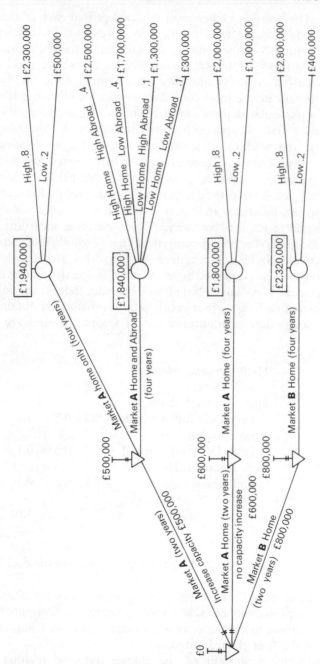

FIG. 43. The decision tree for two alternative products with chance outcomes.

outcomes. The decision maker must first accept that each of these is feasible and that the total problem is represented in sufficient detail. As before, contributions are shown against the appropriate activity (note the net £500,000 shown against marketing product A and increasing capacity) and these are accumulated at the final outcome to indicate the total contribution which could arise from following a particular sequence of alternatives. Again, the decision to be taken initially is approached by considering the final alternatives first and working back through time to the first decision point. In this procedure, chance events are encountered and some means of evaluating these must be developed in order that the initial decision may be taken. As the decision maker was prepared to recognise the various outcomes arising by chance, it is not unreasonable that he should be required to "weight" each outcome according to the likelihood he places on its occurrence. This weighting is of course the subjective probability encountered in Chapter 3, and for which assumptions have been made above. As it was suggested that eventual demand at home and abroad will be independent, the joint probabilities of each of the four combinations possible are obtained from the simple law of multiplication of Chapter 3, and are as follows:

High Demand, Home
    and Abroad $= 0.8 \times 0.5 = 0.4$
High Demand Home,
    Low Demand Abroad $= 0.8 \times 0.5 = 0.4$
Low Demand Home,
    High Demand Abroad $= 0.2 \times 0.5 = 0.1$
Low Demand, Home
    and Abroad $= 0.2 \times 0.5 = 0.1$
                                          _____
                                          1.0
                                          _____

These values will also be seen to have been entered on the decision tree.

Given the value of the outcome of every sequential set of alternatives and the probability of each chance outcome, it is now possible, *using expectation*, to calculate certainty equivalents (*see* Chapter 1) for each of the four chance outcomes.

The certainty equivalent of the chance outcome relating to

product B (and hence in this case the certainty equivalent of marketing B and not A) is therefore:

$$(.8 \times £2,800,000) + (.2 \times £400,000) = £2,320,000$$

This is shown in the box adjacent to the chance event. Similarly, the certainty equivalent of marketing A at home only without increasing capacity is:

$$(.8 \times £2,000,000) + (.2 \times £1,000,000) = £1,800,000$$

Also the certainty equivalent of increasing the production capacity of A and marketing at home and abroad is:

$$(.4 \times £2,500,000) + (.4 \times £1,700,000)$$
$$+ (.1 \times £1,300,000) + (.1 \times £300,000)$$
$$= £1,840,000$$

Similar calculations indicate that marketing A at home only with an increase in capacity gives £1,940,000. The effect therefore of incorporating chance outcomes which give the decision maker opportunity to use his expert knowledge to provide more discriminating estimates is that the decision to increase the production capacity for product A is now not favoured. Instead, the alternative with the greatest expected total contribution is that which involves the production of product B.

Again, it is important to emphasise that the "best" alternative should not be selected automatically. Rather, a logical basis for taking the decision has been provided. In the first instance it will be recognised that although in the case of product B the *expected* total contribution is £2,320,000, the final outcome will be either £2,800,000 if demand is high or only £400,000 if demand is low. (The wide variation between the latter two amounts arises because of the decision to restrict demand to just two categories.) Nevertheless, the figures used convey something of the attitude of the decision maker and it should be the case that consistency will occur in the evaluation of each of the alternatives included. The decision maker may then note that if either A or B is marketed at home only from the outset, there is apparently no flexibility. Demand will eventually be established at a high or low level, with the consequent inevitable financial outcomes. Again, there may be thoughts on alternatives which were not included and a preference may be expressed for some flexibility. This may favour the alternative to expand production capacity for A despite smaller expected total contribution. In the first place this may require the solution to be tested for robustness through sensitivity analysis and in addition questions of the company's attitude towards utility may be raised. This latter aspect will be discussed in a later section of this Chapter.

In respect of sensitivity analysis, it will be appreciated that two sets of estimates have been made: one of costs and receipts leading to contribution and the other of probability. The effect of varying both contribution and probability estimates simultaneously *could* be studied, but this would make interpretation difficult. Preferably, changes in contribution or probability should be considered separately. There is certainly a place here for the "What-if?" type of question. For example "What if the annual contribution arising from a high demand both at home and abroad for product A from year 3 onwards should be £600,000 instead of £500,000?" By recalculation, the appropriate certainty equivalent is now increased to £2,000,000 compared with the previous value of £1,840,000. Despite an increase in estimated contribution the production and marketing of product B is still favoured. As an example of a change of probability, consider that the probabilities of high and low demand for product B from year 3 onwards are now both 0.5. Recalculation indicates that the certainty equivalent relating to product B is now £1,600,000 compared with the original £2,320,000. Thus by comparison with the other certainty equivalents calculated initially, product B is now the least attractive.

It will be apparent from this brief discussion that sensitivity analysis carried out in this way is somewhat arbitrary. But it may be that the decision maker has quite firm views on the range within which his original estimates may vary and in this case the implications of such variations may be taken into account. A major difficulty which remains however is how to assess the effect of changes in several estimates simultaneously. It is at this point that sensitivity analysis tends to become self-defeating. Its major advantage insofar as decision trees are concerned is to enable changes to be made in important variables one at a time and to compare the effect with the basic analysis.

An alternative approach which can be of considerable value when a decision maker does not feel able to place limits on variations from an estimate is to determine by how much an estimate must change in order that a new alternative becomes favoured. Although this may be approached from two directions, either by down-grading estimates relating to the "best" alternative or upgrading estimates from one of the inferior alternatives, the former is recommended as being more systematic. Thus by reference to the alternatives of Fig. 43 and on the basis of expected values the adoption of product B is the best alternative, whereas the marketing of product A with an increase in production capacity is the next best. It is readily shown that in order for the latter alternative to become favoured, the probability placed on a high demand for product B (£500,000 contribution per year) from year 3 onwards would need to fall from 0.8 to about 0.65. If the decision maker feels this to be out of the question, then the decision to proceed with B will be maintained. If the decision maker feels that despite his initial estimate such a change is by no means out of the question then he may well broaden the decision base to bring in other factors (*e.g.* flexibility) mentioned above.

It should however be remembered that in the case of variables which are largely uncontrollable, such as sales, the original estimates were at the time seen as being the "best." Sensitivity analysis on the lines just described serves to focus the decision maker's attention on the more important alternatives, enabling the effect of variations from the estimates made to be studied. In some cases, variables are not mainly uncontrollable, as for example prices or bids. In the latter instance, for example, it may be possible to assess by sensitivity analysis how much a tender should be reduced in order that its acceptance would be anticipated.

THE VALUE OF PERFECT AND IMPERFECT INFORMATION

In the example used above precise estimates were assumed for demand and hence contribution for the first two years. After that point in time, however, it was felt that the level of demand could only be viewed probabilistically. It was conceivable that marketing should be discontinued after two years if so desired, for whatever alternative was selected. However on the basis of expected values the continuation of marketing was preferred in each case, although it was appreciated that the actual eventual outcome might be unsatisfactory. More specifically, the decision to market product B throughout the six years was suggested, leading to a total contribution of either £2,800,000 or £400,000. As the latter is inferior to the £800,000 which would have been achieved by the discontinuation of marketing, the question naturally arises as to whether or not the decision to continue marketing after two years could be made more discriminating. It will be shown that this may be possible by the provision of further information.

Assume in the first instance that the organisation has access to a prophet who is able to foretell with perfect accuracy the ultimate level of demand for product B. By reference to Fig. 43, it will be apparent that if he states that demand will be high then the organisation may proceed confidently with the marketing of product B. If, however, the forecast is that the demand for product B will be low then the preferable alternative is to withdraw the product after two years. This is demonstrated diagrammatically in Fig. 44. The values

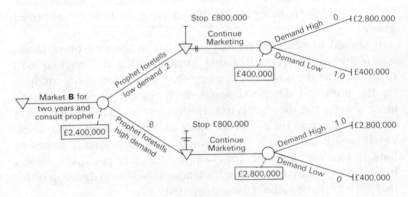

FIG. 44. The effect of perfect information.

of the final possible outcomes are unchanged from Fig. 43, but it is evident that their associated probabilities will have altered. If the prophet says demand will be low then demand will be low, and the probability of it being high will be zero; similarly for the converse. This will have the effect of changing the certainty equivalents (still using expected values). It will then be seen that the marketing of product B is only favoured to withdrawal from the market if high demand is forecast. The consequences of the chance outcomes arising from the prophet's forecast (it is not *known* what he will forecast) will therefore be valued at £800,000 and £2,800,000. As the prophet's forecast is a chance event, it is necessary to compute the certainty equivalent for this. This requires the placing of a probability on him forecasting high and low demand. It will be shown below that two possibilities must normally be taken into account, namely the probability of the informant being correct when the

underlying situation is, say, one of high demand and the probability
of his being in error when the underlying situation is not one of high
demand (that is, low demand). Both of the conclusions drawn by
the informant will be that demand is at a high level. In this instance,
however, as the prophet is never wrong the probability that he will
indicate high demand (the organisation's probability, not his) is
therefore 0.8 and the certainty equivalent is, as shown in Fig. 44,
£2,400,000. By comparison with Fig. 43 it will be seen that the
expected value of selecting product B is increased by £80,000.

In real life prophets supplying "perfect" information do not
exist and if they did it is hardly likely that they would be so altruistic
as to provide their services free. Assume however that in the above
situation perfect information was available at a price. How much
would the organisation be prepared to pay for such information?
It will be apparent that any fee incurred in this way will be set against
the certainty equivalent and therefore the maximum amount which
could be paid to the prophet is precisely £80,000. For any fee less
than this amount it would benefit the organisation to obtain the
advice of the prophet.

In practice, it is often possible to obtain information which will
enable the analysis to be more discriminating. This may be achieved
by physical or market research carried out by the organisation itself
or some external agency. Two important aspects need to be considered, however. On the one hand it is improbable that the information will be perfect (this will certainly apply in the case of market
research) and on the other hand the research itself will both cost
money and take time. Again using the example above it is assumed
that a market survey may be undertaken at some time during the

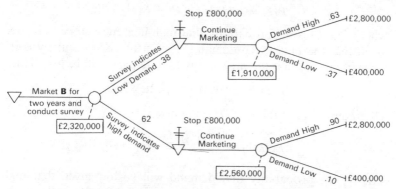

FIG. 45. The effect of imperfect information.

two years before the next decision is taken. Further, assume that experience has shown that the particular agency which is selected to undertake the market survey has successfully predicted the outcome on 70 per cent of occasions. The decision points and chance events and value of outcomes of Fig. 45 are identical with Fig. 44, but in this instance the first chance event will involve the prediction of high or low demand following the market survey. In this case the probabilities are not computed so readily. Bayes' Theorem, as developed in Chapter 3, is useful at this point, as it is necessary to evaluate, for example, the probability of demand being high given that high demand is predicted by the survey. More formally if $P(H|I)$ is the latter probability then:

$$P(H|I) = \frac{P(I|H)P(H)}{P(I)}$$

where $P(I|H)$ is the probability of predicting high demand given that the underlying demand is high, $P(H)$ is the prior probability of demand being high, and $P(I)$ is the probability that the survey will indicate high demand. In this context $P(I|H)$ may be taken as the probability that the survey will indicate correctly, namely 0.7. $P(H)$, as used already, is 0.8 and it only remains to calculate $P(I)$ in order to evaluate $P(H|I)$. It was implied above that the survey could indicate high demand in two ways. First the underlying demand could be high, and the survey indicates this correctly, or the underlying demand could be low, in which case the survey would fail to measure this and would indicate the only other alternative, namely high demand. As these two events are mutually exclusive, the simple law of addition may be used to determine $P(I)$ as:

$$P(I) = P(I|H)P(H) + P(I|L)P(L)$$

where $P(I|L)$ is the probability that high demand will be indicated given that the underlying demand is low (that is, the survey is incorrect), and $P(L)$ is the probability that demand will be low. Thus:

$$P(I) = (.7)(.8) + (.3)(.2) = .62.$$

The required probability $P(H|I)$ is now:

$$P(H|I) = \frac{(.7)(.8)}{.62} = .90$$

$P(L|I)$, the probability that demand will be low given that high demand is predicted, is the complement of this, .10, and the remaining two probabilities $P(H|I^*)$ and $P(L|I^*)$ relating to the final chance outcomes may be shown to be .63 and .37 respectively. (I^* indicates that low demand is predicted by the survey.) Note that the probability that the survey will predict low demand is:

$$P(I^*) = P(I^*|L)P(L) + P(I^*|H)P(H)$$
$$= (.7)(.2) + (.3)(.8) = .38,$$

which is the complement of $P(I)$. Figure 45 enables the calculation of new certainty equivalents to be undertaken.

We have now calculated three expected values for the outcome of marketing product B, and these are:

(a) Without obtaining any further information (Fig. 43), £2,320,000.

(b) Obtaining perfect information (Fig. 44), £2,400,000.

(c) Obtaining imperfect information (Fig. 45), £2,320,000.

It will be seen that perfect information increases the expected value over no information whereas the imperfect information of the market survey (30 per cent chance of being wrong) does not increase the expected value (quite apart from any consideration of the cost of the survey itself). The reason is that in the latter case the product will continue to be marketed whatever the outcome of the survey. This point is frequently overlooked; for information to have any value it must lead to a conditional change in decision making when compared with a situation in which no information is obtained.

In order, in this instance, that information should have a value it must have a success rate in excess of 70 per cent. The break-even point at which there is indifference towards obtaining the information may be shown to be a survey success rate of rather more than 90 per cent, assuming zero extra cost. Reliability of this nature is unlikely in practical market situations, and there would seem little scope for conducting a survey in these circumstances.

One of the reasons why in this case obtaining imperfect information is unattractive is the highly discriminating prior probabilities. These, being established by the decision maker, are quite independent of any conclusion reached by the agency (whether internal or external) providing the additional information. If, for example, prior probabilities of 0.5 had been given to both high and low demand for product B, imperfect information would begin to have a value if a reliability of 85 per cent could be achieved. Another feature is that in this case the continuation of marketing after two years is not seen as leading to disastrous consequences whatever the outcome. If, for example, low demand would involve a heavy negative contribution the attractiveness of obtaining imperfect information would increase. Each project will involve different financial outcomes, prior probabilities, and the confidence placed in additional information. The value of the additional information will depend on the increase in the expected value if the information is used. The only overall limitation is that the reliability of imperfect information can never fall below 50 per cent if it is to have any positive value. At the level of 50 per cent it will be appreciated that there is no revision of the prior probabilities.

Quite apart from modifying a decision in the future, additional information may influence the alternative *initially* selected. In the example used in this chapter, calculations will show that the latter situation would not arise as the expected value of marketing product B is significantly greater than the expected values of the product A alternatives of Fig. 43.

THE EFFECT OF UTILITY ON THE SELECTION OF THE ALTERNATIVE

Statistical expectation of contribution was the means of determining certainty equivalents in the example used above. Consideration of organisational circumstances in which a decision is to be taken returns us however to the subject of Chapter 1. For in practical decision making it is necessary first to examine more closely the consequences of unfavourable outcomes (risk) and secondly to ensure that the opportunity cost of proceeding with a project on any basis is not positive.

The use of expected money values in establishing certainty equivalents is tantamount to the assumption that the project (or others like it) will be repeated many times within the organisation. If, however, this is not the case then the question of utility must arise. The *concepts* of utility as discussed in Chapter 1 are straightforward and undoubtedly play a part in decision making. Also if utility functions can be obtained for individual decision makers then these may be brought into the evaluation. The major problem is however the quantification and stability of individual attitudes towards risk. It is not proposed here to discuss further the difficulties involved in deriving utility functions. Rather a function will be assumed in order that its effect on the evaluation may be studied.

Referring again to Fig. 43, it will be seen that the range of values of possible outcomes are as follows:

1. Market product A at home and
   abroad: £2,500,000–£300,000
2. Market product A at home
   (increase capacity): £2,300,000–£500,000
3. Market product A at home only
   (no increase in capacity): £2,000,000–£1,000,000
4. Market product B (at home): £2,800,000–£400,000

The ranges of alternatives 1, 2 and 4 are broadly similar and intuitively it would probably be felt that utility considerations would not affect their standing, one with the other. The situation may however be different in respect of alternative 3 as compared with other alternatives. Assume that the utility function of the decision maker is that shown in Fig. 46. Although change from the current

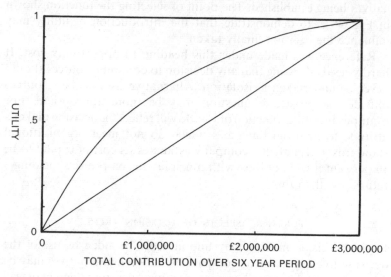

FIG. 46. The decision maker's utility function.

position (measured by total contribution) is positive only, it is evident that the decision maker is very conservative in his attitudes. If maximisation of expected utility is now the criterion for selection among alternatives these may be evaluated by determining the utility of the various contributions and hence determining expected utility. There are four utilities involved in alternative 1, corresponding to the amounts £2,500,000, £1,700,000, £1,300,000 and £300,000 and two in the remaining three alternatives. For example, the total contribution of £2,500,000 seen as being one of the possible outcomes associated with alternative 1, possesses a utility of 0.95, whereas the utility of the contribution £300,000 is 0.25. Expected utilities are as follows:·

1. $(.95)(.4)+(.82)(.4)+(.73)(.1)+(.25)(.1) = .806$
2. $(.93)(.8)+(.40)(.2)$ $= .824$
3. $(.88)(.8)+(.65)(.2)$ $= .834$
4. $(.96)(.8)+(.31)(.2)$ $= .830$

Therefore, on the basis of maximising expected utility the alternative to market product A at home only without an increase in capacity is just to be preferred. Naturally any number of utility functions could be hypothesised, leading to a preference for any of the alternatives being established. The point of selecting the function shown in Fig. 46 is to demonstrate that the introduction of utility may influence the decision finally taken.

Reference was made under this heading to opportunity cost. It hardly needs stressing that any decision to commit resources should never be undertaken in isolation. Alternative uses of the resources outside the project in question may be more appropriate. For example, the utility function of Fig. 46 will reflect the decision maker's attitude to financial outcomes which do not meet organisational standards. Certainly if a company estimates its cost of capital to be 10 per cent it will not look with much favour on projects yielding a return less than this.

FURTHER ASPECTS OF DECISION TREES

Logical decision making may undoubtedly be aided by use of the decision tree approach, as comparison between alternatives may be made quite readily. It will be apparent, however, that there may well be a tendency to oversimplify the problem in order that the tree may not appear too complex. Insofar as the first decision to be taken is concerned, each alternative specified and the subsequent chance events and decision points are brought into the analysis. But the question may then arise as to whether sufficient information has been taken into account to enable the decision reached to be described as truly logical. With reference to Fig. 43, there are 4 initial alternatives and it may be that for example the possibility of marketing product A at home without an increase in capacity is simply not adequately described by one subsequent decision point and one chance outcome. If this alternative were selected, it is surely probable that during the course of six years more than one significant decision would have to be taken. There may be possibilities of a change in marketing strategy, product improvement, competition, change in customer attitude, production costs and so on. None of these, if thought to be of possible significance, should be omitted solely in order that the decision tree should remain as simple as possible. In addition, there arises the problem of how uncertainty should be quantified. Remaining with the same alternative, demand is presumed to be adequately described by a "high" level of demand resulting in a contribution of £350,000 per year with a probability of 0.8 and a "low" level of demand leading to a contribution of £100,000 per year with a probability of 0.2. The graphical representation of this discrete variable is shown in Fig. 47 by the vertical lines.

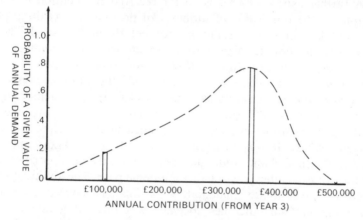

FIG. 47. Continuous and discrete representation of demand for product A.

The broken curve is a possible representation of how the decision makers may have viewed contribution from year 3 onwards as a continuous rather than a discrete variable. And although the expected value of the continuous function may turn out to differ little from the expected value of the discrete contribution (£300,000 per year), there are significant utility considerations in respect of contribution as low as zero (or even negative) and as high as £500,000 per year. It would have been possible to have employed more than two chance outcomes in this instance, as this would not have significantly affected the size of the tree, but the proliferation of the tree in more detailed situations arising from the combination of numerous alternative/outcome paths was mentioned earlier. In Chapter 7 a method of comparing alternatives will be described which is more able to take account of variables described by continuous distributions.

The opportunity of studying the implications of imperfect information using Bayes' Theorem can be an important advantage of the decision tree. This approach is however dependent to a great extent on subjective probability, and "estimates" of probability must be treated with just as much caution as the deterministic estimates which are so frequently criticised. This aspect was examined more closely in Chapter 3, but it is worth emphasising that even if a meaningful "accuracy" can be assumed for the information gathering procedure the outcome is heavily dependent on the prior probabilities.

A further aspect which has so far received no mention in this chapter is the time value of money. All projects of any duration should take account of this factor, although the method used varies from organisation to organisation. In an increasing number of instances discounted cash flow (D.C.F.) or some variation of it is employed. When decision trees are used, the most convenient method is to discount at an assumed cost of capital to achieve net present values. In this way cash flows, changes in net equivalent liquid asset position, etc. may be included in the decision tree at current values. It was mentioned earlier that the figure shown against the final chance outcomes represented the net contribution arising for each alternative chance-outcome path. The ability of the decision maker to see immediately the financial consequences of the range of final outcomes specified was thought to make this approach preferable to the more usual one of indicating cash flows or contributions at the point at which they are estimated to occur. Thus for example the consolidated outcome of high demand at home and abroad in Fig. 43 is £2,500,000 but this is made up of amounts located at different points in time. If the time value of money is to be taken into account it is necessary to specify the point in time at which the component contributions occurred. Assuming that the expenditure on meeting plant capacity may be located at the end of year 1 and all other contributions fall at the year end the various timings are as shown in Fig. 48. The N.P.V. of this sequence using the

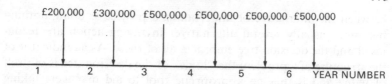

FIG. 48. The timing of contribution (Fig. 43. Product A—home and abroad alternative).

method of Chapter 3 and at an assumed cost of capital of 10 per cent is £1,700,000 as compared with £2,500,000 without discounting. By adopting this approach the N.P.V. of the certainty equivalent of each of the alternatives involving positive action in Fig. 43 is obtained. Table XIV demonstrates the effect.

TABLE XIV: THE EFFECT OF DISCOUNTING AT 10 PER CENT PER ANNUM
ON THE CERTAINTY EQUIVALENTS OF FIG. 43

Alternative	Certainty equivalent without discounting £m	Certainty equivalent with discounting £m
Product A—home and abroad	1.84	1.29
Product A—no increase in capacity	1.80	1.28
Product B—home	2.32	1.68
Product A—home with increase in capacity	1.94	1.38

Ranking on the basis of certainty equivalents is not affected. A major factor in this instance is that the duration of each alternative project is the same. It will be appreciated however that there are possibilities of decisions being influenced by discounting if alternatives are of different duration and if high discount factors are employed.

SUMMARY

Many decisions required to be taken by managers in order to achieve goals or objectives are seen to involve chance outcomes, following which alternative courses of action are possible. In some instances the latter are conditional upon the gathering of information which is not available initially. The decision tree provides a simple means of representing and evaluating decision point-chance outcome sequences. At the most restricted level, comparison is possible between the alternative of undertaking a project or doing nothing but more usually several alternatives involving action are recognised and the decision tree embraces all of these. As an indicator of the structure of a problem the "logic" of the decision tree is of itself of value and is thus an appropriate tool to aid managers taking decisions at a high level. In this respect it is similar to the deterministic network used in planning a project. But similarly there arises the question of the level of detail to be adopted. For senior managers the number of final outcomes should not be excessive and the problem arises as to how many chance outcomes should emanate from each chance event. The minimum number is of course two but even then three cycles of three alternatives and two chance outcomes will produce 216 final outcomes. Furthermore, the number of alternatives available in a practical situation are virtually unlimited if a fine level of detail is adopted and care is needed to ensure that an attractive alternative is not overlooked. As in any model building procedure, if the decision maker is not constructing the model himself, appropriate dialogue is necessary between manager and model builder to ensure that the correct level of detail appropriate to the decision is incorporated.

The power of the decision tree is that it assists selection among alternatives. As however many of the decisions to which it is most appropriately applied are medium to long term, difficulties arise in making estimates and assigning probabilities. As the decision is profoundly affected by these it is necessary that full use is made in arriving at them of the maximum expertise available within the organisation. Again the decision maker should fully approve of all values written into the decision tree.

Further scope is available for the decision maker to exercise his expert knowledge through sensitivity analysis, by which means he is able to study the degree of change needed in his original estimates to cause a new alternative to be selected.

The selection among alternatives using decision trees can be made more discriminating by introducing the concepts of utility and the time value of money. It was demonstrated in the former case and suggested in the latter case that their inclusion could affect the alternative selected. It is recognised insofar as utility is concerned that problems exist in reliably quantifying utility attitudes, but even if these are not formally introduced into the analysis they will play a part in reaching the final decision if only when the decision maker scrutinises the final outcomes. Given the financial policy of the organisation, it is anticipated that decision makers would wish to take account of the time value of money, probably by discounting to realise N.P.V.s.

Finally it might be said that decision tree analysis involves no computational assumption. It simply enables attitudes held by the decision maker towards alternative courses of action to be assessed together with probabilistic estimates of variables to a greater or lesser extent outside his control. Given the level of detail adopted a logical selection may then be made from among the courses of action considered.

Chapter Seven

THE ROLE OF SIMULATION IN DECISION MAKING

INTRODUCTION

As opposed to some of the terminology which has evolved to describe techniques and tools of management, simulation has a generally accepted meaning in the English language of mimicking some tangible activity or acting in like manner to it. In the business context the meaning is precisely as stated but it is necessary to propose a less general definition in order that its role in logical decision making may be more readily examined.

> SIMULATION: A process in which a model of an organisational system or procedure is used to aid assessment of the response of the system or procedure to specific inputs either externally or internally determined.

A prerequisite of simulation is the model, and whenever a model is used simulation is implied. The effectiveness of simulation as an aid to logical decision making is dependent on the nature of the model and the manner in which it is used. The major requirement is that components of the model shall accurately reflect the corresponding areas of the actual situation. A second requirement is that areas of the actual situation which are significant to the decision which is to be taken shall be adequately represented in the model. In summary, these comments require that models should meet minimum standards of relevance and detail.

The actual construction of a simulation model of all or part of an organisation is not the particular concern of this chapter. The building process is facilitated by the skills and experience of systems analysts and a good deal has been written about their activities.* These normally involve decisions on the extent and level of the model,

---

* See JOSEPH ORLICKLY, *The Successful Computer System*, McGraw-Hill, New York, 1969, Chapter 6.

the establishment of relationships within the boundaries so defined and their representation by a system of flow charts,* the collection of information and finally the translation into a computer based model. During this procedure they will be in consultation with management and will be concerned with the implementation, monitoring and modification of the model. The emphasis in this chapter will be on the concepts of the simulation model, insofar as these need to be appreciated by the manager, with the objective of promoting the use of simulation as a basis for logical decision making.

Models were discussed in Chapter 2 and the categories indicated in Fig. 8. The shortcomings of mental models were discussed at some length. The main difficulty in assessing the consequences of varying inputs was stated to be due to the inability of the human brain to cope with sequential operations on data. It was suggested that physical models did find some use, but it will be evident that any decision for which they provide the major basis must be limited in nature. In order to aid a decision involving the many aspects of a real life situation using a physical model there would be an increasing tendency to make the model similar in nature to the physical structure of what it seeks to represent. Some models do, in fact, stop not far short of this situation but these are generally in the scientific and technological field. If circumstances involve personal safety or national prestige (witness flight simulations and space training programmes) the necessary finance for complex physical models is often forthcoming. It is not realistic, however, for organisations to adopt this policy, as quite apart from considerations of finance the uncertainty inherent in long term planning is much greater than in individual technological ventures, usually of shorter duration. It should perhaps be pointed out at this stage that certain experiments conducted by organisations to compare alternatives and which require the involvement of the organisations themselves over a period of time should not be classed as simulation. Excluded from consideration as examples of the use of physical models are therefore such exercises as the test marketing of a new product or the temporary adoption of an appointments system in a hospital.

If written models are seen as having similar limitations to mental

---

* See D. N. CHORAFAS, *Systems and Simulation*, Academic Press, New York, 1965, pp. 35–43.

models, and if the above comments on physical models are accepted, it is evident that for effective business simulation resort must be made to mathematical models (including, from time to time, graphical models). It is planned to indicate how flexible and relatively inexpensive (at least compared with the alternatives) simulation using the mathematical model can be.

Reference was made in the definition of simulation to both systems and procedures. Organisational systems may be recognised as including manpower, materials, financial and investment systems and may be represented at operational or corporate levels. Within these systems numerous procedures may exist, for example stock control, forecasting and accounting. Decisions in respect of these systems and procedures are at the focus of managerial activity and again it is aimed to demonstrate how simulation may provide a suitable basis for decision making in these circumstances.

If a simulation model is to be of maximum value, it must afford the opportunity to accept as inputs all variables which are significant to the decision which is to be taken. The decision may be of a design nature, in which a system is to be studied to assess whether it may be reorganised to function in a more efficient manner, for example, routing, locational and scheduling problems. Alternatively, it may be wished to take a planning decision, in which it is necessary to accommodate uncontrollable variables such as inflation or demand.

It is not always the case however that a model of a specific system or procedure is used to assess the effect of input variables. On some occasions it may be more appropriate to consider the system or procedure as the variable and test this against constant input data. If historical data are available in suitable quantity and detail and it is assumed that the operating environment will remain substantially unchanged then the model may be varied to aid the decision. For example, a number of alternative forecasting procedures may be examined in this way. At a much higher level a possible acquisition or merger may be studied by testing different organisational configurations against actual or planning data.

The concept of simulation may be studied under a number of separate headings according to the type of model which is used. Referring now to the classification of models used in Chapter 2, it is proposed to consider deterministic and probabilistic simulation using both positive and normative models. It should be stressed again at this point that a decision making situation does not necessarily demand a specific type of model. It may be that one type is favoured by the decision maker but that others are not excluded. There is therefore no suggestion here that one method of using simulation is inherently superior. The results of a simulation will require different interpretation according to the type of model which is used, but the actual process of simulation is common. The latter will be demonstrated by reference to a simple example.

It will be assumed that a manager needs to take a decision on whether to market a new product for which demand occurs seasonally once per year. Further, it is assumed that both production and distribution are sufficiently rapid to ensure that demand is met whatever the level may be. By a little imagination the situation could be seen to apply to such products as toys, fireworks, Easter eggs and fashion goods in general. Assumption of spare production capacity enables the problem to be confined to estimation of gross profit or contribution to overhead. Four variables will be used to structure the problem, namely selling price, direct labour and material costs, and demand. These variables will be assumed to be independent one of the other. Deterministic simulation, that is a process in which uncertainty is not handled within the model, will be considered first.

AN EXAMPLE OF DETERMINISTIC SIMULATION

A Positive Model

It will be remembered that a positive model contains only relationships which are known to hold. The variables which are to be included in the model and which are on an annual basis are defined as follows:

G = Gross profit
S = Total sales
D = Direct costs
N = Number of units sold
P = Price per unit
L = Direct labour cost per unit
M = Materials cost per unit

Note first that the common unit is a monetary one. The structural equations of the model are then:

$G = S - D$
$S = NP$
$D = N(L + M)$

From which the predictive model for G is simply:

I. $G = N(P - L - M)$

Gross profit G, is now expressed in terms of the 4 variables referred to above. In order to arrive at a figure for G, it is necessary to place values on N, P, L, and M. There will be an element of uncertainty in L and M but estimates can usually be made with a fair degree of confidence. Assume therefore L to be £6 per unit and M £7 per unit. Selling price P must obviously exceed £13, but it is clear that any decision on P cannot be taken without considering the effect on the number sold, N. Many factors must be taken into account by the decision maker at this stage. These would include production capacity, the availability of labour with the requisite skills, the potential total market and the price and quality of competing products. All of these may be consolidated into a rough price elasticity of demand by the decision maker, which will lead to various levels of demand according to the price set. Assume, however, that the price is largely determined by the market price of competing products, and that currently this is set at £20 per unit. It is recognised that demand will be influenced by sales policy and promotion, but for average performance in these areas the number sold, N, is estimated as 10,000. By substituting values for N, P, L, and M in equation I, gross profit G is now:

$$G = £10,000(20 - 6 - 7) = £70,000$$

The simple model may be used to assess the effect of changes in L, M, and N, either singly or taken together. It may be desired to consider the effect of a special promotion, the cost of which will be allocated wholly against the item under consideration. For example, it is estimated that as a result of a promotion costing £10,000 the demand will increase by 20 per cent to 12,000. From equation I, gross profit will be seen to increase to an estimated £84,000, suggesting that the net effect of the promotion will be valued at £4000.

This example is of course trivial, but it should serve to demonstrate that deterministic simulation using positive models is straightforward, as the decision maker is not placed in a situation where he is dependent on assumptions about relationships made by others. He will know, for example, that accounting procedures used within the organisation are the basis of a financial model and that if he wished to compute the consequences of placing values on input variables such as demands or costs by traditional procedures he would eventually arrive at the figures which would be generated almost immediately by a computer based model. For it is evident that if simulation on these lines is to be carried out in a real life situation the only practicable way of evaluating a series of "What-if?" questions is by resort to a computer, either in the on-line or batch mode. However, whilst the process of simulation is straight-forward it will be apparent that the onus is very much on the decision maker to approve the values put on all the variables within the model. He will no doubt use all the evidence and expertise available in arriving at values for variables but there is no "black box" component of the model (*see* Fig. 9), he is himself in this case the black box.

A Normative Model

Although the process of simulation using a deterministic normative model is precisely that of using a deterministic positive model, each is given separate consideration on account of the important implications involved. The purpose of normative components within models is to seek to include historical explanatory relationships which are expected to apply in the future. By these means it is hoped that the model will be more effective and will remove from the decision maker the need for placing values on some variables, saving time and perhaps achieving greater efficiency. This implies therefore the introduction of a black box element into the model itself which, as has been mentioned on several previous occasions, needs to be wholly acceptable to the person using the model as an aid to his decision making. The normative components may be forecasting routines using regression or tracking techniques on times series or may be equations in which a dependent variable is derived from values placed on independent variables which may or may not include time explicitly.

The example used above may be extended by assuming that analysis has enabled the number of items demanded in the past, N, to be satisfactorily explained by the following relationship:

II. $N = 6000 + 0.25Y + 0.1A$
where Y = Annual value of G.N.P. in £000,000
              A = Advertising expenditure in £

Thus for instance if G.N.P. is £12,000,000,000 and advertising expenditure is £20,000 the number demanded annually is estimated to be 11,000. Practical models will be normative in nature if just one relationship of this type is included. In this case, the input variables to be determined or approved by the decision maker will differ from the input variables which would be employed if the model were wholly positive. In the simple example just employed the same requirements would exist in respect of direct cost and selling price, but additionally there would be one uncontrollable variable Y, and one controllable variable A in the place of the one uncontrollable variable N. Y would probably be obtained from national forecasts and in fact the value used may not be specifically brought to the notice of the decision maker. He would however be required to take a decision in respect of advertising expenditure (assumed here to be a direct cost). As before, the facility for answering "What-if?" questions by using the simulation process is now available. But whereas in the case of the positive model there is no need for the decision maker periodically to question the way in which the output figures are achieved, it is vital that this be done if the model is normative. If equation II is seen as a normative forecasting model for demand, it will be appreciated that regardless of whether the equation was determined statistically or empirically, as actual values for N are recorded the additional information may require that the equation should be modified. This may involve a change in the parameters or the dropping or inclusion of explanatory variables. It is therefore desirable that if normative models are employed to aid decision making there should be a report on each normative component, with a frequency depending on the significance of the decisions taken.

In using deterministic models of both types, the decision maker need not necessarily be ignoring the uncertainty surrounding uncontrollable variables. The deterministic model will enable him to assess the consequences of changing input values as frequently as time and the cost of using the model permits. The changes may on the one hand be arbitrary in the sense that the decision maker recognises a range within which a particular value may fall and within which he has no strong preference for adopting one value rather than another. On the one hand, he may wish to use an approach which has been referred to before, namely sensitivity analysis, and which is now formally defined as follows:

SENSITIVITY ANALYSIS: A study of the change in the output of a model which arises from making changes from previously used values of one or more input variables.

The key words in this broad definition are "changes *from* previously used values." Usually the decision maker will first incorporate his best estimates of the input variables, and hence any additional use of the model will not involve the adoption of arbitrary input values but values which as they differ (in either a positive or negative direction) from the best estimates will become less likely as the magnitude of the change increases. Sensitivity usually implies small changes, but reference to the size of change was not included in the above definition as in practice an output may be insensitive to a major change in an input variable or alternatively a small change in an input variable may create a major change in the output. In adopting this approach to uncertainty, the decision maker is still using a deterministic approach, even though in arriving at the decision which he finally takes he may have used a range of single figure estimates.

In an attempt to overcome the obvious limitations of the single figure approach, some managements have supplemented "most likely" estimates by "optimistic" and "pessimistic" estimates of each uncontrollable variable. By combining in turn the three values of each variable one with another, many outcomes may be generated. There is, however, no indication of the likelihood of each output. At first sight the decision maker may attach some importance to the best and worst outputs, but a little thought will indicate that if a number of input variables are involved then the likelihood of *all* eventually assuming either the optimistic or pessimistic estimates will be very small. This will be examined further in the discussion of probabilistic simulation which follows.

AN EXAMPLE OF PROBABILISTIC SIMULATION

The single figure basis for decision making suffers the major disadvantage that risk is not "quantified." Naturally in the process of reaching a decision and selecting among or between alternatives (remember that retaining the *status quo* is always an alternative) a manager will consider risk. But in situations of complexity the potential risk involved in a decision may not be appreciated if a manager places reliance solely upon his ability mentally to weigh up the implications of the possible outcomes which may arise. Risk may however be formally assessed if the decision maker is prepared to view the uncontrollable variable not as a set of arbitrarily assigned values but as a random variable conforming to a probability distribution. The problem of ascribing probabilities was dealt with at some length in Chapter 3 and will not be discussed in any depth again at this point. Suffice to repeat that even though at the outset a manager may feel that it is quite impossible to put a value on, say, bank rate in four years' time he would, if pressed, ultimately generate a subjective probability distribution of the discrete or continuous form for this variable. It is worth stressing, though, that if bank rate were an input variable to a model it would be assumed that in arriving at a probability distribution for it the manager would take note of any expert advice available to him in arriving at his own final distribution. The note that he would take of the "expert" advice would depend upon the esteem in which the expert was held.

Discrete Distributions

Consider the example used earlier in the Chapter in which a predictive model for gross profit G, was developed (equation I). Best estimates of 10,000 for the number of units sold, N at a selling price of £20 per unit, £6 per unit for direct labour cost L, and £7 per unit for materials cost M, led to an estimated gross profit of £70,000. Assume now that probability distributions are generated for N, L, and M and that P being (at least in the short term) controllable is specified as £20. The distributions finally accepted by management are suggested in Table XV, from which it will be noted that the probabilities are presented in the discrete form. The implication of using continuous distributions will be examined later in this Chapter.

TABLE XV: PROBABILITY DISTRIBUTIONS FOR DEMAND, DIRECT LABOUR COST PER UNIT AND MATERIAL COST PER UNIT

Demand		Labour cost		Material cost	
Units (000)	Probability	£	Probability	£	Probability
7	.10	5	.25	5	.10
8	.20	6	.40	6	.20
9	.25	7	.20	7	.50
10	.30	8	.10	8	.10
11	.10	9	.05	9	.05
12	.05			10	.05

Six levels of demand and material cost are included in Table XV, whereas five levels of labour cost are given. It was mentioned in Chapter 3 that discrete distributions may be presented in a number of ways. For example, the variable may be single numbers as shown or may include class intervals, when the mid point of the class would be given the probability ascribed to the class. The number of combinations of demand, labour and materials which arise from Table XV is $6 \times 5 \times 6$, namely 180. The best and worst of these together with the combination of most likely values of each is given in Fig. 49. The presentation of these combinations in a tree form must not

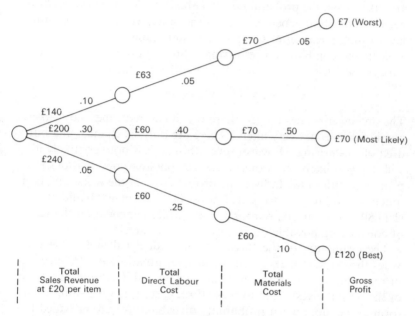

FIG. 49. An evaluation of best, worst and most likely combinations of demand and labour and materials costs (£000).

be confused with a decision tree in which several alternatives may be included. The decision tree in this situation would contain only two alternatives namely "proceed" or "do not proceed." The probabilistic simulation is concerned solely with an evaluation of the former alternative. The worst outcome is evaluated by subtracting maximum total costs from the worst sales revenue. The latter would arise at a sales level of 7000, generating receipts of £140,000. The highest labour cost envisaged of £9 per item would lead to a total labour cost of £63,000. Similarly, the total material cost at £10 per item would be £70,000, leading to a gross profit of £140,000 less £133,000, that is £7000. The gross profit associated with the extreme outcomes is markedly different from that suggested from the combination of most likely outcomes. It would in fact be quite likely that such possibilities would not be considered if a sensitivity analysis based on single figure estimates were carried out. The probable reaction of a manager to the three combinations shown in Fig. 49 would be to question the "likelihood" of each combination.

The decimal fractions incorporated in the branches of Fig. 49 are taken from the probabilities of Table XV. As the variables have been stated to be independent one of the other, we may use the simple law of multiplication of Chapter 3 to determine the probability of a particular combination occurring. Thus the probability that each variable will together assume its most likely value is:

$$(.30) \times (.40) \times (.50) = .06$$

The manager's question is therefore answered; the most likely combination is not very likely! There are only six chances in a hundred of this arising. However, even though it is not very likely it is still the *most* likely. No other of the 180 possible combinations is as probable as this one. In fact, the probabilities of the worst and best outcomes will be seen to be as low as .00025 (1 in 4000) and .00125 (1 in 800) respectively, reinforcing an earlier comment on the value of considering possible outcomes of this nature.

The evaluation of the three outcomes depicted in Fig. 49 provides the decision maker with further information, but the process of reaching a decision is not greatly facilitated. Certainly the form of the output if restricted to these three cases is not the same as the form of the input when probability distributions were provided for each variable. If the manager had accepted the need for probability distributions to be input, then it is realistic that he should be provided with an output probability distribution, in this case of gross profit. It is apparent that if the series of calculations described above were repeated for all 180 possible combinations of sales, direct labour cost and material cost it would then be possible to build up a probability distribution of gross profit. The calculations would however be tedious, and if more than three input variables were included the number of individual calculations would become enormous. Clearly a method which would give a reasonable approximation to the probability distribution of gross profit would be welcome. This is provided by the so-called Monte Carlo method of simulation, when values of random variables are combined, the combination evaluated and the process repeated many times. The purpose of the many repetitions is to avoid an output which might be unrepresentative of the true probability distribution. The process of sampling from a distribution was introduced in Chapter 3 and will be used here to demonstrate how a probability distribution of gross profit could be generated.

Table XVI indicates the random numbers (R.N.) corresponding to various levels of demand, labour cost, and material cost, and which are allocated according to the probability of each value of the variables.

TABLE XVI: ALLOCATION OF RANDOM NUMBERS TO THE VARIOUS LEVELS
OF THE INPUT VARIABLES

Demand units (000)	R.N.	Labour cost £/unit	R.N.	Material cost £/unit	R.N.
7	00–09	5	00–24	5	00–09
8	10–29	6	25–64	6	10–29
9	30–54	7	65–84	7	30–79
10	55–84	8	85–94	8	80–89
11	85–94	9	95–99	9	90–94
12	95–99			10	95–99

We refer again to the random number table of Appendix II. The random digits are conveniently arranged in pairs so that a column of paired digits will suffice for the purpose of sampling from each of the distributions. Three columns will be required, as an important assumption here is that the three distributions are independent one of the other. If the same column of paired digits were used to sample from each distribution, then for the random number allocation of Table XVI low demand would always be associated with low costs, high demand with high costs, and so on. This would obviously conflict with the requirement for independence. Assume that random selection has resulted in the choice of the third, eleventh, and seventeenth columns which are headed by the paired digits 42, 02, and 92 respectively for the distributions of demand, labour and material costs. The process is to select the particular levels in the distribution corresponding to these and subsequent random numbers and evaluate the combinations in each case. We have seen from Fig. 49 that gross profit will fall within the range of £7000–£120,000 and a probability distribution of the output may therefore appropriately be broken down into the six groups (in £000) with upper boundaries £20, £40, £60, £80, £100, and £120.

TABLE XVII: TWENTY SIMULATIONS WITH AN EVALUATION OF GROSS PROFIT IN EACH CASE

1	2	3	4	5	6	7	8	9
Simulation	R.N.	Demand units (000)	R.N.	Labour cost per unit £	R.N.	Materials cost per unit £	Gross profit per unit £ (20 − (Col. 5 + Col. 7))	Total gross profit £000 (Col. 8) × (Col. 3)
1	42	9	02	5	92	9	6	54
2	04	7	11	5	94	9	6	42
3	49	9	40	6	48	7	7	63
4	78	10	15	5	38	7	8	80
5	12	8	50	6	12	6	8	64
6	77	10	69	7	85	8	5	50
7	99	12	06	5	08	5	10	120
8	91	11	27	6	26	6	8	88
9	65	10	55	6	99	10	4	40
10	17	8	22	5	08	5	10	80
11	59	10	20	5	39	7	8	80
12	00	7	19	5	27	6	9	63
13	95	12	51	6	33	7	7	84
14	90	11	60	6	01	5	9	99
15	33	9	89	8	85	8	4	36
16	49	9	91	8	93	9	3	27
17	74	10	20	5	26	6	9	90
18	37	9	01	5	03	5	10	90
19	22	8	47	6	97	10	4	32
20	77	10	22	5	97	10	5	50
Average		9.45		5.75		7.25		66.6

An evaluation (in £000) of the first combination of three random numbers is as follows:

(a) Demand equivalent to R.N. 42 is nine units which at a selling price of £20 per unit produces revenue of £180.
(b) Labour cost equivalent to R.N. 02 is £5 per unit.
(c) Material cost equivalent to R.N. 92 is £9 per unit.
(d) Total cost for a demand of nine units is thus £126.
(e) The gross profit for this combination of sales and costs is £54.

Table XVII indicates the procedure for the first twenty such combinations (simulations). The averages in Table XVII enable a comparison to be made with the expected values obtained from the three distributions of Table XV. It will be remembered from Chapter 3 that expected values are obtained by multiplying each value of the random variable by its probability and summing for the whole distribution. It may be shown therefore from Table XV that expected demand is 9.25 (thousand) units, expected labour and material costs per unit are £6.30 and £6.95, and expected gross profit per unit is £(20−(6.30+6.95)) or £6.75, and hence expected total gross profit is £62.4 (thousand). The result of the simulation is that average total gross profit is rather higher at £66.6 (thousand). This will be seen to be due to average demand obtained from the sample being higher than expected demand, whereas total average costs arising from the simulation are rather less than total expected costs.

The output presented in the form of a relative frequency (experimental probability) distribution broken into the six class intervals suggested is given in Table XVIII.

(It is interesting to note in passing that the expected value of the

TABLE XVIII: THE OUTPUT PROBABILITY DISTRIBUTION
OF GROSS PROFIT

Gross profit £000	Relative frequency or experimental probability
0 below 20	0
20 below 40	0.20
40 below 60	0.20
60 below 80	0.30
80 below 100	0.25
100 below 120	0.05

distribution of Table XVIII is £65 (thousand), demonstrating the bias which results from grouping individual values.)

No values of gross profit fall into the group 0–20 and it is evident that the distribution obtained is skewed more to the right than would be expected. This, together with a study of individual values and their averages suggests that the number of simulations taken was not large enough to generate a sample output of sufficient precision. The question naturally arises as to the size of sample necessary to achieve this precision, particularly as when many random variables are involved it is difficult to assess the form of the output distribution. It will be evident that simulation is a feasible proposition only if a computer is available, but it will be recognised also that a simulation of hundreds or thousands of trials is costly and hence some guidelines are necessary as to the size of simulation which is most economic. Procedures are available (variance reducing techniques) which enable a form of cost/benefit analysis to be undertaken, but it is not essential that non-specialists should know more than that they exist.

There have been many computer software developments which assist in the use of simulation. Routines enable probability distributions to be handled efficiently, modular approaches to be adopted and sensitivity analyses to be effected. Computers are able also to generate their own random numbers as required, a more efficient procedure than carrying in store sufficient random numbers for large simulations when thousands of sample runs may be necessary. As the numbers are generated mathematically they do not qualify for the description of "true" random numbers, but are described as "pseudo-random numbers." The generating process provides a cycle of many millions of such pseudo-random numbers before repetition of the cycle occurs. Within each cycle each number occurs once only and enables the basic requirement of random numbers to be met, namely that a population is made available in which the digits 0–9 are equally likely.

It is therefore assumed that in the case of our example the manager would eventually be furnished with an output probability distribution of the form of Table XVIII which would be of sufficient precision to enable him to take his decision knowing that proper account will have been taken of his input probability decisions. The manner in which he would interpret the output distribution will be discussed following an examination of the approach using continuous distributions.

Continuous Distributions

A difficulty with discrete distributions arises from the frequency and size of discontinuities. It was mentioned that the values of the variables included in Table XV could be thought of as representing class mid points, but managers often respond more readily to questions designed to aid the construction of continuous distributions. Taking as an example distribution of demand, the first questions would request the level of demand which would not be exceeded and the level below which demand would not fall. Suppose that these were specified as 13,000 and 6000 units respectively. These would then define the range of the distribution and would determine the probability points of zero and one respectively of the cumulative distribution shown in Fig. 50. Next the manager

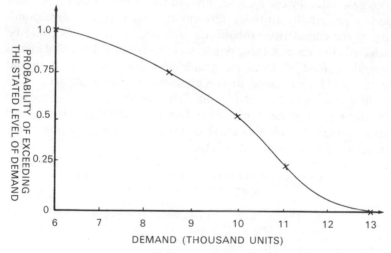

FIG. 50. The cumulative probability of demand.

might be asked to specify that level of demand which in his opinion would have a 50 per cent chance of being exceeded (and conversely a 50 per cent chance of not being reached). This may be 10,000 and would enable a point to be graphed with co-ordinates of demand equal to 10,000 and probability equal to 0.5. The three points obtained would be insufficient to give more than a rough indication of the decision maker's attitudes, but two further questions would probably suffice. These would take the form of asking for levels of demand with, in the first instance, a probability of 75 per cent chance of being exceeded and in the second instance a probability of only

25 per cent of being exceeded. Assume that the values suggested were 8500 and 11,000. By drawing a smooth curve through the five points now available, the decision maker's attitudes are reasonably described.

The process of sampling from information presented in the above form is not as straightforward as is the case with discrete distributions. Two steps are required, the first being the fitting of a curve through the points provided by the decision maker, the second being the sampling procedure from the curve fitted. A number of computer routines have been developed to meet both of these requirements, and the manager can have confidence in them without being acquainted with the precise details of the process involved. Manually, the procedure may be described using Fig. 50. Having in this case fitted by eye a curve through the points arising from subjective probability attitudes, ten equally spaced points corresponding to the cumulative probabilities .05, .15, ... , .95 could be selected. For each of these points a corresponding level of demand would be read off from the graph. For example, 11.8 thousand units would correspond to the cumulative probability 0.05, 11.3 thousand units to 0.15, and so on. Ten points were selected because in this way sampling from the random digits numbered 0–9 would be possible. The full allocation of random digits to various levels of demand is given in Table XIX.

TABLE XIX: ALLOCATION OF RANDOM DIGITS TO THE
VARIOUS LEVELS OF DEMAND

Demand units (000)	Cumulative probability	Random digit
12.5	.05	0
11.5	.15	1
11.0	.25	2
10.6	.35	3
10.2	.45	4
9.7	.55	5
9.1	.65	6
8.5	.75	7
7.8	.85	8
6.7	.95	9

It will be apparent that a discrete distribution has again been created, but the form is somewhat different from the distribution of demand included in Table XVI. In the first place the range is greater

(6.7–12.5 as opposed to 7–12) and secondly the number of individual levels is greater (ten compared with six). Improved definition is therefore obtained from the continuous approach. The possibility also exists of increasing the number of equally spaced points above ten. An advantage of doing this is that more account will be taken of the tail ends of the distribution. It will be remembered that the decision maker originally saw the range of demand rising from a minimum of 6000 to a maximum of 13,000. On occasions it is important to take full account of the potential occurrence of extreme values, and most simulation routines ensure that this is done. Similar cumulative distributions may be generated for the input variables of labour and material cost per unit. Samples may now be taken from all three distributions using the Monte Carlo method described and combined to produce an output distribution of gross profit similar to the one included in Table XVIII. This may then be accumulated and an example of the results in graphical form is shown in Fig. 51.

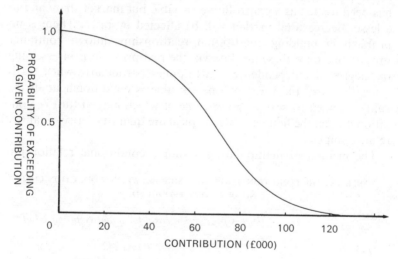

FIG. 51. An output distribution of contribution.

Returning to the choice of proceeding with the introduction of the new product or taking no specific action, it is now the responsibility of the manager to interpret the output. Whereas when considering most likely values only, evaluation of a contribution of £70,000 could be undertaken readily, the decision maker is now obliged to think in probabilistic terms. Assuming that he identifies himself with his organisation the manager concerned will take account of organisational utility. If the spare productive capacity may not be put to alternative use then as there is zero probability of making a negative contribution the decision may be to proceed with the new product. If, however, a second product may be manufactured, then a comparison between the two alternatives becomes necessary. Such comparisons between alternatives and sets of alternatives will be considered in the sections which follow.

Conditional Relationships

An important factor which must not be overlooked in constructing models is the conditional relationship. Some variables are not independent of other variables, whether these are controllable or uncontrollable. For example, total market and market share will be influenced by the controllable variable promotional expenditure. Similarly economies of scale may be evident which result in lower production costs for increased units made and sold. Price has been treated as a controllable variable but market share and to a lesser degree total market will be affected by price. There is no problem in building conditional relationships into a computer programme once these are known, the real problem is in assessing the degree of independence. This applies particularly when (as is often the case) the value of one variable is conditional upon the value assumed by several others, one of which may in turn be conditional upon the first variable. Typical are quantity–price–quantity relationships.

The method of manipulating a simple conditional relationship

TABLE XX: THE CONDITIONAL RELATIONSHIP BETWEEN PRODUCTION COST
AND QUANTITY PRODUCED

Quantity produced per month	R.N.	*A 200–220* £/Unit	R.N.	*B 230 and 240* £/Unit	R.N.	*C 250* £/Unit	R.N.
200	00–09	16	00–04	18	00–09	24	00–19
210	10–29	17	05–19	19	10–39	25	20–39
220	30–59	18	20–59	20	40–69	26	40–69
230	60–79	19	60–89	21	70–94	27	70–89
240	80–89	20	90–99	22	95–99	28	90–99
250	90–99						

Direct production costs for quantity produced of:

may be demonstrated by considering direct production costs and production quantity. Assume that random numbers have been allocated to production quantity, and that three ranges of production cost are recognised, to each of which random numbers have been applied. The various distributions are shown in Table XX.

It will be noted that two of the cost distributions overlap; the location and dispersion of the distributions will usually be determined by a mixture of experience and opinion. The simulation procedure may be demonstrated by reference again to the random number table of Appendix II. Assume that the final column of paired digits in the random number table is used to select production level, and the preceding column the cost level. The total production cost will be built up as follows:

1. Random number 25 implies a production level of 210 units in the month and selects the cost distribution A.
2. Random number 44 implies a unit cost of £18 (distribution A).
3. Hence total monthly production cost is £3780.

The reader may wish to check that total production costs are successively generated as £3960, £3740, £6000, and so on.

SIMULATION AND THE ANALYSIS OF RISK

The previous examples were used to indicate the technique of probabilistic simulation. It is proposed now to study more general concepts which are involved in providing a logical basis for selection among alternatives. Organisational utility attitudes and hence implicitly attitudes towards risk may be quantified and formally incorporated in the analytical procedure to the extent that in some instances selection may be automatic. In most cases, however, ultimate managerial involvement is required not least so that the manager may study the implications further. The latter may involve sensitivity analysis being carried out; this is just as feasible with probability distributions as with single values.

It is perhaps apposite to repeat that the objective of an organisation may not be maximisation of some financial criterion such as internal rate of return but may be cost minimisation (for example, a local authority transport programme) or welfare maximisation (for example, central government policy). There is the need therefore if numerical analysis is to be undertaken to quantify the objectives and the inputs which are significant to the decision. Thus, potential competition will obviously be of significance in many cases and the likelihood of varying degrees of this must be assessed. Or, the transport system must satisfy to some degree the needs of the community it purports to serve, and account must be taken of such factors as accessibility, travelling time and prices. Despite initial difficulty decision makers eventually are often able to suggest some method of quantifying apparently "unquantifiable" factors. One of the problems is of course that the values proposed are generally subjective, and it is therefore dangerous to permit quantification of amenities, unemployment, inflation, school selection, etc. by third persons. (This problem will be studied further in Chapter 9.)

In order to study the concepts, it is proposed that maximisation of internal rate of return (I.R.R.) is the goal of an organisation in respect of individual projects, whereas maximisation of earnings per share (E.P.S.) is the overall corporate objective. Before examining the possibility of using simulation in making decisions about the *total* allocation of resources in an organisation, the problem of selecting from a limited set of alternatives will be examined. The latter is currently the situation facing most organisations when periodic investment decisions are more or less imposed for political reasons (for example, local authorities) or for economic reasons (private industry).

A Limited Set of Alternatives

It is assumed for the purposes of discussion that a number of ways of investing capital exist, which through the production and marketing of a product lead to the generation of revenues. The variables introduced into the analysis are taken as direct production costs, selling costs, general overheads, total market, market share, product life cycle, interest charges and plant residual values. Other variables may be thought to be significant, and in addition the analysis may involve more than one product. In this case, there are eight variables, and even if single figure estimates were used the determination of rates of return, cash flows, and other financial reports over a number of years would involve heavy computations.

A deterministic model once constructed would enable decision makers to make as many simulations as they wished in order to examine the consequences of changes in the inputs* and the same

---

* It is worth noting that some simulation models have the facility for fixing an output variable and then by operating in the reverse direction establishing the values of the input variables which are necessary to achieve the output value specified.

model modified for probabilistic inputs and outputs would provide similar opportunities. In the latter case, having specified probability distributions for each variable within the model the Monte Carlo process will produce an output (of I.R.R.) in the form of a cumulative probability distribution. Such outputs may be used to assess whether potential projects satisfy certain decision rules. For example, the rules may require that there is:

(a) Not more than a 5 per cent probability of a negative I.R.R.
(b) Not more than a 50 per cent probability of an I.R.R. less than 10 per cent.

Figure 52 gives in graphical form two probability distributions, only one of which passes the screening requirements. This latter is A which, it will be seen, just satisfies the two criteria. B, on the other

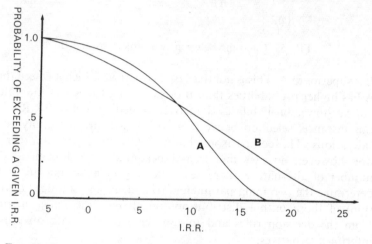

FIG. 52. Cumulative distributions of I.R.R. for two projects A and B.

hand, suggests a one in ten chance of a negative I.R.R. However whereas the probability of exceeding 15 per cent I.R.R. is very small in the case of A, the corresponding probability for B is about 40 per cent. The decision maker would perhaps be ill advised in the circumstances to reject an output of form similar to B, and he may feel on reflection that the screen was not constructed very efficiently. If the utility attitude is such that high values of I.R.R. should carry a reasonable probability, then a third decision rule may require, say, a 20 per cent chance of exceeding an I.R.R. of 15 per cent. If this had been the case then A would have failed to satisfy requirements also.

Similar reasoning may be applied in making a choice between alternatives. For example, consider the alternatives shown in Fig. 53, both of which are assumed to pass any screening test for acceptability. From (a) it is immediately apparent that at all levels of I.R.R.

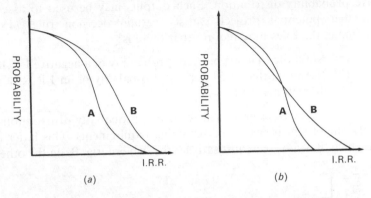

Fig. 53. Choosing between two projects A and B.

B is superior to A. This is not the case in (b), from which it is seen that A has higher probabilities than B of exceeding I.R.R.s of low value but has lower probabilities than B of exceeding higher I.R.R.s. In this instance, selection between A and B will involve utility considerations. The comparison of one distribution with another is not, however, an easy matter and becomes more difficult as the number of alternatives increases. One way of achieving this is to determine the two main parameters (the mean and standard deviation) of those output distributions which pass the screen arising from the decision rules and to use these to eliminate obviously inferior alternatives.*

The ratio of the standard deviation to the mean is termed the *coefficient of variation*, and if this is plotted against the mean itself each alternative is represented by a single point rather than a full distribution. Figure 54 indicates how ten alternatives designated A–J, may appear if this approach were used.

It is possible to reach certain immediate conclusions in respect of a number of the alternatives. For example, E may be compared directly with A and C. For a given expected I.R.R., E is more variable and hence more risky (in terms of the probability of low

* *See* D. B. HERTZ, "Investment Policies that Pay off," *Harvard Business Review*, Vol. 46, January–February 1968.

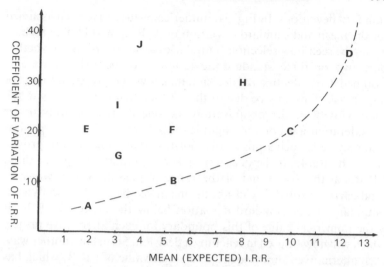

F<small>IG</small>. 54. Ten alternatives summarised by their means and coefficients of variation.

I.R.R.s) than A. Also, for a given level of variability the expected I.R.R. for E is much less than that for C. Hence E would not be preferred, nor in fact by following the same reasoning would be any of the alternatives lying within the boundary drawn through A, B, C, and D. On the assumption that only one alternative is to be selected, it remains to choose from among A, B, C, and D. These four alternatives range from the low risk, low return A to the high risk, high return D. If the attitude of the decision maker is one of extreme conservatism, then A may be adopted. If the opposite is the case, then the selection may be D.

As assumption made at this point is that the output distributions approximate to the normal. This is more nearly true if the number of independent variables used in the simulation is large. If this is not the case, then the final stage of the discussion which follows requires qualification.

Consider first a risk-averse decision maker who demands a confidence level of 99.9 per cent, that is there would only be one chance in 1000 of I.R.R. falling below a particular level. This level of confidence implies that attention will be focussed on that value of I.R.R. which is three standard deviations below the expected I.R.R. Conversely, levels of confidence (97.7 per cent and 84.4 per cent respectively) may be accepted which relate to two or even one standard deviations. In Fig. 54, numerical values have been assumed for the mean and standard deviation of A, B, C, and D, from which it may be seen how selection boundaries arise according to whether one, two or three standard deviations are the risk equivalents assumed. Consider first the decision maker who is prepared to accept higher risk. This may be due to the attitude that compared with the total activity of the organisation the one or two projects under consideration are not very significant. Alternatively, the organisation may be in such a precarious position that a high return project is very desirable. If the decision maker is prepared to ignore those I.R.R.s at the lowest end of the range of possible values which in total carry a probability of about one in six, he will be specifying a boundary at one standard deviation below the expected I.R.R. It is the numerical value of this boundary for each alternative project which will now be used in reaching a decision. Stated in another way, each alternative is now viewed as a single value of I.R.R. which has a probability of about five in six of being exceeded.

In order to demonstrate how the selection boundaries are determined, calculations made for the alternatives A, B, C, and D are given in Table XXI for one, two, and three standard deviations. On the basis of expected I.R.R. (and most probably calculations using single figure estimates only) alternative D is obviously preferred. When, however, the full output distributions of I.R.R. arising from the probabilistic inputs are used, the selection is changed. Even at the higher risk level of one standard deviation, C will be preferred to D (and A and B) as in its case there is a probability of about 84 per cent of exceeding an I.R.R. of 7.94 compared with a probability of 84 per cent of exceeding 7.87 in the case of D. It will be seen that in fact C dominates at all levels of risk with B becoming more preferred as risk aversion increases. In practice, a minimum expected I.R.R. would most probably be included in any screening test. If this had been 9 per cent, then alternatives A and B in Table XXI would have been excluded. The cost of capital recognised by the organisation would be an important consideration in arriving at a required expected return.

In addition to considering carefully his attitude to risk, the decision maker will probably ask for sensitivity analysis to be undertaken. With probabilistic simulation this may involve changing the location and/or dispersion of the input probability distributions. The results of these additional as well as the original analyses will enable the manager to consider further aspects of the problem

TABLE XXI: CALCULATION OF SELECTION BOUNDARIES

Alternative	Expected I.R.R.	Standard deviation of I.R.R.	Selection boundaries		
			1 S.D.	2 S.D.	3 S.D.
A	2.00	0.12	1.88	1.76	1.64
B	5.50	0.61	4.89	4.28	3.67
C	9.80	1.86	7.94	6.08	4.22
D	12.30	4.43	7.87	3.44	−0.99

confronting him, but it will be obvious that no ready-made answer exists. Sight should not be lost of the fact that the analysis is only providing a basis for managerial decision making. It is the manager identifying himself with his organisation who must bear the responsibility for selection. He will know that an eventual post-completion audit may indicate that the 4 per cent I.R.R. achieved following the selection of C (the "logical" choice) could well have been 20 per cent if D (an "illogical" choice) had been selected.

It will be appreciated that the process of Monte Carlo simulation may be adopted to generate year by year income or cash flows quite independently of the financial criterion which is then used to evaluate the output. It is for the decision maker to decide whether he wishes to take account of time by discounting to achieve I.R.R.s, or N.P.V.s or whether he prefers other approaches such as accounting rate of return or payback, which take no account of time. Such matters are discussed at length elsewhere* but whichever approach is used Monte Carlo simulation will provide an output of I.R.R., N.P.V., payback, etc. in probabilistic form. Alternatively, instead of consolidating estimates for all future time periods into one criterion, it is possible that the manager may prefer the year by year distributions of income or cash flow on which to base his decisions.

The Total Set of Alternatives

The appraisal of individual projects is an ongoing feature of major organisations whether they be in the public or private sector. Whatever the method adopted, which may be deterministic or probabilistic in nature, it is not too difficult to compare the anticipated outcome of a project with some benchmark of acceptability. If an attempt is made to appraise the total activities of an organisation a number of difficulties arise, not least of which is the volume of information and computation required. In the first place there is the

---

* See EZRA SOLOMON, The Theory of Financial Management, Columbia University Press, New York, 1963, Chapter 10.

problem of trying to relate the activities to the corporate objectives, which for a company may involve E.P.S. which ideally is to be maximised. Simulation employed to answer "What-if?" questions could lead only coincidentally to such an optimum in situations where many alternatives are feasible. Secondly, whereas in the case of individual (or a small set of) projects resource constraints may not be a major problem, this would certainly not be the case when the total set of alternatives are under consideration.

Of course, forward planning and corporate performance estimation is undertaken by most organisations but in many cases in a deterministic and somewhat arbitrary manner. Projects are agreed at sub-corporate level, brought together, and if the anticipated outcome is seen to meet minimum standards as likely as not the set will be accepted. The possibility of undertaking a different set may not be pursued. If there exists a model of the organisation (necessarily computer based) then a less restricted approach may be adopted by the decision makers. By considered use of the model different sets of total activity may emerge from which one set is to be selected; the advantages of simulation in these circumstances is attractive. Although the construction of a model may be expensive* this approach is probably justified in that corporate decisions are by definition of much greater significance than decisions taken at sub-corporate level. And although also some degree of commitment will be required by chief executives and senior managers, the advantage of being able to assess a full range of alternative outcomes should provide sufficient motivation for this process of decision making to be favoured.

Although no new concepts are involved in a corporate simulation the various outputs are generated in a different way. Proper account will need to be taken of year by year performance. That is, if E.P.S. is the criterion, an average over a period of five years would not be as meaningful as would the individual values of E.P.S. estimated for each year. In the public sector there may be some purpose in being able to estimate that, for example, British Rail or the National Coal Board would on average break even over the next five year period but again the individual annual performance would be of greater interest. Insofar as local authorities are concerned it is difficult to see great value in estimated average annual rating requirement calculated over a number of years. Therefore cross-sectional

---

* Comments will be made later in this chapter and in Chapter 9 on the specialist resources needed to develop corporate models.

sampling of individual activities on a period by period basis is called for, by which means net earnings from all operations are combined and set against unallocated overheads. This would enable private sector organisations to be provided with a probability of achieving yearly certain levels of E.P.S., or, for example, a probability distribution of annual total rate requirement to be established for local government decision making. A further point which may be mentioned is that the time value of money is now computationally of less importance. Comparisons between alternative total sets of projects at intervals of time would be independent of any discount rate and would satisfy the needs of organisations primarily concerned with performance in the short term. For those organisations adopting a longer term view of profitability, it is however likely that major investment decisions will be taken following the discounting of cash flows.

It may be found that none of the total sets of activities satisfies corporate objectives (the "planning gap" again). In this case, relaxation of resource constraints involving funding or recruitment may be suggested, or a search for further alternatives incorporating an alteration in the structure of the organisation through divestment or acquisition may be pursued. It will be apparent that considerable planning and analytical effort is involved, but as computer software grows increasingly flexible and is designed to meet the needs of the non-specialist the possibility of adopting a corporate approach based on simulation becomes very much a practical proposition.

SIMULATION IN PRACTICE

The objective of simulation, which is to provide a basis for decision making through the use of a model of all or part of an organisation, should be attractive to managers. In particular, the opportunity to gain rapid answers to the "What-if?" type of question enables management to resist the feeling that the model is the master of the situation. The three major problems to be overcome are:

1. An understanding of the concepts of model building and the procedures which result in outputs being generated from the various inputs.
2. An appreciation of the role of the computer.
3. The practical problems of building and using simulation models.

This Chapter has so far been concerned with point 1, and little has been said about the practical problems which arise. Insofar as point 2 is concerned simulation, because of the amount of computation involved, virtually necessitates computer usage. Many managers will be aware that simulation has been used for a number of years to aid decision making in respect of certain aspects of an organisation's activities. They will know that work flows and distribution systems, for example, have been simulated using a computer, but as the decisions have been more of a design or control nature relating to existing resources managers will perhaps have accepted without too much question the advice of their specialists. If, however, simulation is to be used to aid higher level decisions of a planning nature the managers concerned can no longer afford too much detachment.

It would be attractive to think that decision makers could build their own models and programme them for the computer. It is a fact that a few senior managers have done this. One answer to the inevitable comment that such involvement must lead to neglect of their other managerial duties is the response that by so doing they gain a greater insight into the structure and workings of their organisation. Account may be taken of the possibility of an extension of the manager's responsibilities and authority as a result of this greater insight. It must, however, be accepted that senior managers prepared to involve themselves in this manner are very much in the minority and that a more realistic aim for these persons must be a full appreciation of the structure of the model proposed and the role of the computer. As mentioned in Chapter 2, there is a slow but discernible trend in the use of computers by higher management. Instant and objective response to questions is the aim of every manager and the ultimate in this respect is provided by real-time computing, preferably with visual display. The nature of the model will to a large degree dictate whether real-time computing for senior managers is feasible. Some models are of such a size that simulations require a number of minutes to complete. In these circumstances, the software and computing facilities of a large free standing system would be preferable. Senior managers would prefer decisions to be taken away and processed rather than sit for minutes awaiting the visual output of an on-line computer terminal. Nevertheless, higher level decisions requiring cash flows, balance sheets and other financial reports may often be appropriately based on models which may be manipulated in real-time.

The third point mentioned above made reference to the practical problems which arise in the construction of models for simulation. Having established the purpose for which the model is to be used the first conclusion to be reached will probably be that certain information is either unavailable or unreliable. Most model builders aim to construct as small a model as is possible but the pressure to expand the model and hence data requirements is difficult to resist. Information on categories of manpower, utilisation of resources, allocation of overheads, stock levels, and so on may be seen to be necessary for the creation of an effective model. If estimates have to be made because of a lack of basic data it is important that records are then maintained in order to upgrade the estimates as soon as possible.

It will be evident that for any model which is to be of practical value the time taken for its construction will not be small. This will depend on the number of persons involved and in some instances ten man-years has been quoted. Even in terms of the model building period, times approaching two years have been recorded. In these circumstances, it is imperative that the model structure is not rigid as an investment of substantial resources in its construction will tend to militate against significant amendments to it. This is recognised by designers of computer software, who through appropriate programming languages and routines attempt to provide some measure of flexibility.* Sometimes this is achieved by using a modular approach which enables part of the model to be accessed, modified, and reintroduced. The modular approach will usually imply that the overall model comprises sub-models (for example, manpower, overhead, financial) and that certain routines may be changed (for example, different financial ratios may be required). Quite apart from the possibility of the nature of the organisation changing through time the questions for which management require an answer will also change. It may be that a company which was seeking growth through acquisition when work on the model began has turned its attention to potential short term profits by the time the model is supposedly complete. The problems of adaptation and updating must be accommodated within most planning processes but they can be particularly acute in the case of something as complex as the corporate simulation model.

The difficulty which often arises in achieving an appropriate use of the model by the decision maker has been mentioned before. The specialists are often criticised for this but the responsibility must

* See J. C. HIGGINS AND D. WHITAKER, "Computer aids to Corporate Planning," The Computer Bulletin, September 1972, pp. 434–439.

be shared with the managers who they are seeking to assist.* The manager may be confronted with a multi-equation model and a computer print-out several inches in thickness which will inevitably create an adverse reaction, but if he is not prepared to make some attempt to understand the technical jargon the efforts of the model building team may well be fruitless. If on the other hand he is prepared to consider himself part of the model building team, taking that instruction which is necessary for his eventual use of the model, then the problem of communication can be reduced. It is suggested that despite the opinion of many senior managers that they are ineducable in numerical techniques, this is not necessarily the case. Reasonable application can soon equip many persons of professed non-numeracy with a sufficient understanding of the computational aspects of construction and usage of models.

GENERAL COMMENTS AND SUMMARY

The mathematical model provides an opportunity for the representation in symbolic form of relationships which exist or are thought to exist within an organisation. Included within the model are variables which are mainly within or mainly outside the control of a decision maker. Simulation is the process of using models in order to assess the consequences of variables of both types taking certain values. The values will be known to the decision maker in the case of controllable variables or forecast if the variables are uncontrollable.

The implications of positive and normative relationships are stressed. The latter in particular must be approved by the decision maker using the model, as although they may adequately describe the past there is no guarantee that such relationships will apply in the future. Having approved the structure of the model the decision maker will need to choose between deterministic and probabilistic use. Deterministic "most likely" estimates, although being highly likely individually, may combine to produce a single figure output of low probability. Sensitivity analysis can however be of assistance in studying the response of the single figure output to changes in the input variables. Although conceptually more demanding, probabilistic simulation will take account of the full range of a decision maker's attitudes towards particular variables, but selection among

---

* For an entertaining view of a senior manager, *see* J. HARRY GOLDIE, *Simulation and Irritation*, supplement to *Corporate Simulation Models*, ed. Albert N. Schrieber, University of Washington, Seattle, 1970.

alternatives may then not be as straightforward as in the deterministic case. If the probabilistic approach is used the selection of an alternative will be influenced by the particular utility attitudes of the decision maker. Thus, for example, a risk-averse manager will avoid selecting a project with a significant probability of making a loss.

Probabilistic simulation involves sampling at random from individual distributions and combining the results. In order to reduce the sampling error to acceptable limits many simulations will be necessary. Although techniques are available to achieve maximum precision with minimum computation the latter will be very much greater than that required by a deterministic simulation. Sensitivity analysis is possible with probabilistic simulation but it may well be that due to the computation required and problems of interpretation deterministic simulation with sensitivity analysis will be preferred.

Simulation has been used fairly extensively for the appraisal of large investment projects covering a period of several years. In these circumstances, the analysis generally incorporates discounting procedures. The possibilities of studying the consequences of making planning decisions for the total activities of an organisation have not yet been exploited. The facility to generate year by year performance by combining either deterministically or probabilistically the various activities would seem to be attractive. This process could be seen as part of an iterative procedure involving the setting of corporate objectives and the determination of the level and type of activity needed to meet these objectives.

It will be noted that there is no claim that simulation will lead to the optimum course of action. Optimisation is the subject of the next Chapter, and it will be seen that in this context simulation has a role to play. In the main, however, senior managers will continue to view simulation as a means of providing answers to "What-if?" type of questions (that is, the model will be viewed as being of the "descriptive" type).

Virtually all decisions for which simulation provides a basis necessitate the use of a computer. Senior managers will never in general operate batch computers, but there are indications that substantial use will be made of on-line units to provide on the spot answers to planning questions.

There are a number of problems which arise in practice in connection with the construction and use of simulation models. In the first instance the level of detail needs to be agreed, and following this appropriate data gathered. The lack of information is often highlighted at this stage. Again the time involved in building the model may be great, amounting in some instances to several years. This creates the danger that by the time the model is supposedly finished it no longer truly describes the organisation which it purports to represent, raising the general question of flexibility and adaptability. Only a certain variance from real life can be tolerated and the large investment in the construction of a model may tend to oppose its modification to meet altered circumstances.

Finally it is suggested that there can be a real advantage to the decision maker in using a simulation model. The process is a simplification of anticipated real life events and the concepts should, with a little application, be understood even by managers who see themselves as being non-numerate. Understanding of this nature can facilitate the total decision making procedure, mainly through the greater insight which is gained into the workings of the organisation.

Chapter Eight

THE OPTIMISING APPROACH TO PLANNING DECISIONS

INTRODUCTION

All organisations have objectives even if these are not explicitly stated. In addition, the stability of objectives will be greater when organisational performance can be measured easily within the terms of reference which the organisation sets for itself and less when there is difficulty in evaluating output. Thus in the private sector a company's objective over the years may be to maximise profitability, whereas at national level government objectives will vary according to the importance attached to inflation, unemployment, growth rate of the economy and other socio-economic factors. Optimisation in the latter context will therefore be to a certain degree subjective, and it will be noted that in the private sector social pressures are causing some companies to include within their range of objectives those which are of a non-financial nature.

Although corporate objectives have in some instances been quantified for many years, examination will often reveal that these are arbitrarily related to past performance or future expectation. The setting of objectives can present little difficulty; a quick look at performance over the last few years may for example result in next year's objective being a 10 per cent growth in profits. At government level a much publicised arbitrary, although not necessarily unrealistic, objective was to double the standard of living within twenty-five years. This is not a criticism of the decision makers. Planning and analytical skills were (and are) simply not available to enable decision makers to know what might be achieved.

The aim must however be to maximise something (even if this is a "composite" of a set of objectives) and hence ideally every organisation should subject itself to the analytical process of Fig. 55. It will be readily apparent that the real problem arises in meeting the requirements of the two centre boxes of Fig. 55. Even in retrospect, and knowing precisely the environment, most organisations would find it an extremely difficult and in some cases an impossible task to establish what the potential resources might have been and how they may "best" have been utilised. Thus in planning for the future,

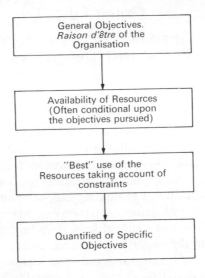

FIG. 55. The ideal method of setting objectives.

when the environment is uncertain, does the approach possess any realism whatsoever? Recent experience suggests that some advantage may be gained by organisations in pursuing the matter. Chapter 7 assessed the value of providing a basis for decision making by estimating values of uncontrollable variables at various future dates. Using a model to simulate how the organisation would react with the environment, the decision maker was able to go far beyond intuition and study in depth the likely consequences of policy decisions taken by him. In this Chapter the decision maker is again required to specify the environment, but in this case analysis will take over and attempt to achieve the optimum within the *framework set by him.* Many and varied have been the techniques developed to optimise, and most for a detailed understanding require more than the "reasonable application" mentioned as being appropriate for the non-numerate manager in the last chapter. This immediately raises the problem of communication between the manager and the specialist, but again it is suggested that sufficient understanding can be achieved, without too much difficulty, to enable the decision maker to have an awareness of the nature of the technique and confidence in the recommendations arising from the analysis.

Before proceeding to examine some of the procedures involved, it is proposed to give some consideration to the second box in Fig. 55, namely the availability of resources. One of the by-products of an optimum position in a situation of resource constraint is that the marginal value of providing extra resource may be determined. It is therefore important to assess the availability of resources (for example, manpower, funds, time) over and above what would normally be expected. Consider for example local government decision making, in which resources are difficult to assess because of uncertainty as to central government's policies in the short, medium and long term. On the assumption that the aim of a local authority is to provide a "service" a resource-service matrix may be proposed on the lines of Fig. 56. Assuming also that all costs are

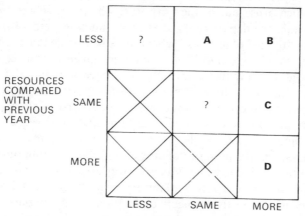

FIG. 56. A resource-service matrix.

at constant prices it is unlikely that any local authority would accept as objectives the implications of the three cells marked with a cross. The centre cell would not be indicative of a progressive authority, but the cell implying less service for less cost is a possibility if a reduction in government grants is forecast because of the state of the economy. An improvement in operating efficiency is suggested by cells A, B, and C and of these cell B implies performance nearest to the optimum. Cell D indicates the case where more services are provided as a result of more funds being made available but without being able to conclude whether greater efficiency is or is not involved.

Attempts to use this approach to set the framework for optimisation in a private company would normally result in a matrix of "performance" against resources reduced to cells A, B, C, and D only. In all circumstances mentioned, in addition to considering the marginal value of resources, the possibility of significant changes in resource availability must be recognised. This would take account for example of large government grants to local authorities, loans to public corporations and increased equity and acquisitions in the case of companies. Therefore in pursuing an optimising approach a decision maker should not confine his attention to the marginal value of resources but should also study the effect of a large increase in the availability of resources, creating perhaps a change in the structure of the organisation itself.

In Chapter 2 mention was made of the goals within the organisation which arose out of the corporate objectives. These would be seen within the departments, divisions, functions, etc. of organisations as "limited objectives" which must be satisfied in as efficient a manner as possible. Decisions which are taken in respect of these goals will in many instances influence other activities and what in fact amounts to optimisation in a specific part of an organisation may lead to sub-optimisation overall. The control of stock provides an example of this. Costs due to holding and procuring stock may be minimised, but at the expense of uneconomic production schedules, and the presence of stock on shelves at retail outlets may have a promotional value which is overlooked. One would expect that an efficient corporate planning procedure would involve an attempt to ensure that objectives and goals are compatible in the sense that optimisation of the goals would lead to optimisation of the objectives. The problems of achieving this ideal in an organisation of complexity, say a multi-national company, will be apparent.

Given that the decision maker accepts that the methods of achieving goals are both determined and dominated by the overall corporate objectives, the question arises—what objectives? In the first place the organisation may well as suggested have several objectives. In the private sector a company may aim to achieve a stated volume of profits, to become the largest operator in its field, and to achieve a certain level of earnings per share. At government level the objectives may be to maximise per capita G.N.P., to reduce inflation and unemployment to a minimum and to maintain a favourable balance of payments. It will be evident that in both cases the objectives are not independent. In the private sector, it would be expected that as most objectives are financial in nature then improvement in one financial criterion would be concurrent with improvement in another financial criterion. This is often the case, but it by no means follows that the value assumed by each criterion is identical with the optimum value which each would have assumed as single objectives. In the short term, profits may not be significantly affected by the method of capital gearing employed, whereas this would not be so with E.P.S. For such objectives as becoming the major company in the field "political" as well as economic objectives are implied. The adoption by a company of political objectives could well have a profound effect on traditional financial performance criterion, and may lead to new objectives of which the maximisation of share price is an example.

In the discussion which follows a number of examples will be used in which overall objectives are assumed. It will be proposed that national government is concerned with maximising "welfare," that local government aims to maximise "service," and that industry and commerce seeks to optimise some financial criterion. Before this stage is reached it is however necessary to examine the framework required for optimisation and to gain some understanding of the techniques which may be used.

THE FRAMEWORK FOR OPTIMISATION

In Chapter 7, the process of simulation using descriptive models enabled "What-if?" questions to be answered by assigning values to both controllable and uncontrollable variables. The decision making environment was however seen to be to a large degree unbounded in consequence of future uncertainty and hence the likely effects of significant changes in both types of variable were studied. The role of the model was to provide the manager with a greater insight into the working of his organisation by indicating and explaining relationships and hence enabling him to concentrate on the major implications of uncertainty. The model is therefore in these circumstances very much the tool of the manager.

If optimisation is to be attempted, then uncertainty does not play so prominent a role. It is of course still recognised to exist and in fact in one instance to which brief reference will be made below the environment may be bounded by variables which are not deterministic but probabilistic in nature. In the main, however, our concern will be with variables, both controllable and uncontrollable which are assigned deterministic values. Uncertainty is then taken into limited account through the medium of sensitivity analysis. The framework in the private sector will be one in which uncontrollable variables such as demand, costs, overdraft facilities, etc. are given specific values and in relation to which the company's resources of capital and manpower are to be allocated in such a way that optimisation of the overall objective (or set of objectives) is achieved. Given this framework (in which the values of uncontrollable variables are specified) it will now be apparent why in Chapter 2 the dichotomy optimising *v.* descriptive was preferred to optimising *v.* simulation. For if the decision maker is prepared to permit very many "What-if?" questions in respect of a particular set of controllable variables, then the optimum use of resources may be achieved by trial and error. In fact, a directed method of search usually described as *hill-climbing* and which is described below is more efficient than trial and error. Simulation may therefore be used to achieve an optimum *given the initial assumptions*, but a high cost may be incurred due to the computing time which will be required.

OPTIMISING TECHNIQUES

For a specific objective (or combined set of objectives) and an environment which is also specified and deterministic an optimal allocation of resources will exist (coincidentally, there may be two or more optima). The possibility of a solution derived by analysis as opposed to search is therefore an attractive proposition. Over the last two decades there have been many examples of analytically derived optima in organisations of many kinds. Solutions have been obtained to problems of queueing, stock control, replacement, etc. and the operational effectiveness of organisations in very many cases has been improved significantly. A common feature of the application of the techniques referred to, with a notable exception which will be mentioned shortly, has been that decisions of a *design* nature as defined in Chapter 4 have been involved. In many cases, constraints have not applied and capital has been invested in anticipation of an improved return. For example, additional service facilities have been provided in order to reduce time spent in queueing or a new depot has been built to achieve overall economy through reduced transportation costs. This class of problem includes costs which are inversely correlated, that is a reduction in one cost may be achieved but at the expense of an increase in another. Minimum total costs are often not apparent but they can be determined mathematically (usually by the calculus). The economic batch quantity, of some note in the field of stock control, is an example of a mathematically derived result which implies, given certain assumptions, minimum stock-holding cost. As problems become larger and constraints must be taken into account, the possibility of using more advanced calculus remains, but practical applications have been very limited.

The "notable exception" referred to in the last paragraph is linear programming, the widely used member of a group of techniques termed *mathematical programming*.

> LINEAR PROGRAMMING: A mathematical iterative procedure which for a problem formulated in a specific manner will determine the allocation of limited resources among competing ends in order to optimise an objective function.

Optimisation may involve either maximisation (*e.g.* of profits) or minimisation (*e.g.* of costs). The reference in the definition to "competing ends" implies that the objective function will derive its value from a number of sources. If the objective were dependent on one source only (for example, a single product company) the solution would be trivial given a bounded environment. Assuming that each individual item could make a positive contribution, the number produced would be determined by demand or resource availability, whichever were lower. Thus, in linear programming the objective (or "objective function" as it is usually described) contains at least two terms. Although in practice the objective function may include hundreds of terms, the principle is identical to that when only two terms are involved. The name of the technique implies linearity, that is the formulation will not include variables in exponential form. At first sight, this requirement would appear excessively restrictive. This aspect will be examined after the procedures and properties have been examined. Suffice to state at this point that means have often been found of "fitting the technique to the problem" and many successful instances of the use of linear programming have been recorded in practice.

It is possibly true that the number of hypothetical examples of this technique which· have appeared in books and articles exceeds the number of pràctical applications (and, as was just mentioned, there have been many of these). This is in part due to the ability, in the particular case of two competing ends, to convey the basic concept by reference to graphs. Circumstances in which two competing ends are involved are sufficiently close to the practical situation to enable the potential of the technique to be demonstrated. If each competing end is considered as involving one dimension in space it will be appreciated that examination of the technique graphically is trivial in one dimension, feasible in two, difficult in three (three dimensional drawing is required) and is impossible in more than three. The mathematical iterative process, some part of which will be presented later, will accept as many competing ends as is allowed by the capacity of the computer (for this is essentially a computer based technique). The calculation will then be within multi-dimensional space.

The Problem

A small company manufactures washing machines and markets two types, standard and de luxe. Production is organised in two divisions, electrical and mechanical. Final assembly is undertaken within the latter division. During a two shift week of eighty hours, the electrical division can produce up to 225 motors for the standard model but only 150 heavier duty motors for the de luxe model. The time required to manufacture and assemble de luxe models in the mechanical division is twice as long as that required for the standard model, of which 250 may be produced weekly.

In order to improve its image the company objective has been to maximise its sales of the de luxe model and to use spare capacity to manufacture the standard model. Sales of the latter have not been difficult and it was decided to undertake a market survey in order to estimate the demand for both products. The results of the survey indicated that the weekly demand for the de luxe model was unlikely to exceed the current level of seventy-five but that the demand for standard models could be about 200. Standard costing revealed that contribution to fixed overheads were £40 and £25 for the de luxe and standard models respectively. The problem was that if the policy to maximise de luxe sales was dropped would a change in production mix be indicated? Further, could specific information be obtained about the significance of the individual constraints?

Developing the Linear Programme
The first requirement that must be satisfied at this stage of the treatment is one of linearity. This implies that economies of scale are not involved. Contribution accounting is more likely to meet this requirement than would accounting methods in which fixed overheads are allocated between products. Here two shift working is assumed and hourly wage rates may be taken as the same for both shifts. If therefore the possibility of bulk discounts on purchased materials is ignored, direct costs per unit of production of each model are constant and hence assuming invariable selling price, so will be the contributions. Again, it is necessary to assume that the ratio of substitution one model for the other in each division is constant at any level of production. For example, within the week 248 standard models and one de luxe model could be produced as also could two standard models and 124 de luxe models (one time unit per standard model, two time units per de luxe model). If these requirements are satisfied, the formulation of the linear programme may proceed on the following lines.

(i) *The Objective Function*
In the problem as described, the objective is clear, namely to maximise the contribution to overhead (C) from the two models of washing machine, standard (S) and de luxe (D). The contributions per model were stated to be £25 and £40 for the standard and de luxe models respectively. The objective function which is to be maximised is therefore (in £):
$$C = 25S + 40D$$

(ii) *The Constraints*
These may be grouped into those which have been determined within the company (endogenous) and those determined without (exogenous). In the former category come the capacities of the two divisions and in the latter category the demands for the two products. The endogenous constraints may be seen as controllable variables if the labour supply is flexible but it would obviously take time to increase the size of the plant. The exogenous

variables will be to a large degree uncontrollable but may be influenced by (realistic) price changes and promotional effort. The linear programme does not of course distinguish between the different categories of constraint. In this problem there are four individual constraints namely, electrical and mechanical division capacities and demand levels for the two models.

(*iii*) *The Competing Demands for Resources Within Constraints*
This presumes that competing demands do exist. This is not always the case, as for example the demand or minimum production levels for individual products. We thus have that the weekly supply of standard washing machines should not exceed 200. If S is the weekly production of standard models then S must be equal to or less than 200. This would be represented by the inequality:

$$S \leqslant 200$$

Similar reasoning leads to the inequality for de luxe models:

$$D \leqslant 75$$

The manner of taking into account the competing demands for the capacities of the two divisions is not quite so straightforward. Again inequalities are involved and the general form is:

$$aS + bD \leqslant X$$

where a and b are constants and X is the capacity. Consider first the mechanical division, as this is the more simple case. X may be represented in terms of either standard or de luxe units. If the former is chosen the value of X is 250, and hence:

$$aS + bD \leqslant 250$$

The values of a and b are determined by considering production concentrated, in turn, wholly on standard or de luxe models. If production is wholly standard then S is 250 and a is thus 1. If production is wholly de luxe then D is 125 and b is 2. The mechanical division inequality is therefore:

$$S + 2D \leqslant 250$$

It was possible to obtain the values for a and b without difficulty as the capacity production of de luxe models at 125 was a factor of the capacity production of standard models at 250. When the electrical division is considered, the capacity is 225 in terms of the standard model (motors) and 150 in terms of the de luxe model (motors). The first step is to obtain the lowest common multiple of the numbers 225 and 150, and this is 450. The constants a and b may now be obtained by consideration of the inequality:

$$aS + bD \leqslant 450$$

Production concentrated on S implies that S is 225 and D is 0, and hence a is 2. Production concentrated on D implies that D is 150 and S is zero, leading to a value of 3 for b. Finally, therefore, the electrical division constraint may be written:

$$2S + 3D \leqslant 450$$

The completely formulated linear programme is therefore:

$$S \qquad\quad \leqslant 200$$
$$D \leqslant 75$$
$$S + 2D \leqslant 250$$
$$2S + 3D \leqslant 450$$

Maximise $\quad 25S + 40D = C$

By comparison with many practical linear programmes, this formulation is very small and yet the optimum mix is by no means apparent. Resolution of the problem is aided in this case by representing the constraints and objective function graphically. The procedure was described in Chapter 3, from which it will be remembered that an inequality implies an area of a graph bounded by a straight line not a straight line itself. Whether the inequality is of the "not greater than" or "not less than" type will indicate on which side of the boundary the "feasible region" lies. This may be seen from Fig. 57, in which the boundaries of the four constraints are determined by the four straight lines. The shaded area is the feasible region (six sided) which remains after satisfying all the constraints simultaneously. The weekly production mix may then be any point within or on the boundary of this feasible region. Zero production of both types of model is in this case feasible. In practice, circumstances may dictate minimum production levels. Here minimum

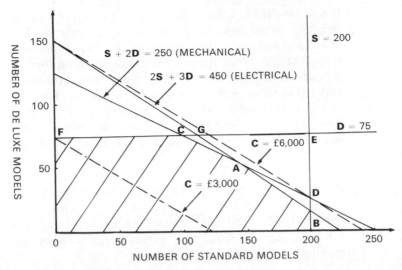

FIG. 57. Graphical representation of the linear programme.

levels of production of the standard and de luxe models could have been fifty in each case. This would have created constraints of the "greater than or equal to" type, and would have produced a feasible region on the graph which did not touch either of the axes.

Zero production would create zero contribution and obviously could be improved on. Contribution C in the objective function will be zero or greater according to the values of S and D, and for any given value of C numerous combinations of S and D are possible. A contribution of £3000 per week could be achieved from either 120 standard models or seventy-five de luxe models, or, for example, forty-eight standards and forty-five de luxes. That is, any production mix satisfying the equation:

$$25S + 40D = 3000$$

would create a contribution of £3000 per week. (It is not proposed at this point to consider non-integer values for S and D.) Thus levels of weekly contribution may be represented graphically by a set of straight lines which, as the coefficients of S and D remain unaltered, are parallel. The further the contribution line from the origin the greater will be the contribution. Two levels of weekly contribution, £3000 and £6000 are represented by the broken lines. All points on the £3000 line lie within the feasible region whereas none of the points on the £6000 line are feasible. It is clear that the higher contribution cannot be achieved. By examination of the graph, it will be evident that the maximum contribution will arise when the contribution line is furthest from the origin and yet contains at least one feasible point, which in this case implies point A. Normally there is a unique optimum solution to a linear programme as the contribution line last touches the feasible region in a point. It is possible, however, that the objective function when furthest from the origin and still within the feasible region coincides with a boundary. In this case, any point on this boundary indicates an optimum. This would have arisen in Fig. 57 if the contribution from standard and de luxe models were £26 and £39 respectively, when the slope of the contribution line would have been identical with the slope of constraint arising from the electrical division capacity.

Point A in Fig. 57 represents the mix of 150 standard models and fifty de luxe models, creating a contribution of £5750 per week. It will be appreciated that the optimum mix arises at the intersection of the boundary lines:

$$2S + 3D = 450$$
$$S + 2D = 250$$

The optimum is the solution of these two equations simultaneously.

Using this latter approach, the contribution which would arise from operating at the points B and C may be determined. The results for these, together with that for point A, are given in Table XXII.

TABLE XXII: THE CONSEQUENCES OF OPERATING AT THE OPTIMUM AND OTHER FEASIBLE POINTS (NEAREST WHOLE NUMBER OF MODELS) (*See* Fig. 57)

Point	Number of standard models per week	Number of de luxe models per week	Contribution per week (£)
A	150	50	5750
B	200	17	5680
C	100	75	5500

Several conclusions may be drawn from Table XXII and Fig. 57. In the first instance, if optimum contribution is to be achieved then the number of de luxe models marketed per week must be cut by 33 per cent. Secondly, the mixes represented by points A, B, C produce contributions which do not differ greatly. (Contribution corresponding to C is about 4.5 per cent less than optimum.) Mix B may be unacceptable due to the lack of balance. Mix C, however, although creating least contribution of the three mixes examined, involves production of the least number of models. If, as probably is the case, distribution costs are treated as an overhead the difference in true cost between mixes A and C will be less than indicated. Again, mix A requires utilisation of the divisional capacities to the full whereas C and B imply unused capacity. If alternative use for this capacity can be found, then again C or B may be preferred. All of this implies tacit acceptance of the original constraints. Even if it is felt that the demand constraints cannot be relaxed, it is possible that the endogenous constraints may be. The optimum mix of 150 standard models and fifty de luxe models is constrained by the capacity of the two divisions only. Sensitivity—or preferably as an initial optimum has been determined—*post-optimality*, analysis may be undertaken to ascertain the value in terms of increased contribution of extra capacity. It may be conjectured as to how this increase in capacity could be obtained. Any combination of such factors as overtime, three shift working (at, say, a night shift rate), additional physical capacity, or sub-contracting may be involved. Whatever the means it will be apparent that little benefit will arise from providing extra capacity in just one of the divisions. An increased contribution of £250 per week could be generated by operating at the limit of the assembly division, when 200 standard models and twenty-five de luxe models would be produced. This would require the capacity of the electrical division to be increased from 225 to 237.5 in terms of standard equivalent models. That is, the inequality would become:

$$2S + 3D = 475$$

and point D in Fig. 57 would be indicated. Costing exercises, or if capital investment is involved an investment appraisal, would be required to assess whether the increased contribution (calculated on existing labour rates) is justified.

The rectangle bounded by the estimates of demand and the two axes of the graph of Fig. 57 is literally the framework within which the production mix must be determined. Therefore, the maximum contribution which could be generated is represented by point E, corresponding to a production volume of 200 standard models and seventy-five de luxe models, giving a total contribution of £8000 per week. Compared with the initial optimum contribution of £5750 per week this implies a potential increase in weekly contribution of

£2250. Various projects may be costed to assess whether advantage may be taken of this opportunity.

THE MANAGER AND LINEAR PROGRAMMING IN PRACTICE

Given the simplicity of the above problem, readers may have been surprised at the extent of the basis which was provided for decision making and the subsequent lines of thought which were suggested. In practice, it is desirable that if linear programming is used for decisions of a planning rather than a control nature (that is if uncertainty is involved) managers should understand the formulation. This should not be taken as suggesting that managers should actually formulate the linear programme. The specialist will be able to do this far more quickly and efficiently in situations of any complexity. The purpose of the manager gaining an appreciation of the technique is yet again to enable a dialogue to be conducted between him and the specialist who will be attempting to create a basis for logical decision making. It is also desirable that the manager should be able to interpret the output arising from optimising the objective function. As in practice the number of variables most usually exceeds two, graphical interpretation is not possible. The mathematical procedure is iterative and may be described by reference to Fig. 57 as a series of steps from the origin 0 through points F and C (or through points B and D) to the optimum A. The value of the objective function and all variables are determined at each step but usually it is only the final (optimum) output generated (usually by a computer package) which is supplied.

As mentioned, there is considerable advantage to be gained by the manager in being able to appreciate the formulation of the problem as a linear programme and to interpret the final output. In a very large problem involving many variables and constraints it is not proposed that the manager should work his way through every constraint or study the output values of each variable. He may, however, wish to see how certain constraints which he feels are significant have been incorporated. Alternatively, he may adopt a sampling approach and select at random a number of constraints which he will ask the specialist to explain. Again, he would be unwise to accept without question the operating conditions suggested by the final (optimum) output or to ignore the potential of post-optimality analysis.

It is not proposed to work through the various mathematical

procedures available: these are described fully in many publications.* From the point of view of the manager, the mathematical technique may be considered to be a deterministic "black box" which always generates the same output for a given input. First a list of definitions will be given and these will then be interpreted by reference to the example used above.

SIMPLEX TECHNIQUE: A general method for solving any linear programming problem.

DECISION VARIABLES: Each end or activity, the level of which is indicated by the optimising procedure.

CONSTRAINTS: Restrictions having upper bounds in the case of available resources and lower bounds in the case of requirements.

OBJECTIVE FUNCTION: The overall performance deriving from the combined levels of the decision variables.

FEASIBLE SOLUTION: The value of decision variables which when taken singly or together satisfy all constraints.

BASIC FEASIBLE SOLUTION: The limited set of feasible solutions corresponding in spatial terms to the "corners" of the feasible region.

OPTIMAL SOLUTION: A feasible solution which optimises the objective function.

SLACK (SURPLUS) VARIABLES: Non-negative variables used to convert "less than or equal to" and "greater than or equal to" inequalities to equalities.

---

* See, for example, SAUL I. GASS, Linear Programming, McGraw-Hill Inc., New York, 1964 and for a less mathematical treatment R. I. LEVIN AND R. P. LAMONE, Linear Programming for Management Decision, Richard D. Irwin, Inc., Homewood, Illinois, 1969.

ARTIFICIAL VARIABLES: Non-negative variables which take zero values in the optimal solution but which enable the basic feasible solutions required by the Simplex technique to be established in the circumstances of "greater than or equal to" inequalities or equalities.

SHADOW PRICE: The value per unit of resource up to which a net improvement in the objective function could be obtained by providing extra units of resource (the quantity of extra units supplied must not cause the levels of other decision variables in the original optimal solution to change).

POST-OPTIMALITY AND SENSITIVITY ANALYSIS: The general study of the effect on the optimal solution of changing the value of input parameters and possibly adding new variables or constraints.

THE DUAL: A reformulation of the original problem (the Primal) by transposition of rows and columns and reversing the inequalities, so that computation and interpretation is facilitated.

A set of feasible solutions was described as "basic." The Simplex method generates a "basic" solution at each of a series of iterative steps until the optimal solution is reached. The earlier linear programming formulation is first restated:

$$S \leqslant 200$$
$$D \leqslant 75$$
$$S + 2D \leqslant 250$$
$$2S + 3D \leqslant 450$$
$$25S + 40D = C$$

Because of the inequalities, this is not a basic solution. Four slack variables are necessary (one for each constraint) to replace the inequalities by equalities. In introducing these, opportunity is taken to present a new formulation (Table XXIII) in which only the coefficients of the decision variables (S and D) and slack variables (K, L, M, and N) are indicated. All variables are non-negative.

TABLE XXIII: THE INITIAL BASIS TABLEAU

S	D	K	L	M	N	C	R.H.S.
1	0	1	0	0	0	0 =	200
0	1	0	1	0	0	0 =	75
1	2	0	0	1	0	0 =	250
2	3	0	0	0	1	0 =	450
-25	-40	0	0	0	0	1 =	0

First it will be noted that ones and zeros are predominant; this is a feature of practical linear programmes. Secondly, excluding the objective function, there are four equations for six variables. For a unique solution as many equations as variables are required. If the number of equations (m) is less than the number of variables (n), then a solution may be obtained by solving for m variables in terms of the remaining ($n-m$) variables and setting these ($n-m$) variables equal to zero. In this case, therefore, a solution will be obtained for four variables with the remaining two equal to zero. A third point to note is that the objective function has been rearranged to bring the terms under the various columns of the tableau. The initial and optimum solutions will be examined.

(a) *The initial basic feasible solution*

By reference to Table XXIII, it will be apparent that if S and D are set equal to zero a solution is obtained for the four slack variables K, L, M, and N; respectively, the values are 200, 75, 250, and 450. This is interpreted as meaning that all capacity is spare (slack) capacity and that none of the demand is satisfied. Furthermore the contribution C, is zero. This is only feasible within the context of the original problem. In practice, minimum production levels would probably be set as constraints.

(b) *The optimal solution*

Reference was made to the fact that the Simplex method generates basic solutions corresponding to "corners" of the feasible region. A further property of the method which has not been mentioned is that the route taken is determined by a search at each step for the maximum increase in the objective function: this economises on the number of iterations involved. From an examination of Fig. 57, it will be seen that whether the optimum point A is approached in a clockwise or anti-clockwise direction three iterations from the initial solution are required. By following the mechanistic rules of the Simplex method, the optimum basis may be derived, and this is shown in tableau form in Table XXIV.

TABLE XXIV: THE OPTIMUM BASIS TABLEAU

S	D	K	L	M	N	C	R.H.S.
0	0	1	0	3	-2	0	50
0	1	0	0	2	-1	0	50
1	0	0	0	-3	2	0	150
0	0	0	1	-2	1	0	25
0	0	0	0	5	10	1	5750

Depending upon requirements and the linear programme computer package used, only part of the information contained in the optimal tableau may be supplied. Every number in the tableau does, however, have a meaning.

Considering first the objective function (the final row) this is now:

$$5M + 10N + C = 5750$$
$$\text{or} \qquad C = 5750 - 5M - 10N$$

As M and N, which are slack variables, are non-negative the maximum value of C, namely £5750, is obtained when M and N are both zero. The latter situation allows a solution for the remaining four variables in the problem, S, D, K, and L, to be determined. The decision variables are S and D and we have therefore from the second and third rows of Table XXIV:

Number of de luxe models to be produced, $D = 50$
Number of standard models to be produced, $S = 150$

Also from rows 1 and 4:

Unsatisfied demand for standard models, $K = 50$
Unsatisfied demand for de luxe models, $L = 25$

Thus a meaning has been given to much of the optimum tableau.

There remain columns M and N in which there are non-zero entries in all five rows. The coefficients of M and N which were encountered in the objective function are the shadow prices (sometimes described as the dual variables) and together with the coefficients in the remaining rows aid quantitative sensitivity and post-optimality analysis.

This analysis may be followed by first noting that values 5 and 10 appear under columns M and N in the final row of Table XXIV (the objective function); these are the shadow prices defined earlier. It will also have been noted that in the initial programme figures of 250 appeared in the electrical division constraint and 450 in the mechanical division constraint. The interpretation is that an increase of one unit in the former value to 251 or in the latter value to 451 would allow contribution to be increased by £5 or £10 respectively. The M column refers to the electrical division and the N column to the mechanical division. The values in the first four rows of the M and N columns indicate how the increases of £5 and £10 may be achieved. Taking the mechanical division column N, the values are $-2, -1, 2, 1$. These may be interpreted by considering an increase in available capacity in the mechanical division from 450 to 451 (that is half a standard model or one third of a de luxe model) and studying the effect of this on the solution variables.

    (i) The value -2 in the first row refers to the slack variable (unsatisfied demand) in the initial demand equation for standard models. The increase in capacity results therefore in unsatisfied demand for the standard model *decreasing* by two.

    (ii) The value in the second row, -1, refers to the number of de luxe models produced which is therefore *reduced* by one.

    (iii) The value 2 in the third row refers to the number of standard models produced which is therefore *increased* by two.

    (iv) The value 1 refers to unsatisfied demand for the de luxe model which is therefore *increased* by one.

Note that (i) and (iii), and (ii) and (iv) are complementary. An extra unit of capacity in the mechanical division permits two more standard models to be produced at the expense of one de luxe model. The net increase in contribution arising would be £50 − £40, namely the £10 corresponding to the shadow price in Table XXIV.

The direction of these changes may be explained by reference again to Fig. 57. Successive relaxation of the mechanical division constraint allows the line representing the objective function to move further from the origin. The optimal basic point will therefore move along AD in the direction of D, implying a decrease in the number of de luxe models produced but an increase in the number of standards. The objective function may be increased in this manner until the point D is reached. Here another constraint (demand for standard models) becomes effective and a new optimal basis would be involved in which sensitivity analysis would be concerned with electrical division capacity together with demand for standard models. It may be noted that if the other constraints are considered to be inflexible, the maximum weekly increase in contribution which may be achieved by increasing the capacity of the mechanical division is £250 (£6000 total weekly contribution from sales of 200 standard models and twenty-five de luxe models). The reader may wish to interpret the electrical division column N of Table XXIV in relation to Fig. 57.

LINEAR PROGRAMMING EXTENSIONS: NON-LINEAR PROGRAMMING

The previous example was dealt with at some length in the hope that the reader may, by following the arguments, have gained a "feeling" for a mathematical optimising procedure in circumstances requiring the allocation of limited resources among competing ends. It will have been appreciated that linear programming as described so far is something of a compromise, in which the variability and uncertainty of the real world is made to fit certain requirements. A manager who has decisions to make in a complex situation involving many constraints and competing ends is ill advised to use linear programming as a logical basis if he feels that too much "fitting of the problem to the technique" is involved. It might be expected therefore that specialists in the technique would naturally aim to increase its flexibility and efficiency and hence its acceptability. This indeed has been the case, and attempts have been and are being made to answer questions of the following type:

(a) Can the linear programming model be adequately descriptive of practical decision making situations? Is the need for all relationships to be linear a prerequisite?

(b) How may uncertainty in the initial values used within the linear programme be taken into account? Is it possible to incorporate a probabilistic approach or should the technique be exclusively deterministic?

(*c*) Is it possible to reduce the costs of computation by more efficient programming methods?

The Adequacy of the Model

On many occasions in this book it has been stressed that a model should, through its structural equations, represent realistically the system or organisation in respect of which a decision is to be made. It has been the case that some managers' initial reaction to the linear programming model is one of some scepticism due to the limited (*i.e.* linear) nature presumed of the relationships. It is certainly true that some relationships are more efficiently modelled in non-linear form. For example, economies of scale, or in the opposite sense increasing marginal cost, imply non-linearity. Much effort has been put into attempts to increase the flexibility of linear programming so that practical circumstances can be taken account of more effectively. In the first instance, the very capacity of the technique enables a micro approach to be adopted. The ability of linear programming routines to optimise when perhaps 6000 equations and 25,000 variables are involved renders the actual non-linearity of one relationship, represented linearly, of less significance than would be the case if only ten equations were employed.

If it is felt that a linear model is inadequate, there is still the possibility that analytical optimisation may be achieved through various "non-linear programming" techniques. It is proposed to make no more than brief reference to the latter, as general applicability has by no means been achieved. That reference is made to them at all is in recognition of the fact that such techniques may be suggested to managers as the basis for decision making and some appreciation of their purpose could be advantageous.

Reference is made first to *separable convex programming,** for which the following definition is proposed:

SEPARABLE CONVEX A technique for optimisation by linear
PROGRAMMING: programming when a non-linear objective function has been reduced to a piecewise linear function.

---

* Several types of programming are mentioned in this Chapter, all of which require a higher level of knowledge of mathematics than is presumed of most readers of this book. A reference for those who do however wish to study these approaches in more depth is FREDERICK S. HILLIER AND GERALD J. LIEBERMAN, *Introduction to Operations Research*, Holden-Day, Inc., San Francisco, 1970, Chapters 15, 16, and 17.

A non-linear objective function will arise if, say, products have to carry a fixed overhead which is allocated over the number produced and the objective is to maximise net profit. A piecewise linear function may arise from price breaks resulting from discounts or as a result of higher wage rates due to overtime or weekend work. An important requirement is that the objective function, which has been approximated by, or is, a piecewise linear function, should be convex if minimisation is the aim or concave if maximisation is the aim. Figure 58 indicates how individual variables of the objective

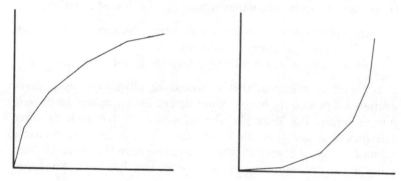

(*a*) Concave function (maximisation). (*b*) Convex function (minimisation).
FIG. 58. Piecewise linear functions.

function may be represented piecewise linearly over the range of levels which they may adopt, enabling optimisation to be effected. It will be appreciated that if for example contribution is to be maximised, then this should decrease on a per item basis as the output level increases. This requires that any economies of scale are more than offset by increased marginal cost.

Analytical solutions have also been developed for the case when the objective function may contain, in addition to linear terms, second degree terms. The name *quadratic programming* has been given to this technique, and has been used for example in portfolio selection.

Some progress has been made in obtaining solutions for the special case of a concave objective function and convex constraints. The feasible region in this case is a convex set of points, that is a line connecting any two points within the region does not cut any boundary. (A full moon in plan is a convex set of points, a crescent moon is not.) Advances of practical usefulness are anticipated in the field of general convex and non-convex programming, but it is unlikely that non-linear programming will contribute more than a small part of the total volume of mathematical programming undertaken within organisations in the near future.

A quite different aspect of the adequacy of linear programming in providing the basis for decision making relates to the significance attached to *fractional* decision variables. If the indicated magnitude of the latter is large (for example, several hundred) it is quite likely that a rounding-off procedure will not create significant practical difficulties. If however the magnitude of the decision variables is small then it is quite likely that rounding off will lead to either:

(*a*) a solution which is not feasible and which in practice could lead to operational problems, or

(*b*) a solution which although feasible is not optimal.

It is therefore apparent that it would be advantageous to have available a procedure which could determine an optimum in pure integer terms. For example, the allocation of ten men to three activities A, B, and C would be indicated as 7, 1, and 2 respectively rather than 6.8, 0.4, and 2.8 which may have been the outcome from using linear programming. Such a procedure has been developed and named *integer programming*.

INTEGER   An iterative optimising procedure for solving
PROGRAMMING: linear (and more recently non-linear) pro-
               gramming problems when the decision vari-
               ables must take integer values.

An important development of integer programming is *mixed integer programming* when only certain variables need to be integer valued. Mixed integer programming is enabling some of the inflexibility of the usual linear programming procedure to be reduced. For example, if only a proportion of constraints need hold (perhaps it is decided to treat in this way the procurement of additional and more costly resources) or two constraints are of an "either-or" nature only one of which need be satisfied, then mixed integer programming provides a possible optimising approach. Also linear programming can only cope with marginal costs and if a fixed cost is incurred (as is the case when a production set-up cost is involved) an alternative means of cost minimisation is required. Again mixed integer programming may be used to assist in achieving this.

As might be expected although the model has greater scope integer programming involves a more complex solution procedure than linear programming and thus the size of the problem which may be handled is relatively smaller. Nevertheless, problems involving several hundred decision variables and several thousand equations have been solved, and the technique is likely to be used more widely as its potential becomes appreciated.

Coping With Uncertainty

To this point optimisation by mathematical programming procedures has been characterised by the deterministic nature of the problems. This is often quite satisfactory when the allocation of resources among competing activities is to be determined within a known framework (for example, all of a given range of products whatever production levels are decided may be sold at fixed prices and produced at fixed costs). But higher level decisions frequently need account to be taken of a planning horizon the distance of which places much uncertainty on the parameters involved. Sensitivity and post-optimality analysis permit changes in the levels of the constraints to be studied either with a view to changing the levels of controllable variables or to assess the significance of various levels of uncontrollable variables. But it may seem preferable in the case of uncontrollable variables to represent them by probability distributions. A procedure termed *stochastic linear programming* has been developed, which allows some account to be taken of uncertainty.

> STOCHASTIC LINEAR PROGRAMMING: An approach in which variables within the model may be described by known discrete distributions. Optimisation is achieved with zero probability of violating a constraint.

As the coefficients of the objective function may be random variables the aim is usually restated as being to optimise the expected value of the objective function. The procedure considers all possible combinations of (discrete) probabilistic parameters and it will be evident that the dimensions of the problem are therefore likely to be very large. Further if zero possibility of violating any constraint is accepted, it may be felt that the final solution may be unduly restricted.

In consequence of this restriction, a procedure has been developed in which some probability (normally small) of various constraints being exceeded is accepted. *Chance constrained programming*, as it is called, is therefore an extension of stochastic linear programming as defined above for which solutions are available in certain special cases.

There have been a number of recorded instances of the successful application of the techniques referred to in this section to allocation problems within an uncertain framework.

Computational Efficiency

Most practical linear programming problems are very expensive in computer time and if it is accepted that before taking action a decision maker may wish to undertake sensitivity and post-optimality analysis it will be appreciated that computational and analytical efficiency will be of considerable importance. The number of iterations required, and hence the amount of time consumed in reaching the optimum, is, as may be deduced intuitively from consideration of the graphical problem discussed earlier, largely determined by the number of constraints involved. The definition of the dual given above provides a clue as to how the efficiency of the operation may be improved in some cases. For a linear programme involving twelve constraints and four decision variables that is twelve rows by four columns could by transposition be converted to four rows and twelve columns which could then be handled by the dual simplex method in a more efficient manner. The dual simplex method is similar to the simplex method in its execution but as opposed to the latter the dual simplex may commence with a "better-than-optimal but infeasible" basic solution from which it works towards the optimum. As it is concerned with the "beyond-the-optimum" region sensitivity and post-optimality, analysis may usually be conducted with computational economy by the dual simplex method.

Reference may also be made to a method termed *parametric linear programming*. This has been developed to study the response to systematic changes in the objective function coefficients or the constraints. For example, if in the example used earlier involving the production of washing machines it had been possible to increase the contribution from the standard model at the expense of the de luxe model by reallocation of resources the possibilities of the trade-off could be rapidly assessed.

Finally procedures have been developed which are more efficient than the simplex method in the manner in which the optimum solution is reached. Notable among these is the *revised simplex* method which may involve much less computation as the quantity of information stored at each iteration may, in comparison with the simplex method, be much reduced. This is especially so when the linear programming formulation contains many zero coefficients as is the case when resource allocation is planned over a number of time periods. Thus production of product A in year N would obviously be shown to be zero in all years other than year N. Other methods which have arisen from the search for more efficient procedures include the *primal-dual algorithm* in which the primal and dual problems are handled simultaneously and *decomposed linear programming* when the total problem is reduced to a number of sub-problems.

It will be clear from the foregoing that mathematical programming is a region of mathematicians' delight! And it is important that the practical possibilities of some of the methods mentioned are not submerged in the depth of sophisticated analysis. The major contribution continues to be provided by the simplex or revised simplex methods operating on straightforward linear formulations. Whilst some of the research undertaken into mathematical programming aimed at optimising has undoubtedly been pursued for purely academic reasons and for which practical application has to date been non-existent much of the research has been conditioned by the inflexibility of the deterministic and linear formulation. There is reason to believe that progress will continue to be made in increasing the scope for mathematical programming,* particularly as more and more organisations seek optimal rather than arbitrary objectives.

THE OBJECTIVE FUNCTION

Pertinent to the discussion to this point and that which follows are a few additional comments on the objective function which is to be optimised. If the objectives are purely financial then it may be possible to formulate an objective function in terms of product profitability (for instance the washing machine example) or return on capital for competing projects if organisational activity is viewed as a mix of possible projects (an example of the use of linear programming in these circumstances is given in the next Chapter). Providing that the problem reduces to one of utilising physical resources to achieve a financial outcome, optimisation presents

---

* For an indication of the breadth of problems to which mathematical programming has been applied, *see* S. M. L. BEALE, ed., *Application of Mathematical Programming Techniques*, The English Universities Press Ltd., London, 1971.

no conceptual difficulty. If the outcome sought seeks to satisfy qualitative requirements of a social, political, or aesthetic nature then an objective *function* cannot be defined, unless quantification is undertaken. For example, how would a company's objective to aid depressed areas by locating certain of its activities therein be incorporated within an objective function? Or how may account be taken of a local authority objective to achieve a high standard of design in its building programme? Or again one objective of national government is to reduce unemployment, how are different levels to be compared?

In some cases, it is possible to incorporate a qualitative objective in an objective function by agreed but arbitrary or subjective quantification. This was done in the national economic model developed by the author to which reference was made in Chapter 2. It was assumed that the "welfare" of an economy could be reasonably represented by the total volume of goods and services produced (the national product), the levels of unemployment and inflation and the balance of trade. The objective function used was:

$$2Y^{.5} - (15(U-2))^2 - 2F^2 + (X - M + 40)/4$$

where
$$Y = \text{G.N.P.}$$
$$U = \text{Per cent Unemployment}$$
$$F = \text{Annual Rate of Inflation}$$
$$X = \text{Visible Exports}$$
$$M = \text{Visible Imports}$$

It is not proposed to discuss the reasons for the values used (or indeed why the particular terms were incorporated). Naturally the objective function must reflect to some degree the subjective attitudes of the ultimate decision maker. Once again, it is implied that the decision maker should "appraise" the model. It would be nonsensical to attempt optimisation of an objective function proposed by another person and which was unacceptable to the individual responsible for reaching a decision. The optimisation of the objective function referred to above cannot be achieved by mathematical programming, but requires use of methods described in the section which follows.

An approach which has been used with some success when difficulties have arisen in incorporating certain objectives within an objective function is to set boundary conditions on these objectives and view them as constraints. This is said to lead to an "efficient" rather than an optimum solution. Thus there may be a minimum quantity of resources allocated to activities within an area where in part the objectives may be social rather than financial. This may be of value in the case of local authority planning. Each department (education, social services, development, etc.) will have its own objectives but these are unlikely to be compatible with overall resource availability. If the council's chief executive or management team is prepared to view the activities of each department in terms of the service provided it may be possible to agree levels of "equivalent service" and use these as the decision variables. Because of resource availability, it will be known that the level of activity which will be possible will be only a proportion of target service. If, however, the minimum acceptable proportions of activity are built into a linear programme along with all other competing demands for available resources (throughout the years within the planning horizon) it may be possible to optimise an objective function in terms of proportional activity for each department during the years for which the plan is being developed.

OPTIMISATION BY EXPERIMENT (HILL CLIMBING)

The reader may well have concluded from the preceding part of this chapter that although considerable efforts are being undertaken to increase the scope of optimisation through mathematical programming an appreciable gap exists between some of the theory and practice. It must be admitted that optimisation through direct analysis in certain circumstances does not appear feasible, at least in the present state of knowledge. The objective function (perhaps because of non-economic and subjective attitudes) may contain non-linear terms, discontinuities may exist, or it may be the wish of the decision makers to treat uncontrollable variables as continuous and probabilistic. If the latter circumstances apply, and as a result analytical solutions are not possible, this does not necessarily mean that the attempt to optimise must be replaced by the *satisficing** approach. On the assumption that the concept of an optimum is meaningful it may be possible to reach the optimum by "trial and error," "search" or other forms of experiment.†

---

* To "satisfice" has been defined as to do "well enough" but not "as well as possible." See RUSSELL L. ACKOFF, *A Concept of Corporate Planning*, John Wiley & Sons, Inc., New York, 1970, Chapter 1.

   † See R. L. ACKOFF AND M. W. SASIENI, *Fundamentals of Operations Research*, John Wiley & Sons Inc., New York, 1968, pp. 113–117.

Optimisation by experiment involves evaluating the consequences of various mixes of the controllable (policy) variables, on the basis of which progress is made towards the mix which is best. The problem is not so much the ultimate determination of the optimum but the efficiency (in terms of the effort expended) with which it is achieved. The example used earlier in this chapter will suffice to introduce the ideas behind optimisation by experiment when the uncontrollable variables are viewed deterministically. Figure 57 was used to represent graphically the determination of the optimum mix of standard and de luxe washing machines. It was pointed out that graphical solution for two policy variables presented little difficulty whereas three policy variables would require considerable skill in draughtsmanship and four or more policy variables could not be manipulated in this way. Figure 57 may however be viewed in a different manner, for instead of being seen as lines the axes of the graph and the constraints may be considered to be vertical planes rising out of the paper. The contribution arising from any mix of the two types of washing machine may then be represented by height above the paper. At zero production of each model the height will be zero (corresponding to the origin). As distance from the origin increases in any positive direction the contribution, and

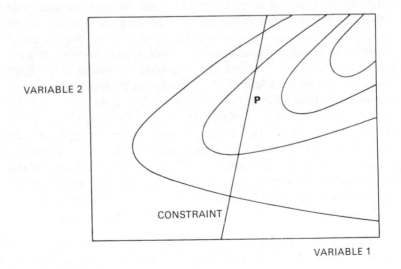

FIG. 59. Two dimensional combinations with constraint.

hence height above the paper, will grow. The contribution line for £3,000 will for example be at half the height of the contribution line for £6,000. It will thus be appreciated that the determination of the optimum is equivalent to finding the "highest" point within feasible region. It is for this reason that the procedure is often described as "hill climbing" (minimisation, when troughs need to be located, may be viewed as the mirror image of maximisation). Although the three dimensional approach to Fig. 57 suggested a plane surface rising away from the origin, practical circumstances may be more truly represented by contours as in Fig. 59 (two policy variables involved). Assuming contours rising to the right of Fig. 59 and the constrained region also to the right of the line it will be evident that the objective function will be maximised in the region of point P. The aim must therefore be to determine by experiment point P with the desired accuracy. A number of methods have been developed in order to do this. Broadly, these may be placed in two categories which may themselves be subdivided:

(*a*) *Multiple iterative:*
   (*i*) Random
   (*ii*) Systematic
(*b*) *Single iterative:*
   (*i*) Single step
   (*ii*) Steepest ascent

These may best be described by reference to the contoured outcomes of combinations of two policy variables as shown in Fig. 60. The multiple iterative approaches involve the evaluation of the objective function at a number of points simultaneously and the optimum used as the centre for a further region of search. The selection of points at random is usually less efficient than the systematic method in which points are laid out on a grid. The initial optima (points A) are shown in (*a*) and (*b*). The problem of locating the true optimum may not be great in respect of a unimodal objective functions involving two policy variables but if ten levels of each variable are evaluated in combination the one hundred computations for two variables rises to one million computations for six variables.

The single iterative methods are of a different type, in which an attempt is made to reach the optimum by successive improvements in the objective function. The single step method of (*c*) commences

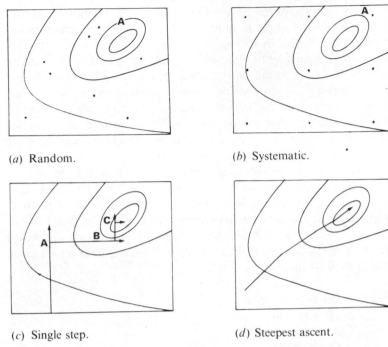

(a) Random.   (b) Systematic.

(c) Single step.   (d) Steepest ascent.

FIG. 60. Optimisation by experiment.

with the variable which gives the most rapid increase in the objective function and follows this until a decrease or a constraint is experienced, when the variable with the next greatest effect is increased in like manner. The steepest ascent method shown in (d) attempts the determination of the shortest route to the optimum by successively estimating the maximum gradient and improving the objective function in this direction.

If the objective function is unimodal, then the single iterative methods are the most efficient. There is, however, no guarantee that unimodality exists. For example, production above a certain level may only be achieved by increased capacity requiring further investment. A section through the evaluated objective function for two variables may then appear as in Fig. 61. In this figure, the unbroken line indicates the improvement in the objective function value which is obtained by selling two products until extra investment is incurred after point X. Thereafter, the objective function value increases to Y when production exceeds demand and stock holding costs are incurred. It is possible that the single iterative methods may fail to

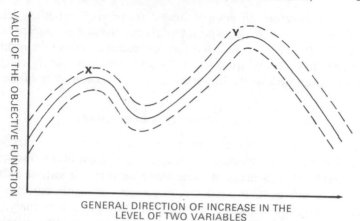

FIG. 61. A local optimum X.

locate Y, which exceeds X. In fact, it may be desirable to combine the multiple and single iterative approaches in the hope that the former will give some indication of the overall configuration following which the latter will be used to explore local optima.

Sight must not be lost in the foregoing discussion of the fact that a deterministic environmental framework has been assumed. The values of the objective function for specific levels of the controllable variables will therefore be determined by fixed values assumed for inflation, demand, and so on. Management may feel disposed to adopt a probabilistic approach towards uncertainty and treat the uncontrollable variables as probability distributions. The procedure is similar, but whereas with the deterministic approach a set of values of the controllable variables would generate a single value for the objective function the analysis now involves the sampling of probabilistic simulation. If the size of the sample taken is large enough and sampling error is minimal then approximations to confidence intervals may be generated. These are indicated by the broken lines of Fig. 61. Decision making would then be carried out as described in Chapter 7, taking account of utility considerations. It will be appreciated however that Fig. 61 represents just one section through the total field of combinations of the two controllable policy variables and in order to determine each confidence interval a sample of perhaps one thousand is necessary. In these circumstances, the already formidable computational effort of deterministic experimental optimisation is increased one-thousand-fold.

Given therefore an environmental framework, whether deterministic or probabilistic, experimental optimisation is conceptually feasible. Whether it is used, and the confidence placed in the results, will be determined by some form of cost/benefit analysis in which a major feature will be the importance of the decision to be taken.

GENERAL COMMENTS AND SUMMARY

If it is assumed that the availability of resources is known precisely and that the total performance arising from the use of the resources is capable of measurement then some optimal allocation of the resources will exist. In such circumstances, the optimum may be determined provided that there is sufficient investment in analytical or computational effort. Decisions of a design nature, as for example the scheduling of a passenger transport system, the location of depots and various blending processes, may therefore be facilitated by resorting to quantified techniques which have been developed during recent decades. If however the decisions are of a planning nature then uncertainty is involved in respect of the availability of resources, the demand for resources, and the effectiveness of their use. Certain planning decisions may be reduced to decisions of a design nature if estimates are made which enable the problem to be structured in a deterministic manner. The estimates will arise from the use of forecasting procedures, and the confidence with which these are viewed will determine the degree of faith placed in the solution. A further difficulty which arises in the case of decisions at higher levels, particularly those of a corporate nature, is the measurement of total performance. This presupposes that the levels of objectives and attainments are capable of being quantified and hence measured. Traditionally the public sector has adopted objectives which are of mixed nature (aesthetic, social and economic) and a like tendency has of recent times been noted in some companies in the private sector. Whilst it is possible to conceptualise the maximisation of an economic objective such as earnings per share it is not easy to conceptualise the maximisation of, for example, overall service offered by a local authority. It is not suggested however that all ideas of optimisation at corporate levels should be dropped, but rather that a less ambitious aid to decision making may be more appropriate. If difficulty exists in quantifying objectives, it may be realistic to specify minimum commitments of resources towards those ends. The resources may be actual expenditure or the opportunity cost of using the cash in a sub-optimal manner (for example, locating plant in a depressed area). An organisation may then be able to forecast deterministically resources and constraints which together with a quantified objective function may enable an "efficient" solution to be obtained by the use of an optimising technique.

One such optimising technique which is analytical in nature is linear programming, and there have been many successful applications of this recorded at various levels within organisations of all types. The advantages and limitations of the technique have been widely discussed but there is one feature of considerable attractiveness which few would dispute. That is its scope, which enables thousands of variables and constraints to be included within the analysis. This permits large parts of an organisation's activities to be modelled and reduces the significance of components of the model which do not conform with the requirements of linearity. Attempts continue to increase the power of this general approach to optimisation by various extensions which are mentioned in the Chapter, but because of the more complex procedures which are necessary the capacity in terms of variables and constraints is reduced. There is no doubt that as larger computers are developed mathematical programming (including both linear and non-linear approaches) will increase in scope and flexibility.

It is not unreasonable that managers should base design or control decisions on the solutions of analysis. The assumption is that the resource availability and environmental framework are known with some certainty. And in some cases there is the knowledge that the decision may be reversed if the new outcomes are unfavourable in comparison with the old. When, however, forecasting is necessary it would be unreasonable for managers to accept without question the solution arising from analysis as this will be totally dependent upon the estimates of the input values used. At the very least, therefore, it is necessary that the decision maker should approve the forecasts and all of the relationships which are included within the model. The latter requires that the manager shall with specialist assistance be able to interpret the formulation of the linear programme. Additionally it is desirable that the manager shall be able to conduct sensitivity analysis on the optimal solution. He has therefore an interest in respect of both input and output and it is suggested that familiarisation with both of these stages can be achieved with little effort (there is of course little necessity for an acquaintanceship with the mathematical procedure). Examples given within the Chapter are designed to satisfy this requirement.

If because of the complexity of the relationships or the desire to use probability distributions to cope with uncertainty the optimising process of linear programming is inapplicable it may still be possible to determine the optimum by experimentation. Again it is required that the framework shall be established deterministically or probabilistically by making assumptions about the uncontrollable variables. The method is then one of making a directed search for the optimum by altering values of the controllable variables. Apart from the cost of this method there is a danger that the search may converge on a local optimum, missing the global optimum. The cost is further increased if a probabilistic approach requiring Monte Carlo simulation is preferred. In these circumstances, the final decision taken will include the utility attitudes of the decision maker.

A final comment is that if decision makers are prepared to structure the problem in quantified terms, then by a process of analysis or experimentation it may be possible, at some cost, to obtain an optimum solution. The value of a solution in a planning context will depend on the confidence placed in forecasts which have to be made and the extent to which the model is descriptive of the real life situation.

Chapter Nine

QUANTITATIVE ANALYSIS AND PLANNING
DECISIONS—PRESENT AND FUTURE

INTRODUCTION

This book commenced with the proposition that decisions of any kind could be classified as being either logical or illogical. In defining a logical decision, it was suggested that account should be taken of "all known and relevant methods of analysis and interpretation." The major part of the discussion has been concerned with certain quantitative methods of analysis which have been found to provide an effective basis for decision making at higher levels in organisations. The main proposition of the book is that over many organisations the adoption of these approaches will lead to a general improvement in the consequences which arise from decision making. Logical decision making which employs analytical procedures of a quantitative nature may nevertheless prove to be less than optimal for two reasons, particularly if only one decision is taken into account.

First, because of uncertainty the alternative selected may prove to be inferior to other alternatives which could have been pursued. For example, actual demand may fall at the upper end of the prior probability distribution which had been proposed for it and hence the potential profits which could have been obtained from another alternative involving increased capacity would be foregone.

The second reason may be developed by referring first to Table II. In this Table, recognition is given to the fact that decisions not based on analysis may qualify for the description "logical." Sufficient has been written it is hoped to avoid giving the impression that "best" decisions will arise automatically from quantified analysis. Although this may be so for decisions of a design nature in such fields as stock control and machine scheduling, this is certainly not true of the planning decision needed at higher levels within organisations. In these circumstances, there will inevitably exist a "decision gap." This gap may be filled with analysis which is non-quantitative, assumed intuition, insight or any other behavioural mechanism which influences the manager in finally reaching a decision. The significance of the gap may in fact exceed the significance of the results of any analysis which might be undertaken. An example may be the examination of alternative national distribution systems for a large company. It may be that quantified analysis suggests that there will be little difference in overall efficiency and effectiveness between a system involving three regional depots and company transport and one in which contract hire is used to distribute from one central depot. In this case, virtually the full weight of the decision must be taken by a non-quantified approach. Again, how significant is the loss of certain amenities arising from locating a new airport? It is evident that the nature and extent of quantification in a decision of this nature, including cost/benefit analysis, will influence the action finally decided upon. An analytical solution may prevent a decision from being taken, which intuitively is to be preferred. No doubt it could quite readily be shown analytically that in terms of national good more effective use could be made of the hundreds of millions of pounds which will be spent on relieving river pollution, but some scope must be left for subjective and political opinion. As companies incline more to objectives which are not wholly in the interests of the shareholders they will need to be able to take account more of objectives which cannot be quantified. It might almost be argued that the approaches described in this book would in fact have been much more relevant years ago and that in some respects the boat has been missed. On the other hand, the argument may be put forward that the creative activity of the entrepreneurs of the nineteenth century would have been stifled by the rigors of working through a lengthy analysis before taking a decision of any importance. Of course, the growth of such quantified analyses as are described over the last quarter of a century has been tied very much to the introduction of the electronic computer. As organisations grow in complexity and size decisions of a corporate nature imply the allocation and utilisation of so many resources that it would be a brave manager who would state a preference for instinctive rather than analytical decision making. The problem is how the latter shall be incorporated into the managerial nest, at the same time avoiding cuckoo-like consequences! Before addressing our attention to this matter, it is of value to give some indication of the current extent of the use of quantitative methods to aid decisions of a planning nature.

CURRENT USAGE OF QUANTITATIVE METHODS WITHIN ORGANISATIONS

Despite a frequently encountered initial bias against the use of mathematical or statistical techniques to resolve organisational problems, nearly all organisations of any size have taken some advantage of those techniques which are available. Operational research units (or generic groups providing service to management) abound in all sectors of the economy in most Western countries. The continuing demand for staff to work in such units is some evidence of the measure of success achieved by adopting a quantitative analytical approach to problems. A large degree of frustration has nevertheless existed, due to the limited solution field of many problems which are put to management services groups. The adoption of corporate planning by many organisations during recent years is however influencing the situation, and has created a demand for the analytical approach at higher levels. This has come about from the rapid recognition by corporate planners that mathematical models of the organisation are a prerequisite if corporate decisions are to be made consistently and effectively. As mathematical model building is almost synonymous with operational research, it is natural that, increasingly, this profession should find itself involved in the construction of corporate and important sub-corporate models.

It is not possible to state precisely the number of organisations which are using the techniques described in this book for major planning decisions. A number of organisations have, for example, a long history of usage of networks for developing and launching new products, forecasting to aid financial planning, and simulation in capital investment appraisal, without having taken the final steps towards corporate model building. A number of surveys have been undertaken to assess the extent of corporate modelling in the United States and other countries. Non-response to survey requests creates problems of estimation, but it would seem that several hundreds of organisations in the United States, several dozens in the United Kingdom, together with isolated instances in other Western countries, are currently using or developing models which qualify to be described as corporate.

In a survey undertaken in 1969 and 1970* in the United States a

---

* ALBERT N. SCHRIEBER, ed., *Corporate Simulation Models*, University of Washington, Seattle, 1970, pp. 26–42.

sample response of 102 companies of nineteen different types indicated the widely differing nature of organisations using or developing a model. Some forty of the companies involved were located in the fields of banking, manufacturing, and electric and gas utilities, but nothing conclusive could be established as to the nature of organisations likely to use corporate modelling. A conclusion supported by the experience of the author in the United Kingdom is that adoption of the approach depends very much on individual initiative. This is to be expected, as high level decisions are usually taken with the knowledge of the chief executive and much will depend on his attitudes. If his management style is positively inclined towards the use of models or is sympathetic towards new decision techniques then it is quite possible that the approach will be adopted. If he is biased against quantitative methods then it is most unlikely that corporate modelling will be established. The situation exists therefore where similar types of organisations use a completely different approach towards corporate decision making. This is evident for example in local government both in the United Kingdom and the United States. An advantage of this situation which will not have escaped readers is that reasonable evaluations of the worth of models in these circumstances will be possible following a few years' experience. It is worth noting that in the survey quoted above over ninety companies felt that the model building effort had been worthwhile. Other points of interest from the survey are as follows:

(a) Sixty-five per cent of models were of the "top-down" type, that is, they were developed by initially considering the whole organisation. The remaining models were of the "bottom-up" type, in which functional parts of the organisation were used as the starting basis.

(b) Ninety-five per cent were descriptive models designed to answer "What-if?" questions. Only 5 per cent attempted optimisation.

(c) Eighty-eight per cent of models were deterministic (the remainder being probabilistic).

(d) The average time required to develop to the working stage a model was three and a half man-years, but the range was as wide as a half–twenty-three man-years.

(e) Ninety-four per cent of models were computerised, virtually entirely for operation in the batch mode.

The second part of point (e) is of interest, as the indication is that there was little use at that time of on-line facilities within the companies taking part in the survey. This situation is changing as evidenced by the claim of one company offering on-line facilities* of having built 300 models for clients in the United States during 1970. This claim is substantiated to some extent, as the author is aware of some half-dozen such systems introduced in the United Kingdom during 1971 and 1972. Reference was made in Chapter 2 to the technological developments which gave impetus to this change. A survey undertaken in the United Kingdom in 1971† of companies in the private sector (engineering, petrochemical, banks and insurances) also found that the average effort expended in corporate model development was three and a half man-years broken down as follows:

Development of the approach	25 per cent
Collection and analysis of data	25 per cent
Computer programming	40 per cent
Implementation of the model	10 per cent

These results were obtained from eleven of the fifteen companies surveyed who were committed to corporate planning. In eight of the eleven companies, corporate planning departments had been set up and in the remaining three cases the chief executive was aided by specialists with other designations. Models described as being of an operational research nature were involved in some part of the planning process in eleven companies.

Most of the above information refers to the private sector, but in addition a considerable number of high level decisions in the public sector are being aided by the use of models. The longest experience has of course been gained at government level, where econometric models have been used to considerable effect in a number of Western countries. Urban planning, with all its complexities and problems of co-ordinating economic, social and political activities, is making increasing use of models to aid decision making. In the United Kingdom some of the public corporations, notably those controlling the supply of electricity and gas, have similarly constructed and used high level models.

---

* See JAMES B. BOULDEN, "Computerised Corporate Planning," *Long Range Planning*, Vol. 3, No. 4, 1971, pp. 2–9.

† See "The Development of a Generalised Computer System to aid the Corporate Planning Process," *IBM Scientific Centre Report No. 0024*, Peterlee, October 1971.

The picture is therefore (in all spheres of economic activity) one of a net upward trend in decision making based to a large degree on quantified analysis. Failures have been recorded on occasions when models have been constructed, but it is not the concept of the approach which has borne the blame, rather the practical implementation of the concept. Some of the reasons militating against the successful adoption and application of the methodology will be discussed in the section which follows.

PROBLEMS ASSOCIATED WITH THE QUANTITATIVE APPROACH TO PLANNING DECISIONS

These may be classified broadly into two categories, termed technical and non-technical. The limitations and associated problems of the techniques themselves are studied first. Following this, reasons why potentially useful analysis is not adopted will be examined.

Technical Problems

A number of problems arising from the shortcomings of techniques have been encountered in the Chapters of this book. These have included the difficulty, following the construction of appropriate networks, of allocating limited resources in an optimal manner, the need to use discrete probabilities in order to reduce the size of decision trees and the handling of non-linear parameters by mathematical programming. In addition to direct limitations such as these, there are a number of associated difficulties which have been of significance. A major feature of decision making is the variation which exists in subjective attitude towards a specific problem. This has implications in respect of utility, the normative equation proposed to explain a relationship to be included in a model, the precise form of the network or programming formulation which is drawn up, and so on. Hence, unless a decision maker is prepared to examine carefully whether subjective attitudes of others are incorporated within the analysis on which he will base a decision, he may unwittingly make a decision which in reality is inconsistent with his attitudes. Despite this, whilst some variation in formulation is often possible, a general defect of many quantitative techniques is their analytical inflexibility. Provided the problem is formulated in a particular manner then a solution may be guaranteed, but a danger may exist in "fitting the problem to the technique," that is, the model used in the analysis may not represent adequately the true situation.

The techniques described in this book, along with many others used at operational levels within organisations, are not new. Most had been developed by the end of the 1950s and since that date dramatic extensions to their power have not been achieved. More complex mathematics has enabled new problem solving procedures to be derived from existing techniques (mathematical programming is a good example of this), but general experience so far has been that the greater scope of analysis afforded by these procedures has not been matched by increased opportunity for their implementation. This is largely due to the considerable increase in computation needed, with which at present even the largest of computers are unable to cope economically. A proposition which will be discussed later in this Chapter is that much of the extension of use of quantitative analysis in the near future will arise from the combination of existing techniques, rather than from the development of new ones.

The major obstacle to a precisely quantified basis for decisions of a planning nature is the existence of uncertainty. As long as uncontrollable variables are recognised, precision will depend on the accuracy of forecasts for these. As most high level planning decisions are unique, the opportunity for forecasting uncontrollable variables on the basis of experience is limited. It cannot for example be estimated with confidence how advantages in medical knowledge will influence health and hence the demand for hospital facilities, or whether new reserves of primary energy will be discovered, or when a competing product will be introduced. Thus, except in the very short term, quantitative analysis can only provide some grounds for logical decision making and any suggestion of accuracy must be questioned. In these circumstances probably the major contribution of quantitative analysis is that the range of possible outcomes may be explored more readily. But even in an organisation which is totally committed to the quantitative approach decisions can only be taken in the knowledge that individual outcomes may be unfavourable. Using the argument of Chapter 1, there is the consolation that the proportion of favourable outcomes realised should be increased by making the best analytical use of information and expertise available. It might be argued that the problem of uncertainty should not imply a technical weakness of quantitative techniques in general. To a large degree this is true, although the difficulty of handling continuous probability distributions is recognised. Nevertheless, the major cause of uncertainty arises from the inability to predict human attitudes and behaviour when acting individually or in groups. Considerable research work is being undertaken at the present time in this area, much of it of a quantitative nature.* It is probable that forecasting techniques will improve as a consequence of this work, and that planning decisions based on analytical solutions should be upgraded.

Non-Technical Problems
The purpose of this section is to examine why it is that analysis of a potentially useful nature is not used within organisations. The most obvious explanation is that senior management is not aware of its existence. The problem in this case is one of education, and explains how this book came to be written. It was apparent to the author from discussion with senior managers that despite the popularity of formal management education in the United Kingdom during the last decade the potential of quantitative analysis at higher levels was not appreciated. Very few senior managers (other than those with formal training in mathematics) knew of the techniques described in this book by more than name. It was evident that in many cases support was given to the use of quantitative methods at lower levels in organisations but little opportunity had been afforded to incorporate such an approach at the higher levels of decision making. Further, many courses in management in universities and colleges offer only limited opportunity for the acquisition of some skill in the quantitative area. Frequently statistics is taught, occasionally mathematics, but the practical usefulness of these disciplines is usually demonstrated by examples of traditional operational research techniques at the tactical level. Perhaps because of the apparent remoteness of students of management from high level decision making it is felt to be inappropriate that part of their studies should be concerned with such matters. Because of this, an opportunity to develop a corporate view of the needs of the organisation may be lost, a defect which may well prove to be of significance to the organisation and the individual as the latter climbs the managerial ladder. It is not proposed to discuss at length reasons why senior managers should not wish at least to undertake a feasibility study of the potential value of adopting numerical analysis in their planning processes. Suffice it to repeat that it is the opinion of the author based on appreciable experience that the "mystique" of mathematical and

* *See*, for example, JAMES H. DAVIS, "Group Decision and Social Interaction: A Theory of Social Decision Schemes," *Psychological Review*, Vol. 80, No. 2, March 1973, pp. 97–125.

statistical procedures and computer usage, which is one of the major reasons, can be overcome by reasonable application. But it is of course recognised that as the world must go on decisions will continue to be taken and objectives will continue to be achieved without making any use of quantitative methods. Nevertheless, if there is any acceptance of the need to use resources in an efficient manner to meet the growing and complex needs of modern society,* there can be little satisfaction in the thought that a given objective may have been achieved more effectively or a higher objective may have been set if the process of decision making had been improved.

The problem of lack of awareness is more easily dealt with than the problem of rejection after trial. In the former case, the proposition is "at least give it a try." But there are many instances when such methods have been tried and satisfaction has not been achieved. This may be due to an unfavourable outcome arising by chance, to which much discussion has been devoted. An important point again mentioned frequently is the much greater ease with which the larger organisation, making many significant high level decisions, is able to tolerate an individual outcome of this nature than is the smaller organisation. There are also behavioural and organisational reasons why decision making based on quantitative analysis is not favoured. Organisations in the United States have probably suffered more from this than their counterparts in the United Kingdom. The main feature here is communication between the decision maker and the specialist undertaking the analysis. The traditional chain of events in the decision process is problem, analysis, solution, implementation, with feedback at any stage. In the United States, as a generalisation, the specialists have tended to be involved in stages 2 and 3 only. That is, they play little part in the formulation of the problem and the implementation of the solution. In many cases, this has led to analysis-orientation which in turn has generated highly sophisticated (and impractical) solutions. A rift has thus grown between the practitioners and theoreticians, of such proportions that in the late 1960s courses in quantitative methods in leading American business schools showed a marked decline in popularity. In the United Kingdom such an acute situation has not arisen, largely due to the conscious efforts of the specialist analysts to retain practical orientation. The problem is however a

* As an example of a viewpoint outside the private sector, *see* editorial, *Local Government Finance*, Vol. 77, No. 11, November 1973, pp. 383–384.

difficult one when high level decisions are involved as the analysts must, to be effective, communicate with the topmost levels in the organisations. Where effective corporate planning departments have been introduced this requirement has in general been satisfied, but other instances exist where quantitative decision making at the higher levels is adversely affected by an unwillingness to grant sufficient status to the specialist groups.

A primary objective of this book is to enable practising and intending managers who have little specialist knowledge to gain an appreciation of the potential value of mathematical and statistical techniques in aiding decision making at high levels. A secondary objective would be to impart to specialists an understanding of the reasons why senior management may not be willing to accept without question methods which to specialists may seem to be obviously and considerably relevant.

FUTURE DEVELOPMENTS

It was mentioned earlier in this Chapter that most of the basic quantitative techniques appropriate for high level decision making processes are not new. During the last decade most research work has been directed towards the extension of existing techniques either independently or in combination. This final section will discuss the potential value to senior management of extensions based on the methods covered in this book, other quantitative and analytic procedures of promise and also what is likely to be demanded by senior management as a support to decisions which they will need to make.

DEVELOPMENTS BASED ON EXISTING METHODS

Many successes have been recorded in the application of quantitative techniques to decision making and research continues into the possibilities of increasing the scope of the techniques. Recognising that management is confronted by two types of decision making situation, namely those of a design nature and those of a planning nature, it is appropriate to make an assessment of developments in these two directions. Following a design decision the costs and benefits of analytic or heuristic solutions may be rapidly assessed by the decision maker. When significant uncontrollable variables are involved for which forecasts have to be made, as is the case for most planning decisions, the assessment is not so straightforward.

Thus the extent to which analysis should be undertaken to support a decision as to whether a warehouse should be located in an entirely new marketing region is by no means apparent. Whilst sophisticated analysis may be of value in siting a warehouse with great precision within an existing market, less specific analysis may seem appropriate when new markets are under consideration. Also of much significance is the manager's preference for deterministic (with sensitivity analysis) or, alternatively, probabilistic decision making, and this will be discussed later. Against this background, a number of developments are worthy of mention.

Of some importance is the role of the network. This has arisen because of the implications of time in all planning decisions. It was speedily recognised that there was little value in carrying out analyses relating to the future unless proper account was taken of the timing of events. In effect, this was the acceptance of the fact that an additional dimension needed to be brought quantitatively into the decision making process. Mention is made first of an extension to network analysis involving the incorporation of mathematical programming or network flow theory. This use of mathematical programming is a good example of interesting research work with (at present) very limited application. Having drawn up a network, it is possible to formulate it as a linear programme* and by use of the simplex method find that path (*i.e.* the critical path) through the network of maximum duration. It is also possible by adopting the concept of the "cost slope" of Chapter 5 and by using the method of parametric linear programming, to develop a piecewise linear variable cost "curve" of the form shown in Fig. 58. The computations involved are very extensive and even the largest computers are unable to handle more than fifty activities. A practical means of generating the total variable cost profile between the "normal" and "crash" duration of a network of several thousand activities is provided by network flow theory† when the required results are achieved through a systematic search routine. It will be evident that the main worth of this analysis is in respect of the individual project. Knowing fixed costs and making assumptions about the effect of completing the project earlier than would be indicated by the normal duration, a rapid means of determining the minimum

---

* *See* GAIL THORNLEY, ed., *Critical Path Analysis in Practice*, Tavistock, London, 1968, pp. 123–130.
† *See* J. J. MODER AND C. R. PHILLIPS, *Project Management with C.P.M. and PERT*, Van Nostrand Reinhold, New York, 1970, p. 218.

total cost of Fig. 37 could be very advantageous. The use of cost slopes does, however, presume that unlimited resources are available so that it would, for example, be possible for a number of activities to be crashed over the same time period. If therefore resource constraints exist for the single project or more than one project is competing for limited resources, the analysis could only be of value as part of a search procedure aimed at determining acceptable compromises.

A combination of network analysis and linear or integer programming which promises to be of greater use in practice is one by which selection is made from among a number of projects competing over time for limited resources. A practical application in the field of local government was suggested in Chapter 8 when it was proposed that "proportions of activity" could be determined on a period by period basis by the maximisation of some objective or welfare function. The same approach could be used to select levels of projects in companies when an objective function may be more easily recognised. By the use of discounting, N.P.V.s of alternative projects may be estimated. The objective function which is to be maximised would then be:

$$\sum_{i=1}^{n} (\text{N.P.V.})_i X_i,$$

where X_i is the proportion of activity of each project, i, which is undertaken and will be in the range of 0–1. The resource constraints of the linear programme will be of the form:

$$\sum_{i=1}^{n} a_{ijk} X_i \leqslant b_{jk} \qquad \text{for} \quad j = 1 \quad \text{to}$$
$$m \quad \text{and} \quad k = 1 \quad \text{to} \quad t$$

where a_{ijk} is the quantity of the jth type of resource required by the ith project during the kth time period, and b_{jk} is the availability of the jth resource during period k.

It will be readily apparent that the major defect of this approach is the assumption that proportionate levels of activity will consume equivalent proportionate quantities of resource and generate equivalent proportionate amounts of N.P.V. Despite this, the general form of solution may well be of value in indicating those projects which are strong candidates for selection and those which appear to be unattractive.

Further extensions of basic network techniques have been directed at handling uncertainty. The latter exists in relation to activity durations, resource requirements, and even the sequence of activities to be followed. Ability to handle all of these simultaneously would be of advantage, but apart from inevitable difficulty in interpreting results much complexity would be introduced into the analysis by the existence of conditional relationships. To date, therefore, each of the three aspects mentioned has tended to be treated separately. The first of these, uncertain durations, has received much attention through the PERT approach described in some detail in Chapter 5. This has many recorded successes in practice attributed to it.

Another means of taking account of uncertainty is to assume that activity durations may be achieved by varying the amount of resource input. Table XI gave a hypothetical discrete distribution of three levels of resource requirement. On this basis, and using a combination of linear programming and simulation Lockett and Freeman* proposed a method of R. & D. portfolio selection which could well have applicability for the general project. In this method, the number of alternative ways of completing activities using different levels of resource are each represented in the network by a different path. Figure 62 shows an activity (1–2) broken down into three paths according to the resource requirements of Table XI.

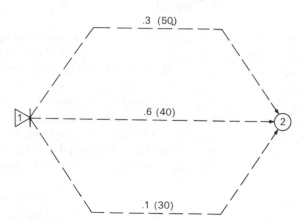

FIG. 62. An activity broken down into three alternatives depending on the quantity of resource consumed.

* See A. G. LOCKETT AND P. FREEMAN, "Probabilistic Networks and R & D Portfolio Selection," *Operational Research Quarterly*, Vol. 21, No. 3, September 1970, pp. 353–359.

The usual circle representing an event is replaced by a triangle at the leading end of the figure, to indicate that the path to be followed is uncertain. The decimal fractions indicate the probability of each alternative being required and the figures in brackets represent the resource levels needed in each case. Assume that a second activity 2–3 may also be viewed probabilistically, and that the various resource levels are indicated in Fig. 63.

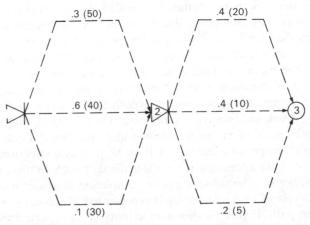

FIG. 63. The nine (3 × 3) paths through a probabilistic network of two activities.

Lockett and Freeman propose that each discrete level of resource requirement should be treated as a separate path. Thus instead of just one path 1–2–3 which would exist for two deterministic activities in series, there are now 9 possible paths from event 1 to event 3. Assuming that each activity is independent, the probabilities of each path arising may be determined by multiplying the probabilities together. Thus the probability of the path implying maximum resource requirement for each activity is 0.3 by 0.4 or 0.12. It is now possible by the use of a sampling process (simulation) to select from among a number of projects. If the network of Fig. 63 represents one of a number of projects, then on average 12 per cent of samples of the two activities will indicate resource requirements during activities 1–2 and 2–3 of fifty and twenty units respectively. If in addition project selection for each simulation is made by the linear programming procedure described above, there will be occasions when a project will be selected and occasions when it will not. In this way, probability distributions of the degree of selection of individual projects and the total outcome arising (say, N.P.V.) will be generated. In the case of some projects, selection will be either total or zero. Using this approach, it is possible to conceive of an organisation testing various mixes of projects against various total levels of constraints and then making a comparison between the distribution of total outcomes which arise. This possibility would need to be assessed against factors already mentioned, for example the returns from projects, and of course whether proportional projects are feasible at all. In addition, it will be apparent that for practical circumstances the number of computations could be enormous. Two activities broken down into three levels depending on resource requirements create nine paths, eight such activities would increase the number of paths to 6561. It is therefore evident that networks of coarse scale would be a pre-requisite if simulation followed by a linear programming solution were to be carried out. For high level planning decisions this may be quite appropriate and the possibility of overall "optimisation" in the use of resources which at the same time provides (through the probabilistic simulation) virtually a complete sensitivity analysis is very attractive.

In the treatment just described, a number of paths were recognised as being possible following the completion of a previous activity. The distinction between the paths was however on the grounds of resources anticipated. Sometimes account must be taken of the possibility of several completely different lines of action conditional upon the outcome of a previous activity. This outcome may, for example, be the development of a new product, the penetration of a market, or the success or failure of measures designed to reduce employment. Thus it will be possible to recognise a number of terminal situations in contrast to the more usual single terminal event which is planned using network analysis. An algebra has been designed* to permit the representation in network form of alternative courses of action which are conditional upon preceding activities and to which probabilities are applied. It will be appreciated that situations of this type have been encountered before and have been analysed with the help of the decision tree. The difference between the decision tree and networks treated probabilistically in the manner described is more structural than conceptual. The former usually involves more terminal events and chance outcomes

---

* See GAIL THORNLEY, ed., *Critical Path Analysis in Practice*, Tavistock, London, 1968, pp. 63–69.

and tends to be less detailed, whereas with networks the converse is the case. Other differences include explicit treatment in the probabilistic approach to networks of activities to be undertaken in parallel and the "inclusive/or" possibility when for example either activity A or activity B or both in parallel are feasible (this would be depicted in a decision tree by three alternatives).

As with previous treatment of uncertainty using networks, the computations are heavy, and it may be desirable to resort to simulation to estimate outcomes. The logic of the probabilistic network makes it much less appropriate for control than planning and for this reason management may prefer to use the basic deterministic approach. If networks are to be used in the control stage of a project it may be decided that uncertainty is best coped with by updating the logic when necessitated by circumstances. That is the network approach will be deterministic but will be applied dynamically (this is the traditional mode of usage).

OTHER QUANTITATIVE AND ANALYTIC AIDS TO PLANNING DECISIONS

Of the traditional technique areas of operational research no place has been found in this book for stock control, queueing theory, replacement and reliability. This is not because they have limited application within organisations. On the contrary, very many suboptimal situations have been significantly improved by their adoption. They are however techniques more useful for the re-design of existing operations and rarely become part of the planning process at higher levels within organisations. Readers familiar with the usual list of techniques which provide most of the basis for a formal study of operational research may be surprised that at no point has *dynamic programming* been mentioned. This method of analysis is useful in determining the optimal policy for a number of sequential and linked decisions. That is, it is a tool designed particularly for decisions of a planning nature. The procedure requires that the planning horizon is split into a number of stages and that the first decision to be taken is arrived at by considering the final decision possibilities first and working backwards. Both deterministic and probabilistic problems may be handled, and in fact an example of the latter has already been encountered in the shape of the decision tree. The advantage of the decision tree was seen to be due largely to the way in which a problem involving a number of decision points and chance events could be made comprehensible to senior management. A limitation of the decision tree was the number of alternatives and chance outcomes which could be accommodated. This restriction in scope applies to all problems solved by the dynamic programming method, whether deterministic or probabilistic. Interested readers who follow up references* in this subject will find that most applications of the technique have been at lower levels in the organisation, for example to resolve problems of inventory replenishment, equipment replacement and production scheduling. Calculations can be extensive and a computer is usually required. No computer package will handle all (or even many) dynamic programming problems, but libraries are being extended. As the method is one concerned with trade-offs between, rather than within, time periods it is anticipated that developments more directly relevant to planning decisions will be achieved. It is also appropriate under this heading to make reference to one area of analysis which conceptually is particularly relevant to high level decision making and bears the name (somewhat inappropriately) of *game theory* (which in fact is the shortened form of the "theory of games of strategy"). As with other techniques which provide the foundation for operational research, basic game theory has been in existence for about two decades.[†] It may in fact prove to be the case that the major part of the effort which has gone into the attempt to translate the competitive element existing in many games to real life situations within organisations is of academic interest only. Nevertheless, competitive situations will always exist and it is proper that efforts should continue to provide a basis on which logical decisions can be taken in these circumstances. A brief discussion follows.

Most of this book has been taken up in discussing various means by which decisions are taken following the placing of values on known or controllable variables against a background of variables which have been estimated as single values or as probability distributions. The problem in competitive situations is that estimates of uncontrollable variables may not be feasible due to the possibility of a competitor being able to follow one of several quite different courses of action. Providing that the latter may be enumerated and

---

* For an applied approach, *see* GEORGE L. NEMHAUSER, *Introduction to Dynamic Programming*, John Wiley Inc., New York, 1966.

† For a non-mathematical description of the area, *see* R. I. LEVIN AND R. B. DES JARDINS, *Theory of Games and Strategies*, International Textbook Company, Scranton, Pa., 1970.

it is assumed that competitors act to maximise expected utility (that is, they are "rational"), it may be possible to define a logical course of action. The latter is true when so called "two-person zero-sum" games are involved. In this case, the loss of one person equals the gain of the other. Even then, the logical action recommended may not be deterministic but may involve a mixed strategy in which selection from among the courses of action available is made at random from a probability distribution which is determined. The consolation of knowing that in some circumstances a continuing opportunity to apply the mixed strategy will be afforded (*e.g.* a game of dominoes), will not extend to a non-repetitive situation in real life such as a war. Further in a real life situation how many examples of conflict exist such that a zero-sum approach is realistic? The gains of one country in war are most unlikely to be seen as being the losses of the other. If future expectations are discounted, the advantage to a company successful in bidding for and taking over a third company is hardly likely to be equivalent to the loss of opportunity assessed by an unsuccessful company. In these circumstances, it may be possible to use a "non-zero-sum" approach to attempt an analysis of situations in which in total a net gain or loss arises. For example, if the promotional expenditure of two companies selling a similar type of product is increased then improvement in the market may outweigh in each case the extra expenditure. Conversely, no improvement may arise, in which case the additional expenditure has been pointless. The circumstances of a desire of two companies to acquire a third may be used to demonstrate additional aspects of the non-zero-sum game. In the initial stages, neither of the companies who are known to be interested in the takeover will be aware of the initial offer the other will make. The analysis at this stage will differ from that which will be used when the situation has become something of a public auction.

As mentioned above, it cannot be said that the early expectations of game theory have been realised. Many aspects of the competitive situation have been analysed but always requiring assumptions to which the solutions are highly sensitive. Rational behaviour of competitors is required, and apart from differing views as to what is rational the possibility that "illogical" rather than "logical" decisions will be taken is always present. Apart from this, payoffs may be viewed differently by different participants. The prospective value of a company for which bids are being made may be in its estimated cash flow to one company seeking acquisition whereas to another it may be the opportunities afforded by a ready made marketing and distribution system. Despite these dampening comments, the objective of game theory to assist in the resolution of competitive situations must be commended. Of all the quantitative analyses which have been developed, it is the one which has attempted to take greatest account of less quantifiable individual and corporate attitudes. For this reason, and the potential rewards of great applicability, research in this area will continue.

An additional method of analysis which has received much attention is *industrial dynamics* which was conceived by Jay Forrester working at the Massachusetts Institute of Technology during the late 1950s.* This approach, which involves dynamic simulation and attempts to take account of feedback operating within and external to organisations, is in concept highly relevant to corporate and systems planning. The procedure extends somewhat beyond the processes of model building described in this book as in addition to the customary cause-effect resource relationships within organisations an attempt is made to model the response of the system to information and stimuli created by the adoption of certain lines of action. The analysis developed makes use of certain aspects of electrical control theory, particularly those involving closed circuit loops.

The need for such an approach became evident from studying over time the inputs to, the outputs from, and the changes within, companies. It was recognised that instability of the latter two (for example, raw material purchases and stocks) arising from a varying input such as demand led to inefficient operation overall. In fact, the amplifying and accelerating effect produced by an oscillatory input could be excessive, leading to companies' frequently being out of step with their economic environment. Whilst no organisation could expect to operate in a stable manner for lengthy periods, industrial dynamics offers some possibility of reducing the fluctuations of internal operations against a background of assumed varying input. The customary problems exist, namely the need to have confidence in forecasts of the cyclical input, the danger of sub-optimisation through the non-inclusion of significant variables, the difficulty of quantifying some variables and the computational effort necessitated by the form and number of the mathematical

* *See* JAY W. FORRESTER, *Industrial Dynamics*, Massachusetts Institute of Technology Press, Cambridge, 1961.

equations used, most of which are non-linear. To facilitate formulation and computation a number of programming languages have been developed, of which the most notable is *dynamo*.

The selection of the name industrial dynamics was unfortunate as the suggestion is that the method is appropriate for industry only. All high level planning decisions in whatever sector of an economy need to take account of dynamic effects. For any system of complexity the time taken for the consequences of a major action to be dampened out may be large. Thus deflationary measures taken by a government may result in a crop of bankruptcies some two years later. Recognition that dynamic effects are of significance in all spheres of managerial activity led to research being instigated at several institutions into the general field of *system dynamics*.

By extending research and application to such fields as governmental and urban planning, it should be possible during the next decade to assess whether a major decision aiding tool has been developed. It may well prove to be the case that, by being able to recognise lagged interactive effects between parts of the organisation and between the organisation and the environment, medium term (say, two or three years) planning decisions will be assisted. It is difficult to accept at this stage of experience that with the exception of organisations with very long lead times (for example, producers of primary energy) planning on these lines over longer periods will be aided.* For many organisations, however, particularly in the private sector, medium term planning is seen by the chief executive to be of paramount importance, and for this reason the development of system dynamics will be observed closely.

SOME FINAL COMMENTS ON THE NEEDS OF MANAGEMENT IN THE FUTURE

One conclusion about the future of management which cannot be questioned is that decision making will always be part of it. Life throughout the world will continue to be determined by the decisions of "managers" defined in the broadest sense (that is "managers" of national economies, armies, trades unions, as well as managers within commerce and industry). Furthermore, pressure on managers to make decisions for the general good will increase as infor-

* See M. J. ROTHKOPF, "An Economic Model of World Energy 1900–2020," *Long Range Planning*, Vol. 6, No. 2, June 1973, pp. 43–51.

mation and communication improves. It is therefore certain that the great mass of managers will wish to avail themselves of any assistance which will improve their decision making ability.

The general nature of progress within those areas involving the reorganisation of resources within a known environment may be forecast without difficulty. In these circumstances, the search for the optimal configuration will be aided by such procedures as mathematical programming and simulation. The major problem will be to decide what level of analysis should be used. It will be necessary to carry out some form of cost/benefit analysis in order to assess whether the increased improvement likely to be achieved by sophisticated and more expensive analysis rather than analysis of a coarser nature is justified. Operational researchers have throughout their existence warned against the dangers of sub-optimisation and have attempted to enlarge the scope of their analyses. As the concept of the "total approach" becomes increasingly accepted and analysis and computers grow more powerful it is anticipated that most design problems within organisations which justify resolution will be overcome. There remains, however, the formidable bulk of problems of a planning nature with which this book has been mainly concerned. As there can never be any guarantee that a particular future outcome will be achieved by the use of the quantitative procedures described in the previous Chapters, it is well to ponder the implications of this admission.

It is easy to adopt the viewpoint expressed in Chapter 1 that by using appropriate analyses and hence taking decisions of a "logical" nature outcomes on average will be improved. That this undoubtedly would in general be the case is no comfort to the manager within a small organisation involved in a major decision or his counterpart in a larger organisation with one or two "logical decision-unfavourable outcome" sequences behind him. In each case, the principals may be unwilling to subject themselves to the discipline required of a logical approach and may prefer to rely on instinct supported by experience. It is in fact difficult to see how the quantitative approach can make a major impact at higher levels unless the initiative comes from senior managers themselves. As there is little chance that they can be prevailed upon against their will to make use of such procedures, it is necessary to place quantitative analysis in its proper perspective. It is important to appreciate that procedures described in this book have been available for use in managerial situations for barely a quarter of a century. Ptolemy's theories of planetary motion and Aristotle's laws of mechanics held sway for centuries before their downfall (caused incidentally by the developing power of mathematics during the seventeenth century). Looking to the future, the need for managerial decisions would seem to extend towards infinity. It is inevitable that as time passes attitudes and responses will come to be explained and even some of the apparently chance effects of life controlled. Together with attendant scientific and technological development, this will lead to the ability to plan with much greater confidence and accuracy. Although this will in given circumstances lead to a progressive narrowing of the decision gap, as defined at the beginning of this Chapter, it would be a foolish man who would anticipate its disappearance. It is therefore appropriate that quantitative aids to decision making should be viewed as just one, but an increasingly significant, part of the total managerial process. Recognition of the need to adopt this attitude is part of an approach termed *synectics*,* which has attracted some interest during the last decade. The term implies the combination of a number of different and apparently unconnected elements. As applied to decision making, this means that as much account is taken (initially at least) of the quantified, which may be analysed mathematically, as the unquantified. The planning process may therefore involve creative thinking, hunches and claimed insight together with any of the techniques which have been described in earlier chapters. A major advantage of synectics is that it should, in theory, operate against "favoured" (and perhaps unjustified) procedures, giving full consideration on each decision making occasion to all means of reaching the desired solution. The advantage of the synectic approach as described cannot be questioned, if only because in the short space devoted to it little more has been said than that every distinctive aid to decision making must be taken into consideration. In fact, synectics has, mainly through examination of the creative process, been concerned with building up a qualitative and ordered counterweight to quantitative methods. Whilst synectics properly applied should lead to a decision procedure which through its logicality should be highly efficient, there is the danger the managers may see in it some "excuse" for being freed of the demands of quantitative analysis. It is difficult to think of major planning decisions which do not necessitate some

---

* *See* W. J. J. GORDON, *Synectics, The Development of Creative Capacity*, Harper and Row, New York, 1961.

numerical analysis, and formal incorporation of such treatment is therefore to be preferred. An approach proposed by Ansoff* and termed the *quasi-analytic method* is of relevance here. This recognises the value of retaining some aspects of the problem in qualitative form, which are then considered together with the results of quantitative analysis which has been employed. The extent of the latter is not haphazard, but is determined by a procedure arising from the needs of corporate planning. These needs may involve multiple objectives (rates of growth, technological development, stability, and so on) which may change with the passage of time. In these circumstances, it is unlikely that one strategy will be superior to others in all respects. As a result, instead of comparing the single outcome (for example, earnings per share) of alternative strategies the effects of each strategy on rate of growth, stability, and other objectives will be considered independently. Ansoff describes the procedure as being "process" oriented as opposed to "outcome" oriented. Quantitative procedures may play a major part in the quasi-analytic approach even to the extent of strategy selection by weighting, but it may well be the case that the final selection of strategies is determined by the subjective preferences of the decision maker. Ansoff points to the need for feedback to take account of the dynamic nature of organisational activity, and although little has been achieved in this respect to date, system dynamics may prove very appropriate if practical application can be achieved. The quasi-analytic method was proposed over a decade ago and was therefore probably before its time. As a total approach widely relevant to high level decision making its resurrection in the near future may be very pertinent.

Both synectics and the quasi-analytic method are concerned with the process of decision making, but in neither case are individual techniques specified. Therefore for management to be able to make use, with confidence, of such methodologies it is essential that they have some understanding of all aids whether quantitative or qualitative. It is likely that in the future, as awareness increases, management will become very discriminating as between those techniques which have potential value and those whose practical relevance are in some doubt.

* This was the subject of a paper titled "A Quasi-Analytic Method for Long Range Planning" presented at the first symposium on Corporate Long Range Planning, College on Planning, The Institute of Management Sciences, Chicago, Ill., June 6th, 1959.

One point of view which accords with Ansoff's earlier quasi-analytic method and which is worthy of examination has been put by James B. Boulden.* Based on the experience of the 1960s he sees a continuing movement away from the optimising model towards (using the terminology of Chapter 2) the descriptive model. Although the optimum is, the ideal, attempts to determine it in any corporate sense have, he suggests (with the significant exception of certain oil companies), been baulked for a number of reasons. These include the difficulty of expressing policy aims in optimising terms, the limited flexibility of the models which are available, and the difficulty which managers have in understanding the models. Boulden attributes the desire to search for an optimum to the involvement of operational researchers in the planning process. Further, he feels that there is a danger that descriptive models, which provide the opportunity to test "What-if?" questions, may suffer the same fate as some optimising models unless model builders (again including operational researchers) resist the temptation of sophistication at the expense of realism.

It must be accepted that the interface between the manager and the model which may be appropriate for aiding his decisions can be a very real barrier. There is, however, no reason at all why if a manager understands the nature and purpose of an inflexible optimising model of the linear programming type and he is satisfied as to its relevance, he should not make use of it. It is of course most desirable that managers should be acquainted with all of the alternative forms of models available and then select from among these. Models were classified according to their structure in Chapter 2 (*e.g.* normative *v.* positive, etc.) and an attractive classification of models according to their flexibility and hence mode of use is proposed by Carruthers† and is given in Table XXV. Although the classification implies that a computer is a prerequisite, a useful basis for considering future attitudes is provided.

As in the last resort senior managers will make their own decisions as to the composition of their "synectic" approach to decision making, it is quite likely that in comparable situations different

* See JAMES B. BOULDEN, "Computerised Corporate Planning," *Long Range Planning*, Vol. 3, No. 4, 1971, pp. 2–9.
† See J. A. CARRUTHERS, "Computer-based Corporate Modelling Programs, Systems and Applications," *Proceedings of the International Conference on Corporate Planning, Management Science and Computers*, Management Centre, University of Bradford, 1971.

TABLE XXV: THE FLEXIBILITY OF MODELS

		Logic	
		Highly flexible	*Little or no flexibility*
Input/Output	Highly Flexible	Type 1	Type 2
	Little or no Flexibility	Type 3	Type 4

managers will not select the same type of model drawn from Table XXV. It may well be that in the future the Type 1 model with its high degree of flexibility will prove to be most suited to the purpose of satisfying management needs. It is difficult to imagine high level planning decisions being clear cut in nature, and the foremost requirement of senior managers is likely to be for flexibility. Even if they themselves do not input data using on-line terminals, it is inconceivable that they would restrict themselves to a procedure lacking flexibility. Carruthers describes Type 1 models as modelling *systems*, and sees these as being highly appropriate to corporate planning. This is not to say that models of types 2, 3, and 4 will not fulfil a useful subsidiary role. Thus Type 2 would typically imply report generators enabling, for example, rapid determination of profit and loss accounts and cash flows. Type 3 models may be exemplified by programmes written for the purpose of evaluating a variety of projects using fairly restricted criteria. Finally, Type 4 models are those of minimum flexibility (for example, forecasting routines) but which may provide a useful contribution to systems of Type 1. Providing therefore that a manager is acquainted with (preferably involved in) the construction of the model and that he understands the method and scope of its use, the problem of overcoming the barrier between him and analytic and computer based aids will be much reduced.

As the philosophy of management at higher levels within any organisation must be the achievement of maximum effectiveness, there is no question but that enlightened management will adopt procedures designed to achieve improved corporate performance. Whether these procedures contain more or less non-quantified elements the general relevance of quantitative analysis will remain.

In order that its potential is realised it is essential that senior management should have a sufficient appreciation of its value and limitations and be sensitive to the situations in which it may be applied. Once this comes about, the importance of the quantitative approach will be neither deflated nor inflated. It will be seen as providing a means whereby managers will be able to remove much that is illogical from the decision making process. And although for any *particular* decision of a planning nature, in which uncertainty figures prominently, a favourable outcome cannot be guaranteed, the overall performance within organisations supporting this approach will inevitably improve.

SYMBOLS AND TERMINOLOGY

SYMBOLS		PAGE
e	A numerical constant whose approximate value is 2.718. It is widely employed in mathematics and serves as a base for an important type of logarithm.	35
$\leqslant$	Less than or equal to.	57
$\geqslant$	Greater than or equal to.	57
$\sqrt{x}$	The square root of x.	61
dy/dx	The first derivative of y with respect to x.	64
$\sum$	The Greek capital sigma (s), being shorthand for "sum of."	65
$\sum_{i=a}^{n} x_i$	The sum of all consecutive values of x_i from $i = a$ to $i = n$.	66

TERMINOLOGY		
Autonomous	In an economic sense implies a change determined and sustained within a system without interaction with the environment.	35
Base	In logarithms represents the number (for example 10 or e) of which powers are taken.	61
Bivariate	Describes the situation when two variables vary jointly (for example, height and weight).	33
Black box	A term used to relate an output to an input without specifying the manner in which the output is determined.	39
Calculus	A branch of mathematics concerned with continuous change and growth.	64
Cash flow	An accounting term usually defined as "profits plus depreciation."	155

Conversational	Applied to computer usage, implies a facility to develop programmes on-line making use of immediate diagnostic responses from the computer.	50
Co-ordinates	The values which locate a point in space by reference to an origin. In 2-dimensional graphs the co-ordinates of a point are usually written (x, y) where x measures the distance at right angles to the vertical y axis and y measures the distance at right angles to the horizontal x axis.	191
Dependent	As applied to a variable, implies that its value is determined by the value(s) of one or more independent variables.	35
Differentiation	A process of the calculus which, when y is a function of x, measures the rate of change of y with respect to x.	55
Dispersion	A statistical term used to describe (through range, standard deviation, etc.) the extent to which the frequency distribution of a variable is concentrated or spread out.	74
Elasticity	In economics, measures the proportional change in one variable brought about by a proportional change in another.	180
Equation	A mathematical relationship involving one or more unknown variables for which unique solutions may be obtained.	56
Ex post	A term in economics used to describe the adoption of a viewpoint looking back at a particular situation when the situation need not necessarily have occurred; the converse of "*ex post*" is "*ex ante.*"	126
Exponent	The power to which a number is raised.	35
Extrapolation	To infer a relationship beyond the limits of the measurements which have been taken (the converse of "interpolation").	100
Flow chart	A diagrammatic representation of information, decisions, and material movements within a system.	177

Function	A relationship between variables in which there is only one value of the dependent variable for each value of the independent variables.	35
Identity	A mathematical relationship which is true for all values of the unknown variables.	36
Independent	As applied to a variable, implies that its value will determine (possibly in conjunction with the values of other independent variables) the value of a dependent variable.	35
Inequality	A relationship between variables of the type "x is greater than y" written $x > y$, or "x is less than or equal to y" written $x \leqslant y$.	57
Inflection	A change in the direction of curvature.	17
Integer	A whole number.	220
Interpolation	To infer a relationship within the range of measurements which have been taken (the converse of "extrapolation").	101
Iterate	To repeat; particularly to advance by steps towards an optimum.	8
Location	A statistical term used to describe (through mean, median, etc.) the approximate magnitude of a frequency distribution.	74
Logarithm	The power to which a particular base is raised. By working in powers of a base as represented by tables of logarithms, certain calculations are facilitated.	62
Lognormal	A skewed distribution of a variable which is transformed to a normal distribution when logarithms of the variable are taken; item sales are often distributed lognormally.	114
Lowest common multiple	The smallest number into which a set of numbers will each divide (for example the lowest common multiple of 2, 3, 4 and 5 is 60).	219

Mathematical programming	A generic title given to a set of optimising techniques, of which the best known is linear programming.	45
Mutually exclusive	A description used in probability theory implying that one random event will exclude another (for example, on the toss of a coin the occurrence of a head will exclude a tail).	79
Net present value	An accounting term used to describe a single composite value of a series of cash flows through time obtained by discounting each to some datum in time.	67
On-line	In computing, indicates a facility whereby the user is able to manipulate the working area of the computer to develop and use programmes for an indeterminate period.	50
Opportunity cost	A term widely used in economics which enables a particular alternative to be valued by comparing it to the alternative which was most nearly chosen instead and which was forgone.	5
Ordinal scale	A method of comparison using rank according to some attribute rather than measured values.	13
Parameters	Constants in a particular function or relationship, but which enable comparisons to be made among *classes* to which the function or relationship belongs. For example, in the straight line $y = mx + c$, m and c are parameters which enable all straight lines to be compared.	76
Population	In the statistical sense, the aggregate of individual units concerning which an inference is to be made.	68
Power	In mathematics, the product of a number of equal expressions. The power is an index placed after and above the expression; it is generalised to include negative and fractional indices.	35

Random sample	A sample of size n drawn from a population in such a way that all samples of size n have the same chance of being selected.	6
Sample	A set of n observations drawn from a population.	68
Skewness	Describes the asymmetrical nature of a frequency distribution.	74
System	In its widest sense, a combination of people, equipment and procedures organised to satisfy a particular purpose or objective.	269
Time-sharing	As applied to computer operation, indicates a system whereby on-line access to a single computer is made available to a limited number of operators simultaneously. The access is often achieved by means of teletype units connected to the computer through commercial telephone lines.	51

RANDOM SAMPLING NUMBERS

20 17	42 28	23 17	59 66	38 61	02 10	86 10	51 55	92 52	44 25
74 49	04 49	03 04	10 33	53 70	11 54	48 63	94 60	94 49	57 38
94 70	49 31	38 67	23 42	29 65	40 88	78 71	37 18	48 64	06 57
22 15	78 15	69 84	32 52	32 54	15 12	54 02	01 37	38 37	12 93
93 29	12 18	27 30	30 55	91 87	50 57	58 51	49 36	12 53	96 40
45 04	77 97	36 14	99 45	52 95	69 85	03 83	51 87	85 56	22 37
44 91	99 49	89 39	94 60	48 49	06 77	64 72	59 26	08 51	25 57
16 23	91 02	19 96	47 59	89 65	27 84	30 92	63 37	26 24	23 66
04 50	65 04	65 65	82 42	70 51	55 04	61 47	88 83	99 34	82 37
32 70	17 72	03 61	66 26	24 71	22 77	88 33	17 78	08 92	73 49
03 64	59 07	42 95	81 39	06 41	20 81	92 34	51 90	39 08	21 42
62 49	00 90	67 86	93 48	31 83	19 07	67 68	49 03	27 47	52 03
61 00	95 86	98 36	14 03	48 88	51 07	33 40	06 86	33 76	68 57
89 03	90 49	28 74	21 04	09 96	60 45	22 03	52 80	01 79	33 81
01 72	33 85	52 40	60 07	06 71	89 27	14 29	55 24	85 79	31 96
27 56	49 79	34 34	32 22	60 53	91 17	33 26	44 70	93 14	99 70
49 05	74 48	10 55	35 25	24 28	20 22	35 66	66 34	26 35	91 23
49 74	37 25	97 26	33 94	42 23	01 28	59 58	92 69	03 66	73 82
20 26	22 43	88 08	19 85	08 12	47 65	65 63	56 07	97 85	56 79
48 87	77 96	43 39	76 93	08 79	22 18	54 55	93 75	97 26	90 77
08 72	87 46	75 73	00 11	27 07	05 20	30 85	22 21	04 67	19 13
95 97	98 62	17 27	31 42	64 71	46 22	32 75	19 32	20 99	94 85
37 99	57 31	70 40	46 55	46 12	24 32	36 74	69 20	72 10	95 93
05 79	58 37	85 33	75 18	88 71	23 44	54 28	00 48	96 23	66 45
55 85	63 42	00 79	91 22	29 01	41 39	51 40	36 65	26 11	78 32
67 28	96 25	68 36	24 72	03 85	49 24	05 69	64 86	08 19	91 21
85 86	94 78	32 59	51 82	86 43	73 84	45 60	89 57	06 87	08 15
40 10	60 09	05 88	78 44	63 13	58 25	37 11	18 47	75 62	52 21
94 55	89 48	90 80	77 80	26 89	87 44	23 74	66 20	20 19	26 52
11 63	77 77	23 20	33 62	62 19	29 03	94 15	56 37	14 09	47 16
64 00	26 04	54 55	38 57	94 62	68 40	26 04	24 25	03 61	01 20
50 94	13 23	78 41	60 58	10 60	88 46	30 21	45 98	70 96	36 89
66 98	37 96	44 13	45 05	34 59	75 85	48 97	27 19	17 85	48 51
66 91	42 83	60 77	90 91	60 90	79 62	57 66	72 28	08 70	96 03
33 58	12 18	02 07	19 40	21 29	39 45	90 42	58 84	85 43	95 67

52 49	40 16	72 40	73 05	50 90	02 04	98 24	05 30	27 25	20 88
74 98	92 99	78 30	79 47	96 92	45 58	40 37	89 76	84 41	74 68
50 26	54 30	01 88	69 57	54 45	69 88	23 21	05 69	93 44	05 32
49 46	61 89	33 79	96 84	28 34	19 35	28 73	39 59	56 34	97 07
19 65	13 44	78 39	73 88	62 03	36 00	25 96	86 76	67 90	21 68
64 17	47 67	87 59	81 40	72 61	14 00	28 28	55 86	23 38	16 15
18 43	97 37	68 97	56 56	57 95	01 88	11 89	48 07	42 65	11 92
65 58	60 87	51 09	96 61	15 53	66 81	66 88	44 75	37 01	28 88
79 90	31 00	91 14	85 65	31 75	43 15	45 93	64 78	34 53	88 02
07 23	00 15	59 05	16 09	94 42	20 40	63 76	65 67	34 11	94 10
90 08	14 24	01 51	95 46	30 32	33 19	00 14	19 28	40 51	92 69
53 82	62 02	21 82	34 13	41 03	12 85	65 30	00 97	56 30	15 48
98 17	26 15	04 50	76 25	20 33	54 84	39 31	23 33	59 64	96 27
08 91	12 44	82 40	30 62	45 50	64 54	65 17	89 25	59 44	99 95
37 21	46 77	84 87	67 39	85 54	97 37	33 41	11 74	90 50	29 62

Each digit is an independent sample from a population in which the digits 0 to 9 are equally likely, that is each has a probability of $\frac{1}{10}$. Reproduced from Cambridge Elementary Statistical Tables by D. V. Lindley and J. C. P. Miller, Cambridge University Press, by kind permission of Professor D. V. Lindley, Department of Statistics, University College, London.

B

Bayes' theorem (*see* Probability)
Black box, 39, 181, 224

C

Certainty equivalent, 14, 160–1, 173 (*see also* Decision trees)
Chief executive, 27–9, 249
Classical approach to forecasting, 98–107
    cyclical effects, 105–7
    seasonal effects, 104–5
    seasonal factors, 102–5
    trend, 99–102
Compounding and discounting, 67–8
    internal rate of return, 67, 196–201
    net present value, 67, 172–3, 175, 201, 256
Computers:
    batch operation, 50–1
    conversational usage, 50–1, 204
    planning languages, 51, 205
    role in model building and usage, 50–1, 190, 204, 244
Corporate planning, 1–2, 8, 25–9, 47, 202–3, 247, 254, 267
    groups, 27
    public sector, 26, 249

D

Decision making, 6–8, 21–3 (*see also* Logical decision making)
    classification, 8
    intuitive, 2, 7, 21
Decision trees, 152–175, 259–261
    selection of alternatives using expected values 156–63
    selection of alternatives using utility, 168–70 (*see also* Utility)
    selection of alternatives with discounting, 172–3
    size of tree, 157, 172, 174
    value of perfect and imperfect information, 163–8
Delphi technique, 94
Design decisions, 93, 214
Differentiation, 63–5, 124
Discounted cash flow, 172

Dynamic programming, 260–1

E

Equations, 55–63 (*see also* Linear equations and inequalities, and relationships)
    simultaneous, 56–7
Expectation, 78–9, 160 (*see also* Probability)

F

Forecasting:
    auto-regression, 127
    Bayesian approach, 127
    bias, 95
    classification of methods, 98
    cumulative sum technique, 119
    econometric, 98
    errors, 95, 114
    horizon, 97–8
    individual values, 95–6
    mean values, 95–6
    trend, 96 (*see also* Classical approach to forecasting, non-linear trend curves, and tracking methods)

G

Game theory, 261–3

H

Heuristic methods, 140
Hill-climbing, 50, 214 (*see also* Optimisation)

I

Identity, 36
Industrial dynamics, 263–4

L

Linear equations and inequalities, 55–8
Linear programming, 215–30, 255–9
    adequacy, 230
    an example, 216–23
    chance constrained programming, 233
    computational efficiency, 234
    constraints, 217–8, 224

decision variables, 224
extensions, 229–35
feasible solution, 224–6
in practice, 223–9
integer programming, 232
objective function, 217, 224
optimal solution, 224, 226–9
post-optimality analysis, 222, 225, 233
revised simplex technique, 234–5
separable convex programming, 230–1
shadow price, 225
simplex technique, 224–9
stochastic programming, 233
Logarithms, 62–3
base of, 62
Logical decision making, 2–3, 6–8, 21, 24, 30, 32, 152, 176, 245, 262

M

Management service groups, 22–3, 247 (see also Corporate planning groups)
Mathematical programming, 215, 235 (see also Linear programming, and non-linear programming)
Maximisation, 31 (see also Optimisation)
Models, 32–51, 176–9, 203–5
classification, 32, 41–50, 268–9
descriptive, 47–50
deterministic, 41, 44–6
dynamic, 41, 46–7
interpretation and construction, 34–41, 203, 205, 247–50, 269
macro, 42–4
mental, 32–3
micro, 42
normative, 41–2, 181–2
optimising, 47–50 (see also Optimisation)
physical, 32–3
positive, 41–2, 179–81
predictive, 41–4
probabilistic, 41, 44–6
static, 41, 46–7
structural, 41–4
symbolic, 32–3

Monte Carlo method of sampling, 186, 193, 197, 201, 244

N

Networks, 128–51, 255–60
allocation of resources, 136–41
analysis, 34, 132–6
bar charts, 134–7
C.P.M. time-cost procedure, 141–4
computer packages, 134–5, 140, 151
critical path, 136
float, 134–6
in combination with linear programming and simulation, 257–9
in combination with mathematical programming, 256
level of detail, 132
origins and construction, 129–32
P.E.R.T. approach towards uncertainty, 144–50, 257
resource levelling, 138
resource smoothing, 138–9
Non-linear programming, 229–35
quadratic programming, 231
Non-linear trend curves, 121–5
life cycles, 121–2
slope transforms, 124–5
use of slope in curve selection, 123–5

O

Objective function, 48, 215, 235–7 (see also Linear programming)
Objectives and goals, 29–32, 47–8
goals, 212
setting objectives, 210
Optimisation, 31, 207, 209–44
by experiment, 237–42 (see also Hill-climbing)
framework, 213–4
problems of, 48–9
techniques, 214–5

P

Perfect and imperfect information, 163–8

Planning, 23–9 (*see also* Corporate Planning)
  bottom-up approach, 2
  decisions, 93
  expenditure on, 22–3
  operational, 24–8
  strategic, 24
  top-down approach, 2
Prediction, 94
Probability, 76–80 (*see also* Probability distributions)
  Bayes' theorem, 80, 166, 172
  classical interpretation, 77
  long-run view, 9, 14 (*see also* Expectation)
  multiplication and addition theorems, 79–80
  quantified interpretation, 77
  relative frequency interpretation, 77
  subjective interpretation, 77
Probability distributions, 45 (*see also* Probability)
  cumulative, 191–4
  for network activity durations, 144–5
  normal, 80–1
Pseudo-random numbers, 190

Q
Quantitative methods:
  current usage, 247–50
  future developments, 254–60
  problems of non-technical nature, 252–4
  problems of technical nature, 250–2
Quasi-analytic method, 267–8

R
Random numbers, 82, 187–9, 190, 192, 194–5
Regression and correlation, 85–92
  coefficient of determination, 89, 100
  correlation coefficient, 86, 90
  correlation matrix, 92
  least squares, 87

multiple regression, 40
multiple regression and correlation, 91–2
partial regression coefficients, 92
regression coefficient, 88, 90
relationship between regression coefficient and correlation coefficient, 90
step-wise elimination of variables, 92
Relationships: (*see also* Models, and Equations)
  assumed functional, 35
  exponential, 60–1
  higher order, 58–60
  non-linear, 41
  normative, 35–6, 39, 42
  positive, 36, 42
Risk and uncertainty, 3–6
  differing views of, 9–11
  risk aversion, 15–18, 199–200, 207
  risk premium, 15–16

S
Sampling and estimation, 81–5
  central limit theorem, 83
  interval estimates, 83, 84, 95–6, 114–6
  non-sampling error, 69
  point estimates, 82, 95
  sampling error, 69
  significance, 85
  standard error, 83
Satisficing, 237
Sensitivity analysis, 155, 162–3, 182–3, 200, 225, 243, 259
Series, 65–8
  arithmetic progressions, 65–7
  geometric progressions, 65–7
Simulation, 50, 176–208
  analysis of risk, 195–201
  conditional relationships, 194–5
  deterministic, 179–83
  in practice, 203–6
  limited set of alternatives, 196–201
  probabilistic, 183–201
  total set of alternatives, 201–3

with continuous distributions, 191–5

with discrete distributions, 184–90

Statistics:
cumulative frequency distributions, 72 (*see also* Probability distributions)
descriptive, 68–76
frequency, 71
frequency polygon, 72
histogram, 71
inferential, 68, 76–92
measures of dispersion, 75–6
measures of location, 74–5
population, 68
presentation of data, 70–3
relative frequency, 72
sample, 68
skewness, 74

Synectics, 266

System dynamics, 264 (*see also* Industrial dynamics)

T

Tracking methods, 107–21
age of average, 112
correction for trend, 109–11, 112–14
efficiency and control, 118–19
exponential smoothing, 111–12, 119–21
forecast errors and interval estimates, 114–16
moving average, 108–9
smoothing constant, 111, 116–18
tracking signals, 119
with limited number of terms, 108–11
with unlimited number of terms, 111–21

U

Uncertainty and risk (*see* Risk and uncertainty)

Utility, 8–19, 49 (*see also* Decision trees)
curves and functions, 14–18, 169
personality implications, 15–19
quantified, 11–15

V

Variables:
controllable, 49, 93, 261
dependent, 35, 38, 40, 59
independent, 35, 38, 40, 59
uncontrollable, 49, 93, 127, 244, 254, 261

W

Welfare, 31
function, 48, 236 (*see also* Objective function)